Remaking the
Sutton Hoo Stone

The Ansell-Roper Replica and its Context

Edited by
Paul Mortimer & Stephen Pollington

Published 2013 by
Anglo-Saxon Books
Hereward, Black Bank Business Centre
Little Downham, Ely, Cambs. CB6 2UA

www.asbooks.co.uk

Printed and bound by
Lighting Source
Australia, England, USA

PL

ISBN 9781898281696

Above all, reconstruction consolidates academic knowledge into practical understanding.

Richard Underwood,
The Early Anglo-Saxon Shield: Reconstruction as an Aid to Interpretation

Contents

Acknowledgments

We would like to record our thanks to the many friends, colleagues and associates who have helped with the research and writing of this book, including:

Noel Adams, Brian Ansell, Angela Care-Evans, Helen Geake, Lindsay Kerr, Kevin Leahy, Wayne Letting, Sonja Marzinzik, Sam Newton, David Roper, Hannah Simons, Angus Wainwright.

Thanks are due to Andrew Morrison, curator at York Museum, who very kindly gave us access to the Uncleby stone.

We would also like to thank the Trustees of the British Museum and the Portable Antiquities Scheme.

We are grateful to Michael Argent and Pauline Sabine-Moore of the Sutton Hoo Society for their support and interest.

Photographs and Drawings

Our thanks to all those who supplied images. A special thanks to Lindsay Kerr for the wide variety of photographs and drawings he has provided for this and other books.

1	T Linsell	78-79	Lindsay Kerr after Arwidsson
2-6	Paul Mortimer	80	David Roper
7-9	Hannah Symons	81	Wayne Letting
10	Brian Ansell	82 -83	PACS
11	Hannah Symons	84	Trustees of the British Museum
12	Brian Ansell	85-89	Lindsay Kerr
13	Hannah Symons	90	Lindsay Kerr after Hauck
14-15	Brian Ansell	91	Wayne Letting after Meaney
16-18	Hannah Symons	92	Wayne Letting
19-22	Brian Ansell	93-96	Lindsay Kerr
23-24	Hannah Symons	97-98	Paul Mortimer
25	Brian Ansell	99-101	Lindsay Kerr
26-28	Hannah Symons	102-106	After Lamm
29	Brian Ansell	107-112	After Lamm
30-60	Hannah Symons	113	Lindsay Kerr
61-62	Brian Ansell	114	After Lamm
63	Paul Mortimer	115	Linday Kerr
64	Brian Ansell	116	After Lamm
65	After Bruce-Mitford	117	Historiska Museet, Stockholm
66	Lindsay Kerr after Arne & Stolpe	118-19	After Lamm
67-68	Matt Bunker	120	Nationalmuseet, Copenhagen
69	After Bruce-Mitford	121	After Lamm
70	Unknown	121a	Lindsay Kerr
71	Ian G. Scott	122	The Trustees of the British Museum
72	After Erä-Esko	123	National Museum of Iceland
73	After Ryan	124-26	Paul Mortimer
74	After Bruce-Mitford	127	The Trustees of the British Museum
75	Holly Hayes, Art History Images	128-130	Hannah Symons
76-77	Wayne Letting	131-134	T Linsell

Glossary

boaster	(or bolster) a broad chisel, 2-4" (5-10 cm) across the blade
boning	A process for achieving flat working surfaces
calque	A direct translation of the words expressing an idea from one language into another, to create a new expression, e.g. English 'to learn by heart' is a calque on French 'apprendre par coeur'
claw	A tool for reducing a rough surface close to the final shape
cleaner	A thin slice of stone for evaluation
compound	A word formed by combining two or more other words, e.g. 'signpost'
coping	A process for splitting a stone to the required size using a large chisel called a coping tool
deuterotheme	The second element in a compound word (e.g. '–post' in 'signpost')
drafting	A process for roughly outlining the stone surface to be removed and establishing the required depth of removal
drop	A rhythmic pattern of blows delivered with a mason's hammer
greywacké	(also *greywacké*) Hard grit stone used for the Sutton Hoo whetstone-sceptre
hard lining	A process for chiselling shallow cuts to the waste side of the marked outline
Indo-European	(IE) A group of related languages of the prehistoric period; descendants of this language group continued into historical times (Hittite, Ancient Greek, Sanskrit) and form some of the major language groups of Europe and Asia (Baltic, Germanic, Indo-Iranian, Romance, Slavonic, etc.)
OE	Old English
OHG	Old High German
OIc	Old Icelandic
ON	Old Norse
OS	Old Saxon
petrography	Scientific study of stone
piriform	Pear-shaped
pitching off	Removing an evaluation piece from an unworked block with a pitching tool
point	A tool for creating an even working surface
pressblech	An embossed metal plate decorated with figures and animals, interlaced patterns, etc., mostly used on high-status objects such as helmets, swords, drinking horns
proterotheme	The first element in a compound word (e.g. 'sign-' in 'signpost')
Proto-Germanic	The hypothetical ancestor of all languages in the Germanic group, including English, Dutch German and the Scandinavian languages, as well as such ancient languages as Old English, Old Norse, Old High German and Gothic
repoussé	A method of working a design into metal by beating it over a die
shake	A fault in the mass of a stone
simplex	A word used singly, not as part of a compound
try-gauge	A template used to establish and check the correct profile of the work in progress
vent	A fault in the mass of a stone
Wuffingas	The royal family of the East Angles, descendants of the legendary figure of Wuffa

About the Contributors

Brian Ansell

Brian Ansell was born in Suffolk in 1950. His career in stone masonry began in 1969 and, as part of the learning process, he attended the masonry training colleges of Cambridge, Bath and Weymouth. Brian qualified at Lincoln Cathedral in 1980 specialising in advanced masonry, stone sculpture and portrait carving. Further study and in-depth practical knowledge of the more complex styles of decorated medieval architecture led him to work on many of our internationally-renowned historic buildings including the re-carving of York Minster's Great West Door. Brian's present work includes interactive experimental archaeology, historic artefact reconstructions and teaching traditional stone sculpture at all levels.

Paul Mortimer

Paul Mortimer is a retired secondary school teacher who now has time to indulge his passion for history, focussing especially on the magnificent ship-burial in Mound 1 at Sutton Hoo. Paul has commissioned museum-quality replicas of many of the finds – the helmet, sword, shield, the stone and other items - which he uses to illustrate his talks. Paul's first book, *Woden's Warriors*, was published in 2011. He has appeared on various media, including a number of television programmes.

Stephen Pollington

Stephen Pollington has been involved in writing and speaking about the Anglo-Saxons for more than two decades. He has appeared on numerous television programmes – most recently with Michael Wood in *The Story of England* and *The Great British Story* – and has written more than a dozen books on aspects of the subject as varied as medicine (*Leechcraft*), runes (*Rudiments of Runelore*), language (*First Steps in Old English*, *Wordcraft*), warriorhood (*The English Warrior*), art and material culture (*Wayland's Work*) pre-Christian religion (*Elder Gods*) and feasting/social structure (*Meadhall*). He is a researcher and translator, a part-time consultant to a London auction house and a member of the Company of Art Scholars, Dealers and Collectors. (www.stevepollington.com)

David Roper

David Roper is a metallurgist with a passion for the art of the British Iron Age and the Early Anglo-Saxon periods. He has worked on numerous film and television projects producing arms, armour, costumes and stage properties. He has recently launched his own bespoke manufacturing company, Ganderwick Creations (www.ganderwickcreations.com).

Foreword

As a member of the Sutton Hoo Society and, in recent years, its Chairman, I am delighted to have been invited to pen this introduction to what is a remarkable record of scholarship, lifetime practical experience and sheer enthusiasm by its joint authors.

The focus of this work was found surrounded by over 300 artefacts in the great burial ship grave unearthed by, amongst others, Basil Brown on high ground alongside the River Deben opposite the town of Woodbridge in Suffolk in the summer of 1939. Among the finds in the burial ship were spectacular items of jewellery made of precious metals and studded with garnets, weapons of war, symbols of kingship and some more mundane domestic items. They were a collection which originated from many parts of the old Roman Empire.

The subject of this volume, despite its important location within the burial chamber, must have seemed comparatively mundane amongst many of the other items. It was not even in one piece when lifted from the soil. Should such a judgement have actually been made in those days - in 1939, when war again seemed imminent - they would be inadvertently doing a great injustice to the ancient craftsmen who created for us a spectacular and highly enigmatic symbol of its time. Yet in basic terms, it is little more than a few kilograms of stone - in fact a very hard mill stone grit known as 'greywacké,' originally adorned with some metal ornamentation none of which has much intrinsic value in itself.

This book sets out to describe the article in great detail from its beginning up to its realisation, not through the eyes of learned academics and art historians, but using the skills of two talented artisans. The first is Brian Ansell, a time served stone mason and subsequent stone sculptor, who spent over forty years learning his trade on some of our greatest ecclesiastical buildings, amongst them York Minster and Lincoln Cathedral. Brian was given special access to the original whetstone in the British Museum where he set about investigating the techniques and detailed planning which lay behind its creation. This enabled him to enhance his own knowledge prior to commencing the actual carving process. The replica was to be made of similar stone, and worked with mason's tools which had hardly changed from Roman times.

The other craftsman involved, David Roper from Herefordshire, is a specialist metal worker and has created the most magnificent replicas of many of the other artefacts from the burial. One cannot help linking him to the legendary Weyland the Smith in the way his skilful hands added the equally enigmatic metal work which adorns Brian's completed whetstone.

In this detailed process Brian was assisted by a third craftsman, but one with the most modern of technical skills. Hannah Simons is an archaeologist and a most accomplished photographer. As can be seen from some of her photographs in the text the definition and detail of the images are undoubtedly the finest yet taken of the stone. As such they were of great help in recalling and checking on the detail of the original during the carving in a way that the original workman could have never imagined.

In reality what has emerged from this inspired partnership is undoubtedly a replica, but that seems to undervalue a modern high quality work of art. I must confess to preferring the view that the modern completed item is simply the second (and there is a third as two were made) of a limited run; there just happens to be at least fourteen centuries between their respective arrivals.

Undoubtedly the major achievement of this work was the insight it gave into how the whetstone was created. It did not stop at that either: there is more to masonry than just cutting stone. To understand the construction process requires a considerable understanding of geometry which clearly abounded in the past, even on a comparatively small sculpture such as this. Our two craftsmen were asked to do what they know best, produce a replica of the Sutton Hoo whetstone, and in the process identify in detail just how it was made. There was no requirement in this brief, just as in the original request one suspects, to understand why it was made, who ordered it to be made, what it was to be used for, what it was intended to represent or who would be using it; undoubtedly our two craftsmen would have had plenty of ideas of their own, both then and now! However its discovery amongst the fabulous Sutton Hoo treasures gives a clear indication of its importance, and seems to place it on a par with the other artefacts alongside which it lay undiscovered for almost fourteen centuries beneath the sandy Suffolk soil on a remote headland overlooking the river.

It is the achievement of this spectacular recreation from the past which has undoubtedly opened a door which will enable others to attempt to answer some of the questions listed earlier. It is an approach, where appropriate, which is highly recommended for the future. At the same time, the construction process has revealed how some of the early attempts to assign it a purpose without understanding its construction, or even in some cases without having handled or seen the original, will be doomed to failure. Despite all this work there is still a long way to go yet before attempts to explain the whetstone's true purpose. In many ways it has become the most fascinating of all the recovered artefacts from the Mound One ship.

In order to move things forward, the authors of this book have researched far and wide to find examples of, seemingly, similar items, a task which will save future researchers some considerable effort, but it dramatically shows how complex a problem this really is going to be.

The meaning of the detail on the whetstone has been meticulously pursued through examination of actual artefacts and numerous literary sources all of which provide useful insights as well as perhaps a few, unintentional, red herrings along the way.

Here in this volume, and in the finished product which is now on permanent display at the National Trust site at Sutton, near Woodbridge in Suffolk, is an outstanding example of modern British craftsmanship which somehow unites those who made whetstone number one with those who made whetstone number two. It is a triumph of inherited skills and acquired experience which has, and hopefully will, continue through the centuries.

You are now invited to consider the remaining questions listed earlier using the tools and guidance in this book. You have at least a sound basis of fact, founded in research and practical effort upon which to base you own theories. Whoever chooses to follow the trail of the whetstone will find it both an interesting and challenging task.

Michael J. Argent

Chairman, Sutton Hoo Society

June 2012

Introduction

This book had its genesis during 2008 when Angus Wainwright of the National Trust decided to ask Brian Ansell to make a copy of the stone from Mound 1 at Sutton Hoo. Angus arranged for suitable stone to be delivered by Tarmac to the National Trust offices in Suffolk and the rest was up to Brian - with a little help from the British Museum, the National Trust and Dave Roper in making the bronzes and iron work. Brian was assisted in his researches at the British Museum by Hannah Simons and together they kept careful records of the progress of his work. It was always intended to record Brian's work formally in images and writing, but we have taken the opportunity to go a little beyond that.

Much was learnt from the process of creating the replica and we hope that we have been able to provide a faithful record of the way in which the work progressed, and what that has taught us. We believe that it has allowed us to look at the stone in new ways. This will in turn help to focus attention on specific aspects of the stone and may narrow the search for answers as to its function and purpose.

Brian Ansell eventually made two replicas: one for the National Trust to form part of the collection at the Sutton Hoo Visitor Centre and another for Paul Mortimer, for his own researches into the artefacts from Sutton Hoo.

The first part of this volume, then, reports on the research and work of the two craftsmen who produced the replicas. We both feel that this is an important end in itself. It has permitted us to begin to understand aspects of the stone that have not been considered before, such as the geometry of the composition of elements and the possible significance of measurements within the design. We think that there is good evidence that the stone, the ring and the stag were all planned and designed together at the initial stages of the original design and that they were, literally, made for each other.

The second part of the book is taken up with some views about 'what it all may mean', the significance of the ring, the stag, the stone faces together and in isolation– and beyond this, some analogues. It begins with a brief review of the most relevant literature and records the ideas of many of the writers and academics who have written about the whetstone. This overview provides many avenues to explore - and a number of assumptions to challenge. We include a summary of some aspects of the linguistic evidence, specifically some important nouns, that the Anglo-Saxons associated with rule and rulers, with a short aside covering the vocabulary of whetstones.

A typical 'factoid' – an opinion voiced early in the history of the subject which has remained virtually unchallenged ever since - concerns the stag-and-ring mounted on the stone bar. It has been suggested that the stag surmounting the stone cannot be of Anglo-Saxon manufacture and that this species was not a cult animal for the early English. This idea appears to begin with the inconclusive connection between the two objects – bearing in mind that the stag-and-ring assembly was for some decades thought to be a finial for the iron 'standard' from the burial chamber. In order to evaluate the evidence, one chapter concerns itself with the cultural importance of the stag to the Anglo-Saxons and whether the animal can be associated with 'royal power' or political authority within the Anglo-Saxon and wider Germanic world-view.

We have also included a section on the place that significant and empowering stones have within European myth. Objects descending from heaven and objects fashioned from stone play an important part in the foundation stories of many cultures and, while no direct proof of such a connection with the *Wuffingas* is ever likely to be available, there is nevertheless an important dimension to Anglo-Saxon kingship alluded to in the creation of this item of regalia.

We have then reviewed the stone afresh in the light of the insights that the process has provided, comparing it to the analogues that have been mentioned by past commentators. Finally, we draw some conclusions regarding the stone's origin and purpose based on our researches.

We conclude the study with an outline of areas for further research so that the book may prove a springboard for future students of many subject areas: the history of English kingship, religion, craftsmanship and symbolism.

Paul Mortimer & Stephen Pollington

Essex, 2012

Editors' note on terminology. The Sutton Hoo Stone has been most frequently referred to as a 'sceptre' or a 'whetstone' in the literature. The authors feel that 'stone' is a safer and more accurate term to use in the light of our researches. However, the reader will note that we have not always been consistent throughout this book when referring to the stone. We ask for the reader's forgiveness.

I. Making and Re-Making

1. The Metalwork

David Roper and Stephen Pollington

The metal fittings for the greywacké stone bar were produced by David Roper of Ganderwick Creations. The fittings comprise: the lower cage and foot; the upper cage and mount; the ferrous ring and fittings; the stag figurine.

Production of these objects posed several problems of interpretation and entailed a considerable amount of original research. The starting point for the project was volume 2 of Bruce-Mitford's report in which the various metal fittings are discussed in detail.[1] The project is broken down into sections for discussion in this paper.

The Stag Figurine

The stag was produced in copper alloy and cast by the lost-wax method and a one-piece mould: a wax model of the stag was made and covered in clay with two channels to the exterior. The clay was gently heated so that the wax ran out through the channels, leaving a void in the shape of the object to be produced, the mould. This void was then filled with molten metal (copper alloy, in this case) which took on the shape of the mould. The clay was broken open and the resultant casting cleaned up, with the runners (sprues) removed.

One of the problems with lost-wax casting in a one-piece mould is ensuring that the molten metal reaches to the ends of the void furthest from the feeding point. As the metal cools it becomes solid and can block the narrower parts of the mould; similarly, air can become trapped inside the mould, leaving bubbles and a pitted surface.

The reproduction stag was cast with the feeder channels entering beneath the feet. The original may have had a feeder to the outer tines of the antlers, although there is no surviving evidence for this on the existing Anglo-Saxon casting. The reproduction was cast with the feet positioned on discoid blocks, which were drilled out to allow the iron ring to pass through them. An alternative method would have been to end the stag casting at the feet, and then to solder on separate annular castings or loops made to accommodate the iron ring. This would have the advantages of hiding the entry-point for the feeders, and of simplifying the mounting process.

Figure 1 The reproduction stone bar and fittings

---

[1] Bruce-Mitford, 1978

The stag figurine has been labelled "Celtic" and it has been suggested that it was a pre-existing heirloom object which was attached to the iron ring at some unspecified period before entering the ship burial. The latter proposition is interesting but unprovable in the light of present knowledge; the metal appears to be in the range of standard Anglo-Saxon bronze alloys and is generally unremarkable. The "Celtic" label has proved to be unhelpful, since there is no clear and usable definition of what this word means in relation to post-Roman metalwork in England. Popular ideas about "Celtic art" often incorporate Hallstatt and La Tène elements with others from Anglo-Saxon stone sculpture and manuscript illustration, which cover more than a thousand years of history and clearly do not all belong to a single culture.

Figure 2 The cast bronze stag and the iron ring

The Iron Ring

The making of the iron ring draws on Bruce-Mitford's report but possibly deviates in one important detail: The report indicates that the ring is penannular and formed from plaited square-section rods, but the reproduction uses round-section ones instead.[2] Notably, the British Museum's own reproduction is similarly constructed. It was decided to follow the British Museum's lead on this aspect of the design, since square-section rods or wire would be technically difficult to achieve and even harder to bundle neatly into the configuration needed to produce the herringbone effect on the ring. Importantly, visual examination cannot determine whether the rods were square- or round-section.

The 'ring' is actual penannular, as shown in the report's figure 276. This feature was incorporated into the reproduction. The two ends come close to completing the circle, and are encased in the supporting mount.

The ring is provided with fluted clips which serve to break up the herringbone pattern. On the reproduction, these are made from swaged strips similar to elements elsewhere on the whetstone, soldered in place. The method of attachment on the original is not specified in the report. The swaged strips are formed by pulling flat-section strips through a shaped slot in a swaging block so that they take on the contours of the aperture.

The Upper Cage and Mount

The upper cage is not made with a cast cage of carinated bars, as found on the lower bulb, but with a complex arrangement of eight vertical swaged strips which were placed over the channels in the stone bulb. The strips used vary in the number of flutes, and appear to have replaced the original fittings; as the channels cut for this replicate those on the other bulb, it is likely that the original intention was to include a second cast copper-alloy cage at the upper end. It is possible that the casting difficulties encountered with production of the lower cage dissuaded the metalworker from pursuing this plan, but the fact that he produced a successful casting for one end demonstrates that he was able to overcome the challenge.

---

[2] Bruce-Mitford does not state that the iron ring was made from square section rods, which is the opinion of Hughes, Oddy and Werner in the scientific report (Vol.2, p. 387). However Mr Roper, who has looked very carefully, is not convinced and maintains that the rod was round in section.

Perhaps more likely is the suggestion that the cage became damaged at some point and either the original craftsman was no longer available to create a new cage, or perhaps the high failure rate for the castings showed that a better solution had to be found. In any event, the cage was replaced by a simpler but durable substitute made from the swaged-strip which was already in production for items such as the Mound 1 helmet. The strips were probably soldered onto each other around the bulb.

Figure 3 The stag figurine, iron ring and fitting, washer (inside ring), mount and swaged strip cage before attachment

Study and interpretation of the images in vol.2 (fig.241) indicates that there is a rusty stain on the upper end of the stone bar, on the small discoid pad which forms its top. Bruce-Mitford suggested that this stain resulted from rusting of the iron bar, and trickling of the rust slurry through the hollow centre of the junction to form a puddle on the stone bar. But examination of the photo (vol.2 fig.256) shows that the rust is confined to this one area – it has not run down the sides of the pad onto the bulb of the bar – and there is a small rust-free area within. It seems that the formation of the rust has prevented oxidation of the surrounding bronze. This indicates that the iron stain results from a small iron washer placed above the stone pad, on the underside of the top mount (vol.2 fig.275a). Nor is it certain that the junction is actually cast hollow. These facts in combination strongly suggest that there was an iron washer on the underside of the mount, and this washer accepted a peg or pivot on the lower end of the ring-assembly. The washer may have allowed the ring to turn in the vertical plane, which may be significant.

Figure 4 The lower cage and the foot

Figure 5 The lower cage seen from above and showing the carinated section of the claw's legs

The Lower Cage and Foot

The production and fitting of the lower cage presented a number of technical challenges. These were overcome in ways which were available to the Anglo-Saxon craftsmen who produced the original although we cannot be sure that the solutions we found were those the Anglo-Saxons used.

The lower cage comprises six carinated legs which enclose the lower bulb of the stone bar, resting on a dished mount. The cage posed a challenge in terms of casting. As mentioned above, it is essential when making a complex casting in a one-piece mould, to ensure that the molten metal can reach the extremities while still in a liquid state. With a single feeding point, it proved very difficult to produce an even flow of metal throughout: it cooled too quickly and failed to reach the outer ends of the mould, or became very porous by the time it did so. Multiple feedings points would have solved the problem, pouring metal from more than one source into the mould, but this technology is not known to have been available to the Anglo-Saxons. The solution used was to position a large ball of wax within the cage formed by the legs and to run feeders from this to the inward faces of the legs. Once the wax model was converted to a mould, the large central void quickly filled with molten metal which then continued to run out into the leg elements. This technology is only an enhancement of the single feeder, lost-wax method and could certainly have been invented as a practical solution to the problem by a competent craftsman of the time.

Assembly

The assembly of the metal fittings can only have taken place after completion of the stone bar: it would not be practical to continue working the stone once the metalwork was in place (but see below for one important modification). The various elements were created separately and soldered into place directly on the stone bar. The solder and heat source must have been applied very precisely in order to avoid damage to the stone.

It is possible – even probable – that a small jet of flame was directed using a narrow pipe in the metalworker's mouth, a technique still used today in some traditional jewellery workshops. Fine pipes were certainly available to the Anglo-Saxons, as the find of a fleam (venesection pipe) has been made at Flixborough, Lincolnshire.

The legs of the cage(s) were opened gently in order to fit over the stone bulb, then closed into the channels around the stone. The cages were already assembled with the foot at the lower end, ring (and perhaps the stag) at the upper end.

Figure 6 The stag and iron ring mounted onto the swage strip cage prior to assembly.

Conclusions

The technical challenges of the reproduction were considerable but the completed object is, as far as is known, entirely consistent with the evidence presented by the original. Some small deviations from the information in Bruce-Mitford's report were necessitated, and it is likely that further investigation will show that these deviations are in fact consistent with the artefact. It was a rewarding project and I am very pleased to have completed it without recourse to technologies which the Anglo-Saxons could not have used.

2. The Sutton Hoo Whetstone-Sceptre Project: Stone Sculpture by Direct Carving

Brian Ansell

(Photographs and illustrations in this chapter supplied by Brian Ansell)

Introduction

Stone carving by its fundamental nature possesses a property that makes it unique among the products of the mind and hand of man. Nothing survives having such comparable command of vivid and intimate communication of ideologies from long-past civilisations, and in a real sense it represents one of the least blurred voices from the past and the only one from societies of remote antiquity. Legends, myths and folklore are probably those things which most nearly approach stone sculpture in this respect, but it is easy to understand how exposed they are to being corrupted in the purity of their record by constantly changing influences through the passing ages.

At the very beginning of the stone carving process it is worth noting that even the best quality iron tool used to carve stone is sometimes at the utmost limit of its capacity to work. This is particularly evident when a hard grit stone such as greywacké is the chosen material, as the mineral deposits from which the fine grit stone is created are considerably more durable than the iron itself. From a stone carving point of view I suspect the greywacké used to create the sceptre would rarely be used as a material for sculpture unless it was intended to give the utmost possible degree of durability at the cost of painstaking labour. In the case of this very hard stone, it is only by exploiting the tools' extraordinary toughness against the stone's superior hardness that carving can be achieved at all.

Considering this as an important principal in the creation of carved stone objects my initial thought regarding the 'whetstone sceptre' was: why go to the extremes of carving this particular piece of elaborate sculpture from this kind of material when other durable stones commonly used for centuries were very well known? As a material, a practical purpose it certainly has and in all probability that was a significant element taken into account at its conception and possibly part of its intended function. These thoughts, together with preliminary study and exploratory tool-work soon revealed that if the stone used to create this meticulously crafted object had been even fractionally less dense, the complex proportions and geometric symmetry of the stone bar together with the small sculptured naturalistic human faces would have been virtually impossible to achieve.

Following a lengthy search for the elusive fine-grained stone, the first stage of the reconstruction began when a pallet was delivered to the National Trust's offices at Westley Bottom, near Bury St Edmunds in early November 2008 carrying a small slab of randomly quarried greywacké. The stone, approximately seven inches thick, thirteen inches deep, and thirty-three inches long was generously supplied by the TARMAC Company and quarried from their Arcow site just north of Settle, in North Yorkshire.

The first consideration, and before any work, was to establish the suitability of the stone, its colour and texture by 'pitching' off a small piece to compare with the original Sutton Hoo sceptre at the British Museum. Following this, we were pleased to learn that after careful inspection and further examination by experts the sample was considered to be very acceptable and as close to the original stone as possible. Having gained approval to proceed, it was then necessary to establish whether the greywacké slab was sound and free from defects whether natural or created by the quarrying process. In order to establish this, it was essential to remove a thin slice, a cleaner, from the surface of the slab enabling a visual inspection to establish the stone's consistency and to mark any 'vents', 'shakes' or other faults as their direction and depth could seriously affect any further work. The greywacké slab was collected from Westley Bottom in early December by stonecutting specialists and taken to their workshops at Abbey Masonry at nearby Glemsford. In their industrial saw sheds cleaners were cut from the face and bed of the stone using a large circular diamond-tipped blade with jets of pressurised water as a coolant. After a great deal of effort to cut the greywacké, the cleaners revealed sound material within a few inches of the rough quarried edges. The size and direction of the larger faults were clearly visible, and the finer ones, because they hold water for longer than the surrounding drying surface, could be easily seen and their position accurately marked.

It is worth mentioning here that stone traditionally quarried using hand tools rarely required cleaning, only squaring-off for use. But as modern industrial-scale quarrying depends on the use of heavy machinery and sometimes blasting with explosives, large enough pieces of flawless stone suitable for carving can be almost impossible to find.

Figure 7 Looking across the width and to the right hand side of the stone after sawing off the cleaner clearly showing the size and direction of a deep 'shake' travelling across and into the slab at ten to twenty degrees towards the centre of the slabs thickness. The shakes showed no visible signs of crystallisation commonly found in ancient faults or calcification caused by percolating water over many centuries, indicating that these faults occurred relatively recently and probably as a result of commercial quarrying. To make absolutely sure the stone bars were free from the minutest of faults they were left outside exposed to the elements of winter (08/09) as a period of damp and frost will certainly expose any weaknesses in the rock.

Figure 8 Masons' Hammer and Pitching Tool

Figure 9 Coping Tool

To keep the project as authentic and as near to its traditional beginnings as possible, the mechanically-produced face and edge of the stone bar were removed by a stone splitting technique called 'coping'. The coping tool, used in this case with a two-pound masons' hammer, is similar in appearance to a large chisel but much heavier in the body; it is forged single-edged and used for splitting stone to its required size.

An ancient technique called 'boning' is still used for achieving the initial flat plane from which all other surfaces are created. The process begins by creating a relatively even surfaces across the ends of a split, rough, or irregular stone. Once that has been done, the boning rods are set into position and checked by eye to estimate any discrepancies. The stone immedietly beneath the 'boning rods' is then levelled down by chiselling away the stone until the rods are aligned absolutely true with one another. Once level, the rough stone between them can be taken off, first by drafting the long edges between the boned ends, then taking off the remaining stone from the middle leaving a flat tooled surface. On large areas, diagonal or cross-drafts are cut to establish the required surface, which often leaves this stage of the work with a zigzag or herring-bone effect.

Figure 10 Boning rods

Figure 11 The Point

Traditional boning rods are made from hardwood with a square section proportional to their length for accuracy. If the uneven surface between the rods interferes with the 'sighting', cubes of uniform size made from wood or bone are positioned on the cut-away surfaces to raise the rods for visual alignment. Similar devices used in carpentry are called 'winding strips'.

The resulting pitched or coped surface can vary - depending on the type or texture of stone, its natural bedding and consistency - from an almost flat surface to unevenly rough. To remove this roughness and create a more even surface (the first stage of roughing-out) it is necessary to use a tool called a point. I belong to that long-standing school of traditional stone sculptors which believes that as much of the roughing-out work as possible should be done with the point, heavy or light, and consider it to be in most cases the mason's or sculptor's main tool.

The tool itself resembles a heavy iron pencil with a drawn-out point forming a narrow cutting edge of about a quarter of an inch wide, and is usually driven with a short-handled masons' hammer weighing anything from two to six pounds; a mallet can be used on softer stones. The technique of working with the point is to hold it with the cutting edge firmly on the face of the stone and the blow struck. The general principle here is that the point is driven in just under the stone's surface and cracks a piece off. Very importantly, the angle to the stone at which the tool is held is decisive and the correct one is only learned by experience: too shallow and the tool will skid on the surface doing no work; too steep the tool will 'draw' or dig in with a strong possibility of damaging the tool, the stone or both. The best cutting angle varies for working different kinds of stone but as a general guide it is usually between forty to sixty degrees to the surface. The more acute angle of forty to fifty degrees is a useful guide for limestones and sandstones, while the slightly steeper or more obtuse angle of around fifty to sixty degrees is needed for very hard or dense stones such as granite and greywacké.

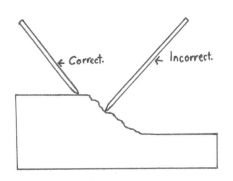

In general, projections, angles, edges, etc. are the difficult surfaces to work, and when carving this principle must be exploited to the maximum. For instance, it follows that the middle parts of flat surfaces or hollows are the areas where the most resistance will be encountered and difficulties can increase in working down if the surfaces become too smooth while there is still a lot of stone to get off.

Figure 12
The correct and incorrect angles for driving the point

An essential procedure when working with the point is never to drive it at an up-hill slope because the stone being removed is all the time buttressed by the main bulk of the stone being worked and will not come off easily causing the tool to draw 'dig' into the stone. It is much more productive to work the other way round - cut at the falling-away slope - as there is little resistance and the stone comes off easily

After the point the next tool to be used is the claw, (second stage of roughing-out). The claw tool resembles a chisel but has a serrated edge and can be used with the hammer or mallet. Its main purpose is to take off the rough surface left by the point to leave the work as close to the final shape as possible. A wide claw is invaluable when it comes to producing a flat surface on large areas of stone and its marks are clearly seen on historic buildings and ancient stonework. The narrower ones are indispensable when rough shaping is necessary as they are able to follow contours in every conceivable direction.

Figure 13
The Claw Tool

The final tooled surface is created by the chisel. Chisels are known by the width of their blade and are usually measured in multiples of one eighth of an inch (3mm) to one inch (25mm), then in steps of one quarter of an inch (6mm) to two inches (50mm). At two inches and above the chisel is known as a 'boaster' and can be up to six inches (150mm) wide. The chisel is generally used with a mallet, resulting in the removal of all previous tool marks.

The action of working with the point, claw and chisel is all basically same. The difference is that, of this range of tools, the point is the one that is held at the steepest angle to the surface of the stone, and the chisel is held at the least steep angle, but careful observation will show little difference between the two. I must emphasise that the universal rule in stone carving is that the stone carver always hammer-drives the tools, never pushes them at the stone. This is a characteristic difference from woodcarving in which chisels are sometimes pushed at the work.

Hammers used by masons and stone carvers are generally heavier in the head than those used by carpenters or engineers and proportionally shorter in the handle; they are also customarily gripped much nearer the to the head than the latter. A distinguishing feature of the traditional masons' hammer is that increased weight is not added by enlarging the overall bulk of its head, as with a general purpose lump hammer, as this would prove too cumbersome and unwieldy for finely controlled work. Instead, the extra weight is applied by elongating the head while roughly keeping the same square section, preventing any loss of force or balance whilst true-hitting the tools.

Regarding the hammer-blow, or more precisely 'drop', for roughing-out or removing any unwanted uneven surfaces one or two blows are applied without repositioning the tip of the tool. Although this is a matter of individual habit, from rough work to more fragile or hard stone the rhythm of work is *tap-tap, pause, tap-tap, pause*. For the finer, more delicate work or creating a surface where relatively less stone is removed and the rhythm, *tap-pause, tap-pause*, ensures the stone is efficiently removed by systematically taking off lots of small pieces. The 'pause' in this description is dual purpose in that it allows for the constant adjustment of the tool's angle dictated by the material and inhibits a build-up of dust at the cutting edge as even a tiny amount can reduce the effectiveness of subsequent blows of the hammer. Any, or a combination, of these working rhythms is commonly heard coming from masons' and stone carving workshops.

As a natural result of many years of continuous practice the mason or stonecarver develops to a state of not being consciously aware of having hands or hitting the tool with the hammer. It is an ability to concentrate and direct all attention exclusively on the tip of the tool, the surface of the stone and its behaviour at the point of impact. It is a necessary preliminary mastery that has to be acquired, together with the ability to continually vary the angle of the tool while all the time true-hitting the butt with the hammer automatically without having to give any attention to it. This proficiency must be acquired through many years of practice in order to be able to adjust the angle of the tool to the differing cutting angles called for by the surface of the stone.

For this particular authentic reconstruction the same timeless process was used throughout to create a rough stone bar approximately twenty four inches (61 cm) long by two and a half inches (6.4 cm) square. The rough bar was then tooled to further square the face, bed, and ends, followed by removing the tooled surface by rubbing it down with a piece of medium-grained millstone grit (Stancliffe) with water as a lubricant to just larger than the actual size of the original whetstone-sceptre stone bar. The resulting surfaces are left flat, square and smooth enough for setting-out of the first stages of masonry.

Regardless of previous experience, a time-served mason or stone carver will experiment by varying the angle of the tool on any new type of stone to establish an efficient method of working. Although stone carving tools may appear very simple or even crude, their size and relative proportions are themselves the outcome of ages of experiment and experience. This basic approach to stone carving, regardless of the different types of tools used throughout history or the abilities of the highly skilled smiths that made them, had until recently remained unchanged for millennia. Some evidence for this comes from studying the tool marks on, perhaps a Greek sculpture from the fifth century BC, or on an Egyptian carving several thousand years old and realising that these ancient tool marks are the same as the ones made in the workshop only yesterday. This is how the routine of the stone carver's life is made up, centred as it must be on the idea of progress towards better work that cannot but involve much study of antique sculpture. It is apparent that proceeding backwards to an improved understanding of some ancient carver's qualities may in fact be quite progressive.

It has been considered many times over recent decades that the working of stone by hand, except for the more complex designs, could be easily superseded by machinery, and now with the ever-increasing use of computer-controlled saws and profiling machines it is still being said, but the traditionally trained skilled banker masons remain the essential heart of the trade. For example, for restoration work where many one-off pieces of complex stonework are required there is very often no substitute. Working by hand is a necessary part of understanding the abilities of the stone itself.

At first view it seems impossible to work stone accurately using a hammer and chisel but the ability to do so is the hallmark of a skilled mason.

The Commission

Before any work begins, it is essential to discuss all relevant aspects of the proposed design to the smallest detail with clients or commissioners. This often lengthy procedure is absolutely necessary and extremely important as every stage, feature and aspect of the proposed project has to be carefully studied, fully discussed and agreed before commencement because any alterations or changes after work has begun will seriously jeopardise the outcome of the project with a strong possibility of it being reviewed, delayed, or even rejected altogether causing the whole process to be repeated.

In the case of the Sutton Hoo whetstone-sceptre project the commission was based on a long standing idea of the Sutton Hoo Society. The aim was to get skilled craftsmen who worked with traditional tools and materials to bring their experience and knowledge to the task of shedding new light on particular artefacts from the Mound One Ship Burial.

Following an interesting conversation with Angus Wainwright, an eminent archaeologist at the National Trust, I was delighted to be invited to engage in a project to recreate one of the most unusual objects ever discovered from the Anglo-Saxon period. Originally created from a very fine-grained millstone grit called 'greywacké', the unique and extraordinary whetstone *sceptre* is certainly one of the most unusual pieces of sophisticated high-quality stone carving I have come across in my forty-year career as a stonemason and sculptor, and of course it was an immense pleasure to accept.

To gain preliminary insights into the stone bar and its design it was essential to read and research as much about the object as possible. The aim was to become familiar with its material, size, weight and design and then to make a working drawing that could be easily modified as the design was refined. Information relating to the overall dimensions of the stone bar and its initial form were gathered from the finely detailed illustrations contained in the comprehensive British Museum report.[3] The scaled measurements where converted to an actual size full-size drawing. To this drawing were added some of the basic elements of the design so as to create a simple lay-out leading directly to the actual working plan that would be used for masonry purposes.

The Design

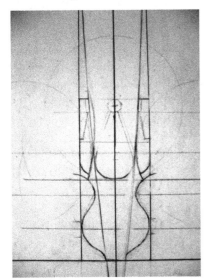

At the beginning of any authentic and pure reconstruction it is sometimes necessary to research tools, equipment or devices that would have been used by the original maker. In the case of stone sculpture the tools are not only well documented but, because of their simple efficiency, they have been in continuous use for centuries and have remained unchanged and unsurpassed.

The setting-out equipment used to form the working drawing for the sceptre reconstruction consisted of a gauge or measure, a straight-edge, a square and compasses. The gauge or measure used here is a twenty four inch rule to measure the work and establish proportions; the straight-edge in this case is thirty inches (76cm) long and is used to check and adjust the flat surfaces of the bar's length and to mark centre lines and edges for squaring off; the square is to make sure all surfaces and ends of the bar meet at a constant ninety degrees to one another, it is immensely important in three dimensional work that the geometry on all faces of the stone meet at the same point on all surfaces.

Figure 14 Working drawing of the bottom end of the stone bar

---

[3] Bruce-Mitford, 1978, p. 310-93

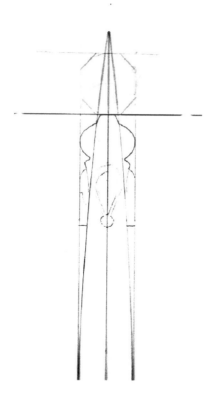

Figure 15 (left)
Working layout of the top end profile of the bar.

Figure 16 (below) Elements of the layout transferred to the stone bar. To the right of the stone bar lies the hardboard template used to mark out the curve of the central section 'body' of the design. The segment used to create this is taken from the circumference of a circle of sixteen feet four inches in diameter.

The compasses are without doubt one of the most important and an integral parts of a mason's tool kit, and have been throughout history. Technically an instrument, the compasses are used for setting-out and establishing the detailed geometry required for forming plans and layouts as well as marking out the actual work whether to scale or full size.

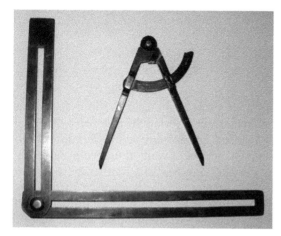

Figure 17 Compass and set-square

Compasses used in practical stonemasonry are made in many sizes and those found in general masons' workshops have legs from nine to thirty six inches (225 to 930mm). For larger circles, an instrument called a bar compass is used by separating the centre and marking points along the length of the rod. The bar is traditionally made from metal or wood and its points are fastened by screws or wedges to set the diameter. It is generally used for setting-out a segment of the circumference needed for architectural work, for example an arch layout or to establish a wide subtle curve.

The Layout

The layout for the whetstone sceptre began by centring a sheet of A3 white card (Fig 19); to this two parallel lines were added, one above and one below the horizontal centre line to set out the exact width of the bar. From the vertical centre line, the length was marked and the ends squared to create the actual overall size of the working plan. It is worth noting the importance of centring because in masonry it is the centre from which all other work is formed, from the initial drawing to the finished work. By marking-out and establishing the design outwards from the centre any adjustments to un-square surfaces, twists, etc are made in the initial stages of the masonry process because they will always be to the outside of the work.

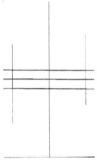
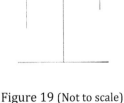

Figure 19 (Not to scale)

Figure 18
The square end with circumferences marked out.
Note that the top surface lies outside the
circumference of the projected circle.

The same method applies to the ends of the bar; they are centred in a similar way to establish a centre point for setting out the circular ends.

This photograph of the actual setting-out shows a slight discrepancy over the length of the stone bar indicated by the circle touching three sides at this end. The opposite end of the bar is perfectly square, but an error during the rubbing down process has caused this face to slope upwards creating a slightly out-of-square surface. This perfectly illustrates the importance of working from the centre lines as the misshaped end is easily corrected at the beginning of the process. If the difference occurred with the surface intruding into any part of the circle no adjustment could be made to correct an undersize section and the entire process so far would have to be repeated.

Templates

Practical stonemasonry is based on the guidance of templates; their shape is cut from a rigid material that embodies the profile of the stone to be worked. They can be made from a variety of materials, with zinc plate most commonly used in masons' workshops as the soft metal is rustproof and suffers little from repeated use. It is however not uncommon for occasional or one-off pieces of work to use templates made from plywood, hardboard, or even thick paper card particularly as they can be easily transferred to a more durable material if required. To set out the curved body of the sceptre, I used a template made from hardboard, not just because it was more convenient to construct but the material from which the hardboard is made remains reasonably stable in workshop conditions. The accuracy of the template would also be unaffected by it being used only eight times, twice on each of the four surfaces and marked with a pencil causing no wear to the marking edge. The arc of the main body of the sceptre is a segment of a circle with a diameter of sixteen feet four inches; the circle was set out by using a set of bar compasses set to a radius of eight feet, two inches.

The complexity of the design at the ends of the sceptre involved a different approach from the methods used to set out the masonry of the main body of the bar. As work progresses at the domed ends all flat surfaces are systematically removed, leaving nothing on which to accurately place an internal template for the more intricate work. To overcome this, external or reverse templates are made called 'try-gauges'; these are taken from the outside of the plan and are offered-up to verify the accuracy of the inner depressions and hollows of the design from the remaining outermost surfaces from the outer circular ends to the centre of the bar. These particular gauges were initially constructed from stiff card, firstly to ensure no damage or marking would occur when physically offering them up to the original sceptre, and secondly because any adjustments could easily be pencilled onto the card and cut for refitting. As a result of this fine-tuning, the adjusted try-gauges were now accurate and applied to the working plan for the actual reconstruction work.

Traditionally, templates were made from thinly sawn, well seasoned hardwood; although this proved very durable as a working material it was susceptible to wear and tear with frequent use, resulting in the need to constantly check the template against the working drawing or layout for signs of wear, damage or distortion of any kind. If cleaning or adjustment of the material was not possible it was not uncommon for a failed template to be put aside for replacing another useful profile.

There is an important principle involved when it comes to the placing of templates on any three-dimensional stonework that requires absolute precision. The template taken from the plan is positioned face up, effectively transferring the shape to be worked the to the upper surface of the stone, aligned with the necessary reference points - in the case of the sceptre this is where the curve terminates at the ends of the bar - and its position marked. This is then repeated on the reverse side, but this time the template is placed face down, in a sense sandwiching the stone between the face-up templates. This method ensures the marked-on shape exactly matches both the opposing sides. This practice ensures the opposite sides, especially at the beginning of work, are consistent and create a perfect section and a flat surface on which to further accurately mark on the design.

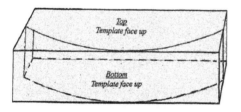

Figure 20 Illustration of how templates are placed. (Not to scale)

Templates are usually kept with other documents relating to the project records: together they are part of the accurate and detailed account of the actual work, and it is then possible to reconstruct anything from the entire work or any part of it if needed at a later date.

Try-gauges

An example of a reverse template or try-gauge (fig.15). The white card bottom section of the illustration is taken from the outside of the plan, keeping to the original surface indicated by the line representing the stone bar. This clearly indicates the outer points of the design while preserving the width of the bar. The white card try-gauge was applied to check the intricate profiles of the original sceptre and to adjust my initial working plan accordingly during the first visit to the British Museum on the 7th April 2009.

Particular attention has to be given to profiles formed using semi-rigid card templates: because of the slight suppleness of the material it is susceptible to distortion during use and therefore has to be constantly checked for accuracy. For example, the necks or hollows of the domed ends form perfect circles at their innermost sections and have to be continually checked with a trammel, depth gauge and bevel compasses, and for double checking it is necessary to use reverse gauges for all sectional interior diameters.

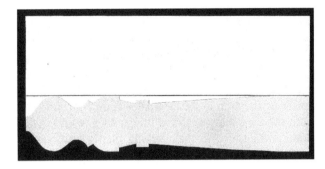

Figure 21 This white card exterior template was used to establish the initial profile of the south or bottom end of the original sceptre.

Figure 22 The actual card try-gauge used to establish the profile of the top or north end of the sceptre.

Bevel compasses are essential for marking out or checking internal diameters that are difficult to access such as the circular hollows and rounded depressions at the base of the finials.

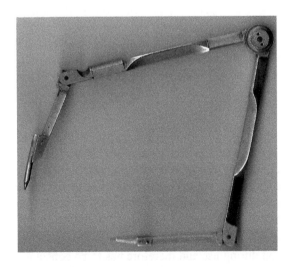

The compass point is placed in the centres of the ends of the bar and the compasses set, a circle is then marked at the required position without being hindered in any way by projections or mouldings.

Figure23 Bevel Compasses

Tool Kit Used to Create the Whetstone Bar

Figure 24 Mason's hammer, Carving hammer, Bronze dummy, Pitching tools, Tooling chisel, Point, Claw, Chisels, Trammel, Boning rods, and Square.

"The tools of the Saxon carvers seem to have differed little from the standard tools in the Roman period, some of which are still in use today (Hodges 1964, fig.22): walling hammers and picks; blunt and sharp points; punches; straight-edges and compasses; wide and narrow-bladed chisels. Parts of the stones surface which were not meant to be visible were 'tooled' dressed with rough, diagonal, scored lines. The more smoothly dressed parts were marked off by a fine point, as were the laying-out lines for ornament. The surface of the stone was further finished by the use of the fine chisel and could be smoothed down to an almost polished surface."

From the General Introduction to *The Corpus of Anglo-Saxon Stone Sculpture. Chapter III, Techniques of Carving* by Rosemary Cramp.

Figure 25 Portrait of the Artist as a Young Man

The Masonry Process

Figure 26 Surface before working

Figure 27 Surface worked on one face

Figure 28 Surface after working

Coping

After creating an initial surface the stone is effectively split to the required size as the coping tool cuts more accurately on a flat surface because its entire edge directs the downward force of the hammer into the stone. After coping, the sides are marked and squared off using a point and chisel.

Examples of tooled and coped surfaces

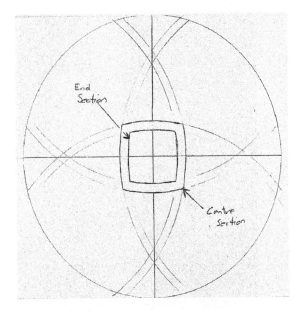

Figure 29 Cross section of central bar.

This diagram was based on actual dimensions taken from the original sceptre; the 'round shouldered' cross section of the body of the bar shows the difference from the middle to the ends. The outermost surfaces are the overall square of the bar.

Masonry

Stone masonry is the methodical process of removing all surplus material from a quarried stone to create a three-dimensional form. It begins by chiselling shallow cuts to the waste side of marked lines, a practice called 'hard lining'. The cut is made by hammer-driving a fine chisel along the surface while guiding it at a slight angle towards the area to be wasted. A general rule is that a cut is made from the edge to about two thirds of the way across a section, then worked in from the other side to meet it; if cut right through there is a real chance of damage because the chisel finds no resistance at the point of exit and will push a larger piece off than intended. Hard lines are repeated on all intersecting marked areas to establish the initial shape of the object; it is then possible to safely remove all unwanted stone between them as the fine cuts double as a safety feature in that they prevent any splintering of the stone during its removal from travelling into the flat surfaces required for further work.

Figure 30 By gently chipping away, the stone is removed to create an intersection called a 'fillet'; this divides the curved surface from the raised area for the more complex work.

Figure 31 The surface prepared and the design marked out.

Close examination of the tool marks created during the various stages of work on this project can be clearly seen on stone sculpture from remote history, giving a valuable insight into similar techniques, methods, and abilities of bygone craftsman.

The gentle curve of the bar's central body is worked inwards towards the centre then repeated from the opposite direction. Working in from opposite ends on the same piece of stone can often reveal subtle and distinct changes in its composition, leading to slight variations in the tool work: this is not unusual and causes no difficulty to the experienced mason as it is just a simple matter of adjusting the angle of the tool until it cuts efficiently.

The way in which most surplus stone is removed is by a process called 'drafting'; it begins by studying the working plan to calculate the largest area of material to be effectively removed leaving a flat surface for marking out further work. This procedure allows for at least two outermost points of the design to be picked up on any straight line and is repeated many times in order to remove as much of the surplus stone as possible.

Figure 32 The radius of the knob marked out on the end of the bar.

Figure 33
Work begins, carefully removing the excess

Figure 34 The quarter circle of the kob is
roughed out and the chamfer below is begun

Figure 35 South or Bottom Finial of the Bar

For reference and subsequent working from the plan, as many as possible of the outer areas of the original surface of the bar are left on as they are necessary to constantly check interior angles and to gauge depths and hollows, especially when working in the round, but most importantly to assist the use of try-gauges or reverse templates as without reference to the surface the setting-out process would inevitably wander with a loss of perspective that would be virtually impossible to retrieve.

When the first curved face of the bar is established, work can begin on the circular ends. This part of the process begins by taking off a chamfer just outside the circle and always working in towards the main bulk of the stone bar; this is repeated on all corners removing as much stone as possible.

It is very important that all marked out surfaces and reference points are clearly visible throughout the entire roughing-out process, as parts of the drawn layout are easily removed by constant handling and brushing off dust created by the work.

The method of creating the cylindrical ends is by cutting away ever diminishing chamfers until most of the material to the outside of the circular area has been removed. This stage shows the surfaces of three chamfers relieving the first quarter of the circle, the remains of the first one is now the centre draft.

The raised square section of stone between the round end and the curved surface of the bar is the section that will eventually allow the more intricate work: carved features in stonework begin once the masonry is established.

The final chamfers are removed to establish a circular section and it is on this new surface the next sequence of draft lines are marked with a trammel from the end of the bar showing the extent of the next area to be removed.

The stone to be removed in this section is cut diagonally from the trammelled line to the outer edge of the inner circle at the end of the bar to create a round chamfer.

Figure 36 An angle of ninety degrees created by cutting the section in square drafts.

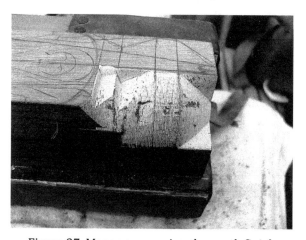

Figure 37 Masonry exposing the south finial

Figure 38 The rounding of the roughed out knob is almost complete (top) versus the facetted surface which were used to construct it (below).

The finial at the top of the bar differs from the one at the bottom in that the domed end is compressed comparatively by almost a third, effectively creating a 'torus' profile and terminating with a short tapering projection - unlike the bottom which flows continuously inwards from the end of the bar to the intersection of the hoods forming a sweeping 'ogee', or cyma profile. To create the top projection the height and diameter were marked onto the end of the bar and, when cut away, the intersection creates the springing point from which the dome below and the projection above can now be worked.

Once the chamfer is cut away towards the top the same sequence is repeated on the inward section effectively removing as much of the waste as possible while leaving a flat section of the surface between the falling away drafts. The centre of this flat surface will become the outer edge of the finial with the diameter of its square section. The diagonal draft lines can be seen marked on the bar from the setting-out (Figure 36) and begin to give an impression of the actual masonry process.

The quadrant section here (Figure 37) has been deliberately worked to explain the process described so far visually; this information would in all cases be lost because draft sections are cut through the entire work.

The same section (Figure 38) showing drafts cut with the existing layout still clearly visible on all three surfaces and from these the first stage of the actual design can begin with very little stone to take off. The fine tooling of the ogee profile of the bottom finial is created by constantly testing the shape with the try-gauge as work progresses, and is at this stage left slightly over-cut in the hollows to allow for any adjustments as work progresses.

Figure 39 Side view showing the layout markings.

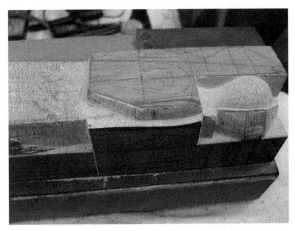

Figure 40 Work has begun on the shoulder.

Figure 41 A finely cut draft establishing the uppermost edge and surface of the hood and the exterior edge of the face within.

It appears here that the worked profile is now slightly undersize which is due to the stone bar being slightly oversize: a marked-out design by its very nature is always a little larger than the actual work because the pencil or scribe makes its line to the outside of templates. Time-served masons are taught at the beginning of their training that the exact form of the work is only achieved by working the line off, enabling consistency and ensuring a perfect fit with other sequential pieces

The upper and lower square sections of the bar are deliberately left to allow a flat surface from which to establish the depth of hollows and to check the evolving shapes with the try-gauges. Having worked the finial profile, it is now possible to move towards the adjoining square section of the bar, the first draft to join the formed end with the square bar is evenly cut along the corner of the box section.

The projection left in the hollow would normally be cut away as the drafts would meet at this point, leaving two intersecting flat surfaces; instead, it is left to show how it is gauged to the actual depth to the centre of the hollow.

With the initial intersecting draft dividing the adjoining sides it becomes possible to see the effect of the newly revealed surfaces. At this stage it is possible to extend the curve of the bar's main body as far as the intersection of the medallions.

Still slightly oversize, the raised edges created by cutting away the curved surface (Figure 41) produce the raised vertical edge on which the more detailed work can be marked.

Further separation of the 'main body' surfaces is established by repeating the work on the adjoining surface allowing the form of the bar to develop by following the layout lines marked out at the beginning of the process. The edges of the hooded shapes can now be revealed by marking the height of their position on the raised edges dividing the upper and lower surfaces and again cutting drafts to establish their form.

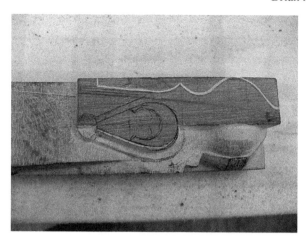

Figure 42 The profile of the hood, shoulder and knob begins to emerge

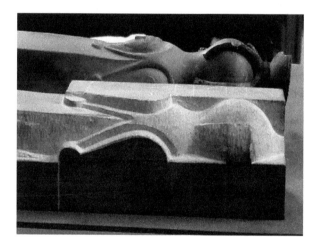

Figure 43 The intersection of the square bar with the bottom finial of the reconstruction compared with the same end of the original sceptre during the first visit to the British Museum study room on the 7th April 2009. The comparison revealed slight differences

A plan view of stone bar showing the work so far which demonstrates the importance of removing the stone methodically as one surface begins to blend seamlessly into another. Essentially, without this method of working, it would be virtually impossible to achieve a precise three-dimensional feature working in from the exterior. Although all work so far is still strictly speaking, traditional craft masonry, it becomes easier to understand as work progresses how these skills with the correct aptitude can sometimes lead to a mason becoming accomplished in the art of stone sculpture.

Even though the stonework is progressing and elements of the design are being revealed, it is now vital to compare the work so far with the original sceptre - this will allow, because the stone bar is still slightly oversize, for any adjustments or fine-tuning.

The worked quadrant illustrates the necessity of thoroughly checking all aspects of the design in fine detail as an undetected mistake at this stage of the work could easily be repeated several times on the adjoining surfaces leading to the project being, at best, started again from the beginning if sufficient material allows or worse, abandoned altogether.

Close examination of the top finial revealed valuable additional information regarding the design at this end of the bar. For example the projection at the top of the domed finial minutely differs in size and proportion in some of the illustrations and photographs taken from previous official reports, possibly because of differing angles from which they are taken. This became evident when squaring-off the bar at this particular point, as the lines did not meet up exactly as the others did in the same section. To overcome these minute differences and for convenience at this stage the working plan was set out by creating an average section to incorporate the misaligned part; it could then be easily altered to match the actual sceptre.

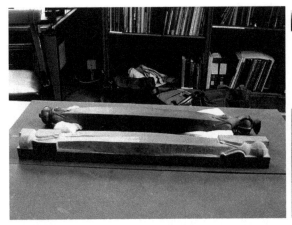 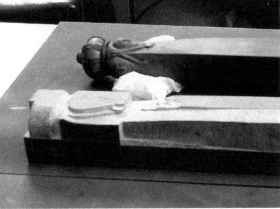

Figure 44 Comparing the newly formed sections of the reconstruction against the original stone sceptre at the British Museum study room

Figure 45 The profile of the average section shown here was subtly altered to match the original, then the information transferred to the working drawing

An invaluable visit, it was from this that the measurements were confirmed, the form established, templates, try-gauges and profiles adjusted to fine-tune the working plan that would be used to create the authentic reconstruction.

In any industry requiring the removal of material to create an artefact - and with stone sculpture in particular - it is worth mentioning the importance of documenting the various stages of extraordinary objects such as this, simply because all the evidence of its creation is lost in the process of making.

Figs 46 & 47 Looking down at the reconstructed top end of the 21st century stone bar (left) it is just possible to make out the centre circle struck at the beginning of the project. Its completed form clearly shows the method of its creation from the evidence left by the working tool marks. Compare this with the Anglo-Saxon original (right).

Figure 46 (left)
Top view
21st century

Fig 47 (right)
Top view
Anglo-Saxon

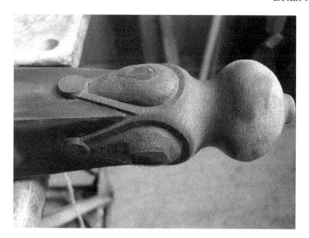

Figure 48 The intersection of the circular sections of the upper hoods meet the circle at the base of the finial. The domed triangle produced by this process flows seamlessly in three dimensions to create the spandrel in which the carved motifs will separate the upper edges of the hoods.

The upper finial is still slightly oversize to allow for the final rubbing down. The scribed centre line can still be clearly seen on the un-worked surface (Figure 49) and is left as a depth guide along with the outer part of the dome.

Figure 49 The finely tooled bottom finial of the bar showing its finished shape with the outer edges of the hood mouldings in their final position. A small flat area of the original surface indicates the original square outer section of the bar and has been essential to establish the complex intersecting forms and angles of the design.

The curved body of the bar is still square in section as it diminishes towards the carved ends.

The square section of the reconstruction is evident here set against the sceptre, the 'shoulder' round section of the original creates a subtle reverse curve as it falls away under the finials, a unique method of integrating the bar with the finials.

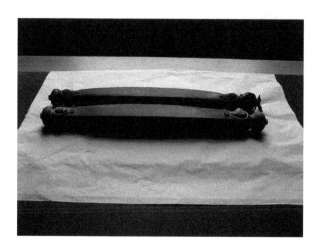

Figure 50   Comparing the reconstruction to the original whetstone sceptre in the Study Room at the British Museum on the 17th August 2009. This was the last opportunity to see the original before it was due to go back on display.The two bars are of exactly the same length and proportions, although the parallax distortion in this photograph makes them appear divergent.

The raised studs below the hood mouldings are still oversize at this stage and will be reduced as part of the carving process.

Carving

With the masonry process complete and the use of templates or gauges no longer required, it is now possible to direct attention to the fine-carvings and associated details at the ends of the bar. The now-raised areas within the medallions clearly show a small patch of the original flat surface at their centres and a part of this will remain as the outermost feature of the carving, picking up one of the five points along the centre of each surface maintaining the original outer size and proportions of the stone bar.

Carving three-dimensional forms in stone - whether abstract, animal, human, or any combination of these - requires decisive planning at the onset. At first view, all eight carved heads are portrayed as human and although they can be represented in a variety of shapes and styles depending on the fashion of the time or the inclination of their creator or commissioner, the faces on this particular object are naturalistically human. From a sculptural and artistic point of view the basic proportions of the human face have always been very well known and setting them out usually begins with the eye line which is always at the horizontal centre of the head.

Figure 51 The upper edge of the 'hood-moulding' marks the final stage of masonry dividing the carving from the finial.

Figure 52 The eye line is finely chiselled across the centre to establish its position. All eye lines on the sceptre faces are in the same position on their relative ends and square the bar on all sides.

Figure 53 (both pictures) The top showing the eye line in the same position on two faces of the stone and the relieved intersection of the hood moulding.

Once the position of the eyes is marked and cut, the feature that will become the nose is relieved by cutting away the stone either side to a depth just above the surface of the face. Towards the top of the picture (below) is one of the fine carving tools with a cutting edge approximately one eighth of an inch wide.

Above the cut of the eye line are light pencil marks showing the rough position of the brow. It is worth mentioning that methods used for direct carving are similar in approach to craft masonry in that most carvings of a similar nature on the same stone are worked simultaneously to similar stages. This allows for adjustments due to any discrepancies in style or form that occur during the carving process.

The roughed-out proportions of the bearded faces at the bottom of the stone bar showing the all-important vertical and horizontal centring; the nose is relieved with the cut continued to the underside of the brows. At this stage of the work the sculptural aspects begin to appear with extra depth created by cutting down as far as the bar's surface to the inside of the hood moulding leaving a raised frame.

Figure 54 (showing bottom of bar) At this stage, characteristics seem to appear but this is only the surface on which they will eventually be drawn.

The principal tools used to create the carved heads on the stone bar are a one pound (450g) carving hammer, a fine chisel, a quirk, small pastry brush and 9H pencil. The 'quirk' is a specialist tool used for masonry and carving. It resembles a standard chisel except the cutting edge slopes at about eighty degrees to a point on one side allowing accurate fillet or edge cutting with a perfect view of the work.

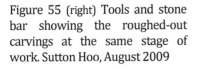

Figure 55 (right) Tools and stone bar showing the roughed-out carvings at the same stage of work. Sutton Hoo, August 2009

Figure 56 (below) The top of the stone bar showing the same stage of work as the bottom

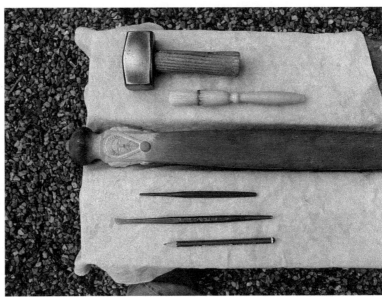

Here the upper edge of the hoods and the arcs of the spandrels form a perfect circle which descends into a groove to hold the bronzework.

This type of motif is a simple but effective device for decorating an otherwise plain space between one or two intersecting arcs or triangles. It is simply created by simple double-cutting with a chisel, the first cut carries the width of the hood mould to its natural termination points, with an opposing cut to a depth equal to its width at the top giving a natural 'V' section. This method of decoration has been commonly applied as a feature in this type of design throughout history and the resulting downward pointed emblem is a natural result of this process.

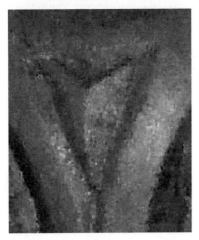

Fig. 57 Detail of the spandrel motif

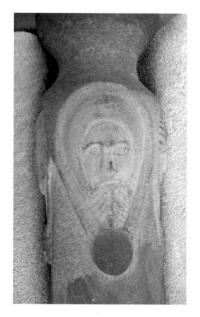

Figure 58 (left) With the final surface established, the position of the facial features can be marked on and cut, the eyes and top lip of the mouth create the basic character of the face with the naturalistically styled hair and beard cut as the last stage of the work.

The hood mouldings are finished roughly rounded from the roundels to the intersections, but the hood is cut as an internal chamfer meeting the tops of the heads and effectively separating them from the bar.

As this project was my introduction to working greywacké, trials of natural abrasives were necessary to discover a suitable material for creating the final smooth surface on the stone bar. This proved to be an interesting experience in that the most of the usual gritstones used to achieve a satisfactory finish on hard stones failed simply because the greywacké itself is a very hard and fine gritstone, and in some cases the greywacké actually smoothed the sandstone blocks used to rub its surface.

Eventually, and after much trial and error the fine finish was achieved by initially rubbing away the tool marks with a small two pound block of Stancliffe millstone grit used at the beginning of the process followed by a piece of greywacké for final finish. All fine rubbing on stone is assisted with splashes of clean water, which acts as a natural lubricant reducing friction but permitting a subtle grinding action between the two surfaces creating a fine abrasive slurry that readily cuts down the surface.

With sedimentary freestone there is no obvious bedding within the quarried slab, making it an ideal material for sculpture as it can be efficiently worked in every conceivable direction. The stone slab's even density is a result of the geological compression of sediments during its creation and, by exploiting the subtle difference between the smooth top and the slightly less smooth side, it is possible, by using a piece of the compressed edge of the stone, to create the fine abrasion required for finishing the whetstone-sceptre.

Although the methods and materials used to create the fine surface finish on the sceptre reconstruction are the result of trial and error, they are based on professional experience. This final procedure is the only part of the project that is speculative in that the materials used to finish the original sceptre, because of their diverse nature and location, will very probably remain unknown.

By the time the final surface on the sculpture has been achieved the visual evidence of previous marks of the making process will have been removed and the piece will have the same overall colour and texture.

Figure 59 The piece of greywacké slab edge used for the final finish.

Figure 60 The completed stone bar (sceptre) with the concentric 'V' cuts to facilitate the bronze clasp fittings on the finials, six at the bottom and eight at the top.

3. The Geometry of the Stone, Ring and Stag
Brian Ansell and Paul Mortimer

Once the replica had been made its dimensions were checked against the original at in the British Museum. The process of remaking revealed some possible errors in the published report by Bruce-Mitford so all the measurements of the original were re-considered very carefully. This checking led us to consider the coincidences of measurement and proportion between the stone bar, the ring and the stag.

The Stone's Proportions
The circle from which stone's segment was set out had the following measurements:

Radius: 8 feet 2 inches (2.49 metres).
Diameter: 16 feet 4 inches (4.98 metres).
Circumference: 51 feet 4 inches (15.64 metres).

The curved length of the segment creating the sceptre equates to 1/27th of the circumference of the circle: 27 x 22¾ inches = 616 inches (51 feet 4 inches.)

The replica was weighed on a number of different Post Office scales – none of them ever displayed exactly the same weight, they always differed by several grams. The average of the results is 3.338 kg. This weight is entirely consistent with the weights attributed to the original by Bruce-Mitford.[4]

The Carver's Training
Bruce-Mitford used the term 'barbaric' many times in his paper on the sceptre-whetstone, contrasting it with the 'classical' proportions encountered in the Graeco-Roman and Byzantine worlds. Yet the carver was evidently as skilled as a 'classically trained' mason and would have served an apprenticeship lasting at least several years before being sufficiently accomplished and confident to attempt a project such as the stone.

The term 'classically (traditionally) trained' is mostly used as an expression relating to architectural work because of the meticulous accuracy of stonework established in the classical styles of Greece and Rome. A mason/carver - then as now - would have been fully aware of the 'classical tradition' of his or her craft. Masons of the Middle Ages, for example, were regarded as practicing a liberal art and not merely a useful skill, as they needed a knowledge of mathematics and geometry. The 'classical' element of stone sculpture, particularly when relating to the human form, is largely one of proportion and balance.

The Underlying Geometry of the Whetstone, Ring and Stag
There is strong evidence from the geometry contained within the plan of the whetstone ensemble that all of its constituent parts were, conceived of by its designer(s) as a coherent whole; that is that the stone, ring and stag were designed to be together.

---

[4] Bruce Mitford, p.312. When Angus Wainwright and Brian Ansell were at the British Museum, the original whetstone was re-weighed and seemed to be much heavier than indicated by Bruce-Mitford. The replica provided a very similar reading on the British Museum scales. However, subsequent re-weighing (of the replica only) on Post Office scales shows that the British Muesum scales were not calibrated correctly.

In order to recreate the separate parts of the ensemble, Brian Ansell and Dave Roper had to go beyond the measurements provided by Bruce-Mitford's *The Sutton Hoo Ship Burial* volume 2 and take some of their own. This was particularly essential for Brian: as a master mason he is used to executing a design from a carefully thought out and drawn plan.[5] As there was no plan left in Mound 1 Brian had to work out all the dimensions and draw a plan of his own, the arc or curve of the bar was originally marked out from scaling up dimensions from the BM report and then adjusted and verified from the original whetstone's dimensions by taking the termination points from the surface to the outer edge of the inner end circles (see Figure 61) using the standard procedure to triangulate the centre of the circle. In basic masonry, this is a method of finding the circle of an arch from a single voussoir.

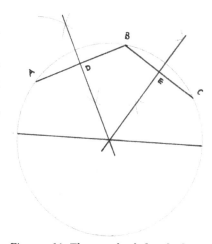

Figure 61 The method for finding the centre of a given circle of which a segment is known. (Not to scale)

Following this templates and profile gauges were created. This exercise was successful and the replicas, despite the appearance in some of the photographs within this book, are of the same dimensions as the original stone.

During the above procedure, Brian established that the curve that determines the shape of each of the edges along the length of the stone bar is part of a circle, the diameter of which is 16 feet 4 inches (4.98 metres). This is a very similar dimension to the old English measure, the *rod, pole* or *perch*.[6] Incidentally, the circle produced by this radius has a circumference of 51 feet 4 inches (14.64 metres) and the arc of the circle that contains the length of the bar is 1/27 of that circle, which may have a significance of its own.[7]

The bar gets its characteristic shape from this curve in four directions; along each edge of the bar. A perfectly square section bar of the correct length had to be created from the stone before shaping and carving could commence and the original width of that square section is still retained in five areas of the finished piece along its centre line, the middle of the bar, the outsides of the knobs/domes, the outermost parts of the carved faces.

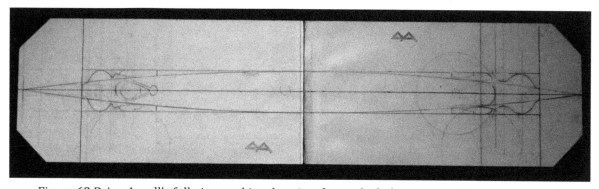

Figure 62 Brian Ansell's full-size working drawing, from which the stoneworking was executed.

---

[5] For full details see Ansell, this volume.

[6] For an exploration of what this measurement may mean, see Pollington's 8. The Anglo-Saxon Rod and the *Sceaftmund* (this volume). The differing names came from different localities and trades.

[7] See Pollington's discussion of the king's number, p.42 (this volume).

It can be determined that each of the two knobs were planned to be the dimensions that they are now, neither have ever been re-worked since the bar was completed, apart from the grooves in the top knob that are there to accommodate the metal components. There will be more to say about this re-working below. If the top knob had been reworked, after completion, to change its shape to a squatter profile, then the width at its centre would have had to have been reduced as the height of the knob changed; its centre would no longer be the same width as the maximum width of the bar. As this is not the case, then it is clear the existing, squat profile was the shape intended at the initial stages of the design. As this is not the case, then it is clear the existing, squat profile was the shape intended at the initial stages of the design. There does appear to be definite and deliberate reasons in having the knobs of different heights and this involve the metal parts. The bottom fitment is a pedestal, an inverted saucer shape, whereas the metal parts at the top, excluding those that belong to the ring are of a different design and have to accommodate the pin from the ring. It would seem that the top knob was shortened in order to provide for a more harmonious design. This can be seen when measurements are taken from the middle of the length of the bar; from the middle line to the bottom, not including the pedestal, is a distance of 12 inches (30.3 cm). From the middle line to the top of the bronze fitment is also a foot (30.3 cm). The squatter knob has been designed to accommodate the bronzes at the top. Incidentally, the top knob is around 1 ¼ inches (3 cm) in height while the bottom is 1 5/8 inches (4.1 cm).

There are, at either end of the bar, two projecting studs that stand proud of the knobs. The diameters of these ends are both ½ inch (13mm). The bottom end is a result of the natural termination of the design at this point. The top (stud) however is created by a deliberate 'stopped' chamfer, a device that leaves the domed section by way of a mitre. Common in stonework the 'joggle' is designed to connect

Figure 63 The replica whetstone superimposed on Brian Ansell's template, the centre of the ring placed at the point of convergence of the stone's sides and the extension of the centre-line marked in red.

with or attach another piece of work whether stone, wood or metal. These studs are invisible when the fitments are added and have not been included in the measurements of the knobs here.[8]

---

[8] The stone is so accurately made that, before the metalwork was added, and provided the surface was flat, the stone would stand upright quite happily on either projection.

Brian Ansell & Paul Mortimer

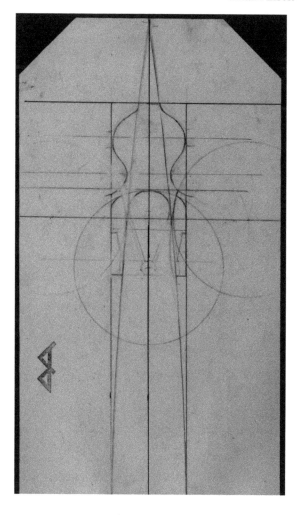

Figure 64 The two different four-inch (2.45 cm) diameter circles associated with each head can be seen in this drawing. The circle that affects the front clearly has its centre in the middle of the small disc below the head 'surround'. This may be another reason for the survival of these discs.

If the circumference of the circle that concerns the curved bar is produced above the bar, when seen in plan, the curves from both sides meet at about 3 inches (7.5 cm) above the bar. When the iron ring is on the bar, where the two curves cross is the centre of the circle formed by the iron ring.

The iron ring has a diameter of 4 inches (10.2 cm). This same size circle is included within the design of the heads on the bar. Each of the heads has similar dimensions from a planning point of view, even though the heads at the top are slightly smaller than those at the bottom, there are still dimensions that they all share. The top of the curve that forms the apparent surround around the head is part of a circle that has a diameter of 4 inches (10.2 cm). This same circle is also seen when each head is considered in profile, and again involves the surround; this time it is the gentle curve that gives the surround its shape in profile at the top. Incidentally, the surrounds are not flat, except once they pass the eyes, towards the middle of the bar. In fact they aren't true surrounds at all; they are a way of accommodating the heads and allowing the curves below the knobs to conform to the shape of the main part of the bar.

Curiously, the heads at the bottom are about 1½ inches (3.5 cm) from the top of the head to the bottom of the chin, discounting the beards. When this is multiplied by seven, it is almost 10 inches (24.5 cm) which takes it just about to the middle of the bar.[9] When I was taught to draw in art classes, I was told that the head is 1/7 the height of the body, so if the head had a body, its feet would be situated in the middle of the bar. It doesn't work quite so well with the heads at the top, as they are slightly smaller.

The eyes of the heads at the top of the bar are all in exactly the same plane, as are the eyes of the bottom heads. Discounting the beards, the eyes are in the middle of the heads when the heads are measured from the top to the chin.

So far we haven't considered the stag but there are areas of coincidence with this, too. The bar has a maximum width of about 2 inches (5.1cm) which is the same as the width of the antlers when seen from the front. It is the same dimension with the antlers when seen from the side, too. The body of the stag, is also about 2 inches long, although when the stag is situated in profile and compared to the bar, it is slightly offset, however, this effect is mitigated by the fact that the hind legs of the stag are slightly angled in such a way that they point towards the centre of the iron ring. The width of the pedestal at the bottom of the whetstone is also 2 inches.

---

[9] The measurement is taken from the top of the head.

The height of the receiving cup above the top knob is 1 inch (2.6 cm), once the stag and ring are in place from the top of the receiving cup to the top of the antlers is 8 inches (20.4 cm). The width of the receiving cup is 1 inch (2.6 cm).

The top knob had been re-worked in the past, and the eight swaged strips that secure the receiving cup in place are, it would seem, not original. The grooves that are present seem to indicate that the original fitting had or was intended to have carinated and facetted arms, like those six that are still present at the bottom. Dave Roper's experience has shown that these are very difficult to cast and the original fitting may have been broken due to a poor cast, perhaps smashed if the whetstone had fallen over, or maybe never put in place due to difficulties in manufacture. However, the swaged strips are now in situ and whatever the situation it would appear that the original intentions of the designer(s) have been preserved in the existing measurements of the finished piece. Incidentally, the very narrow swaged strip which has been used to surround the bottom metalwork may well be there to counter the effects of a poor cast.

One curious characteristic of the swaged strips is that they are all of different widths in different places on the assembly and this is difficult to explain. In two cases, they need to be quite narrow, for instance those situated at the junctions of the knobs with the bar. The junction strip of the top knob has three ribs, while that of the bottom has four. The narrow swaged strip around the six carinated arms of the bottom fitting has only two ribs. Each of the eight swaged strips on the top knob has five ribs. The cast fitting around the iron ring and that around the feet of the stag have been made to give the appearance of swaged strips and they have six ribs each and there are six of them. Of course there may be no significance in any of this but it is strange that you get 2, 3, 4, 5 and 6 ribs on different strips, particularly in the case of the faux swaged strips associated with the ring and stag.

Conclusion

So what does all this mean? As stated at the start of this paper, it would appear that all the parts were carefully designed to be put together: there appears to be a deliberate and co-ordinated attempt at creating a particular aesthetic effect. What the purpose and function of the piece may have been is still a matter for further debate, but it seems that that debate now has some firm facts upon which to progress. It would seem unnecessary to continue to claim that the stag was an heirloom piece and older (or younger for that matter) than the stone, as some commentators have.[10] Wherever and whenever the separate parts were made it is highly likely that they were conceived and manufactured together, not by the same craftsman , there are too many skills involved in masonry and the metalwork for that, but by a team working together with a clear goal in mind. The geometry indicates that a great deal of thought and planning went into the piece; it may even be that Carver was correct when he said, it was the

"....product of a seventh-century 'regalia working party'..."[11]

although he went on to imply that the object was a bit of a mish-mash and 'a ridiculous conceit'. It is true that the metal composition[12] of the stag is different to that of the other bronze elements and it is possible that was deliberate, too, or it may just have been made in a different workshop or by a different craftsman; it doesn't have to have come from a different time and place.

We will discuss origin and function elsewhere in this volume (p.129) and try to move further towards a conclusion.

---

[10] See our *Review of Relevant Literature* and our *Critique of Enright* (both in this volume).
[11] Carver, 1998, p.170.
[12] See Ellis in Bruce-Mitford, 1978, for details.

II The Enigmatic Staff

4. The Sutton Hoo Stone: A Review of the Relevant Literature
Paul Mortimer

In the survey that follows, I have tried to consider the ideas of each commentator according to the chronological order in which their papers were published except for Rupert Bruce-Mitford who wrote the official report for the British Museum. Because of this he has influenced the thoughts of all subsequent writers and is probably the first person turned to by anyone wanting information about the stone. It therefore seems reasonable to begin with his assessment followed by earlier and then more recent papers. Another exception concerns the writings of Michael J. Enright which are critiqued in a chapter of their own (below, p.78). It has not been possible to locate copies of the papers of the earlier German academics Karl Hauck, Adolf Gauert and Percy S. Schramm who published their thoughts and observations on the stone in 1954,[13] but their ideas have been reprised by many of the other writers looked at below, especially Bruce-Mitford. Apart from those particular writers, I have tried to include all the major contributions to the debate about the Sutton Hoo stone known to me.

I apologise in advance for the length of both this section and the *Critique of Enright*, but I hope that it will lead to some valuable and instructive insights.

Bruce-Mitford, Hicks, Ellis et al. (1978)

Rupert Bruce-Mitford wrote the report on the stone for the three volume work, *The Sutton Hoo Ship Burial*; the stone report appears in volume 2. Bruce-Mitford's paper is supported by a report on the provenance of the stag, by Carola Hicks, a technical paper on the petrography of the stone bar by S. E. Ellis and a scientific examination of the stag and bronze elements of the ensemble by Hughes, Oddy and Werner. Together, these papers form the official report of the stone and associated pieces and are the most comprehensive examination of the Sutton Hoo stone assembly. It will be very useful to look at the findings and suggestions that are made by Bruce-Mitford.

Bruce-Mitford begins his examination with a description of the circumstances of the find within the burial chamber and proceeds with a very detailed examination of the stone bar and its condition, he describes the heads and the two knobs at either end and their surviving fitments, the pedestal, the iron ring and stag assembly and follows this with the reasoning why the stag and ring must have come from the top of the stone bar. He then discusses the ceremonial status of the bar and looks at contemporary sceptres and those from the 'Antique Tradition' and considers depictions of later Anglo-Saxon sceptres. Next he considers the stylistic aspects of the heads on the stone bar, and examines other stones from northern Europe and the British Isles. Included within his work is a critical consideration of what some other scholars have suggested about the stone and he also presents us with a set of conclusions based on his own ideas of what the stone is and its purpose and place within his ideas of kingship in Anglo-Saxon England. His analysis is exceptionally thorough and he makes it very clear that his conclusions are his own.

> "Such an impressive, non-functional piece can only have been either an object of religious veneration or the expression of royal power and authority. ... Its aspect and character, nevertheless, seem thoroughly barbaric, and there can be no doubt as to its pagan inspiration."[14]

---

[13] All are included in *Herrschaftszeichen und Staastssymbolik*. 3 volumes, 1954
[14] Both quotes from Bruce-Mitford, 1978. 346.

Thus Bruce-Mitford sums up his feelings about the stone; he believes that it could have had no practical use as there are no signs of it ever being used to sharpen or hone a blade and that the bronzes at either end would have got in the way.[15] The idea that the stone has a 'barbaric origin is something that Bruce-Mitford returns to a number of times during his examination;

> "The Sutton Hoo sceptre, as has been said, has its barbaric aspects and features."[16]

> "The use of red paint on the knobs, and the treatment of the faces, have an authentically barbaric stamp."[17]

He also uses quotes from a number of other commentators to emphasise the 'barbaric' and pagan nature of the object and seems to be very much in agreement with Sir Thomas Kendrick's statement that,

> "Nothing like this monstrous stone exists anywhere else. It is a unique, savage thing; and inexplicable, except perhaps as a symbol, proper to the King himself, of the divinity and mystery which surrounded the smith and his tools in the northern world."[18]

Unfortunately, it is not absolutely clear exactly what Bruce-Mitford, or Kendrick for that matter, mean when they use the word 'barbaric' or similar concepts; do they mean that it is unsophisticated, unrestrained, non- classical, non-Roman or a combination of these? The idea of it being a 'savage thing' must remain with the individual observer, however it certainly isn't unsophisticated and it was surely made by a mason trained in 'classical' methods and perhaps, Roman techniques as Ansell has demonstrated.[19] The piece was carefully planned and carved as Bruce-Mitford admits during the conclusion to his study:

> "...in a new, imaginatively conceived, expertly designed and executed symbol – a sceptre that expressed a freshly achieved political vision."[20]

Here he is referring to his own suggestion that the stone ensemble was a deliberate fusion of Anglo-Saxon, Scandinavian and Celtic symbolism in order to bolster Rædwald's position as Bretwalda. We will look at some aspects of these assertions a little later on.

Bruce-Mitford compares the stone to a number of Roman sceptres but can find no direct parallel and points out the radical design differences between the classical ones and the Sutton Hoo stone.[21] He considers, too, the two presumed wooden sceptres or staffs of office from the boy prince's tomb in Cologne cathedral and once again demonstrates that there are few if any similarities.[22] Finally, he looks at depictions of Carolingian and later Anglo-Saxon sceptres and can find few similarities and actually finds it easier to list the most important differences after saying that

> "...the Sutton Hoo sceptre differs radically from any other known Late Antique sceptre-type. Its significance may have been less mundane than that of the consular sceptre, details of its design being more conditioned by the religion, myth and traditions of the pagan Germanic world."

He then suggests that the differences should be 'especially' studied and lists what he considers to be the main ones:[23]

- Its weight and the fact that it is uncomfortable to hold for long periods of time,
- The material it is made from – stone – no other sceptre is made from such material,

---

[15] Bruce-Mitford, 1978. 315 & 346. See *Critique of Enright*, this volume and conclusion on the validity of this comment.

[16] Bruce-Mitford, 1978. 350.

[17] Bruce-Mitford, 1978. 357.

[18] Kendrick, 1939. 128. Quoted in Bruce-Mitford, 1978. 373.

[19] Ansell (this volume)

[20] Bruce-Mitford, 1978. 376.

[21] Bruce-Mitford, 1978. 350 to 352.

[22] Bruce-Mitford, 1978 353.

[23] Bruce-Mitford, 1978. 357.

- The red paint on the knobs and the treatment of the faces,
- The number of faces and the way they are disposed,
- The almost square cross section of the stone.

Next, he examines the design and treatment of the faces and gives careful consideration to the possibility that those at the top could be female. As far as style and execution are concerned Bruce-Mitford is convinced that the heads come from the Germanic tradition and cites a number of parallels, including the face on the bird's hip from the shield from Mound 1 Sutton Hoo (Figure 122), designs within the shield decoration from a number of shields found in Sweden, other bronze designs from Scandinavia and England.[24] Later, in his treatment he also draws a comparison to the well executed portrayal of a man's bearded face from an Anglo-Saxon lock piece found in Dorchester, Oxfordshire.[25] It is the careful treatment of hair in the images and the piriform surrounds that convince him that the heads on the stone are of a Germanic origin.[26]

Figure 65 Bronze lock from Dorchester, Oxfordshire

Having discussed the style of the faces he then wonders whether there are any other stones that have a resemblance to the stone from Sutton Hoo, either in the material used or in style and function. He comments on evidence from Birka, Sweden, which suggests the ritual or symbolic use of two much smaller stones that show that they once had attachments fixed to them. [27] He also refers to two stones, made of similar material to greywacke, that were found in an Anglo-Saxon grave at Uncleby, Yorkshire (Figure). The larger of these was buried so that it was standing upright when covered, which is how the Sutton Hoo stone is assumed to have been placed in the tomb[28] He looks at two shaped stones that probably had had metal mounts from Colerane, Northern Ireland but these like all the others so far mentioned display no sign of heads

Figure 66 Detail of shield flange from grave XII at Vendel, Sweden, clearly showing the heads of bearded men within a piriform border at the centre-bottom of the flange. The central feature is a four-way knot. This grave is contemporary with Mound 1 at Sutton Hoo. (After Arne & Stolpe)

[24] Bruce-Mitford, 1978. 358 to 360.
[25] Bruce-Mitford, 1978. 369 to 370.
[26] Bruce-Mitford, 1978. 359.
[27] Bruce-Mitford, 1978 361.
[28] Bruce-Mitford, 1978 362.

or faces. However, he then draws our attention to a number of stones that do have heads or faces carved onto them, all from the British Isles. There is a fragment from Hough-on-the-Hill, Lincolnshire, (Figure) a stray find, of very similar material to that from Sutton Hoo, the face carving is comparatively rough and the whole, surviving piece is about 10 cm long.[29] The stone from Lochar Moss, Dumfriesshire, Scotland has a face that is much closer to those on the Sutton Hoo in the level of skill applied to its creation. This, too, is about 10 cm in length and may well have been an object all by itself, or may have been fixed to something else. Again, it is a stray find without context.[30]

Figure 67 Square-section whetstone with bronze fittings from Newtownlow, Ireland.

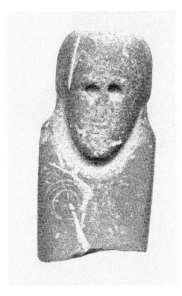

Figure 68 (above) Square-section whetstone of unknown origin, now in Ireland. The metal fitment is of Scandinavian design. Another similar-shaped whetstone, about 45 cms long, was found at Loughpark Crannog in Ireland. It, too, apprears to have had metal fittings and is probably from the Viking age.Cf. Lyttleton, 1998, pp.156, 159.

Figure 69 (left) Whetstone fragment from Hough-on-the-Hill, Lincolnshire

He then considers a number of other stones that may have been whetstones with heads on them, none of which have beards or moustaches or are stylistically close to the Sutton Hoo stone, and says -

"...it seems that there is a context for the Sutton Hoo stone bar in the British Isles, though no real parallel to it. The geological background and the habit of carving stone bars seem to point to Celtic tradition. On the other hand the face *types** on the sceptre and their *style** are paralleled only in the Germanic background and chiefly in Scandinavia."[31]

---

[29] Bruce-Mitford, 1978 364.
[30] Bruce-Mitford, 1978 369.
[31] Bruce-Mitford, 1978 369. * italics in the original.

As many of the stones he uses for comparison have no context, being stray finds, it is difficult to assign them to a particular culture or even a time period, so Bruce-Mitford's use of the term, 'Celtic' is surely a little insecure and as Bruce-Mitford himself points out, there was a Germanic tradition of carving heads on wooden posts, and of casting them in metal.[32] In addition, no other known stone has more than two heads (e.g. Portsoy) and none have them as skilfully carved as on the Sutton Hoo - whatever is said about the allegedly 'Celtic' stones, the Sutton Hoo stone is a radical departure.

Bruce-Mitford does consider the writings of a number of other scholars, some of whom made their comments before it was realised that the stag and ring came from the top of the stone. Karl Hauck, it seems, believes that the stone could be an *Ahnenstab*, an ancestor staff, and that the faces represent the ancestors of the king. He also suggests that the frames around the heads are torcs.[33] Bruce-Mitford points out that the carver could have made them more torc-like, if that is what they are supposed to be, and that, if they are torcs, they are in the wrong place, being around the head rather than the neck.[34] Hauck, along with two other German scholars, W. Berges and A. Gauert, sees the stone as being a dynastic symbol of the *Wuffingas* and their preoccupation with Woden.[35] Bruce-Mitford points out that the three scholars have never considered whether any of the heads represent females, which may upset the ancestor thesis. Possibly, the biggest objections to the idea would be the fact that the king-list of the *Wuffingas* shows many more than eight ancestors and that there are no known *Ahnenstäb*, nor, it seems, were they ever mentioned in literature before Hauck; the idea is pure speculation, albeit an interesting one. Perhaps a firmer hypothesis is one that Bruce-Mitford mentions in a footnote but does not pursue, and that is the idea that the stone is a 'judgement sceptre' and stood upright in front of the king or judge during proceedings.[36] Apparently such things were used in parts of Germany during the Middle Ages and later and it would be very interesting to try and find out where and when such a tradition has its origin.

Bruce-Mitford also considers the ideas of Frances P. Magoun, who does not believe that the stone (without the stag) could be a sceptre; he thinks that it was of dynastic significance and that it was a great phallic symbol bursting with vigour and fertility.[37] Bruce-Mitford is grateful for Jacqueline Simpson's contribution regarding the Icelandic sagas but we shall consider her ideas for ourselves below. Bruce-Mitford dismisses the suggestions of Sydney L. Cohen as "unrestrained speculation",[38] but again we will look at Cohen's proposals later.

Bruce-Mitford also believes that the use of stone as the material for the 'sceptre' is important and says:

> "There is no doubt that the use of stone in the sceptre's design is of paramount significance; even if the stone bar with human faces, and indeed the whetstone with human faces, is in the Celtic tradition, its possible significance in the world of Germanic, particularly Scandinavian, religion and mythology (which already enter into their regalia, it seems in the figural scenes of the purse and which dominate the imagery of figural scenes on the helmet) must also rank high in our consideration of what is, after all, the symbol of an Anglo-Saxon king, whose royal line may have Scandinavian origins."[39]

---

[32] Bruce-Mitford, 1978 360.

[33] Bruce-Mitford, 1978 372.

[34] Bruce-Mitford, 1978 373.

[35] Bruce-Mitford, 1978 372.

[36] Bruce-Mitford, 1978 346, footnote 5. Bruce-Mitford is discussing a suggestion put forward by the German, legal historian H Baltl.

[37] Magoun, 1954. 125 to 126.

[38] Bruce-Mitford, 1978 371, footnote 2.

[39] Bruce-Mitford, 1978 374.

He continues with two possible reasons for the use of stone,

> "The first is that the object fits broadly with a Celtic background, since, as we have seen, whetstones human faces occur uniquely within Celtic contexts, utilizing a raw material that was conveniently to hand, but no doubt having social or religious import. The second, and this must have primacy, is that the whetstone may have been of major significance in the mythology or sacral basis or social function of Germanic kingship. If the saga references to whetstones cited (p. 374) are to be given any weight, the ceremonial whetstone could well be a recognised symbol of power and the dispensing of justice. The Celtic and Germanic elements could very properly meet in a *bretwalda's* regalia."[40]

Carola Hicks thinks that the stag is of Celtic origin and Bruce-Mitford agrees.[41] It has been identified as a red deer stag, a species that ranges throughout northern Europe, including the British Isles.[42] Hicks discusses the stylistic aspects of the stag, looking for analogues from the Halstatt period and Scythian, Celtic, Germanic and Roman art. She considers the stag model, supposedly from Gateholm Island (Pembrokeshire), whose provenance was always doubtful and which has now disappeared;[43] certainly, visually, this is the closest analogue to that from Sutton Hoo that Hicks presents us with. She compares the stag to both the Anglo-Saxon boar from the helmet from Benty Grange and the model of the fish from the cauldron at Sutton Hoo,[44] There would seem to be very little stylistic links between these objects, however, she concludes her paper on the stag with

> "....its stylistic features and the fact that it is a small animal in the round suggests that it is strongly influenced by Roman-British tradition..."[45]

She also feels, as does Bruce-Mitford, that the fact that the bronze the stag is made from is quite different in composition to that making up the other bronze components of the stone ensemble, is of significance.[46]

Bruce-Mitford believes that the stone is a 'sceptre':

> "It must surely be accepted as beyond all reasonable doubt that in this strange and singularly impressive object in the Sutton Hoo ship-burial we have a sceptre, a massive staff of stone crowned with a ring and stag, held in the king's hand to signify his royal title, power and majesty."[47]

That the bronze, saucer shaped attachment at the bottom is for resting on the knee while the king is sitting holding the object and not much else;

> "The saucer fitting will not serve as a foot for the saucer to stand on, because although it will stand erect when balanced on the saucer, as the replica demonstrates it is highly unstable. The saucer does, however, exactly fit the knee cap, and it may be regarded as made to do so, and the sceptre as designed primarily to be held by the king when seated, with the lower end resting on his knee."[48]

---

[40] Bruce-Mitford, 1978 376.

[41] Hicks, 1978. 378 to 382. Bruce-Mitford, 1978. 334. Pollington has dealt with the imagery of the stag in greater detail, elsewhere in this volume.

[42] Bruce-Mitford, 1978 337.

[43] Hicks, 1978. 379.

[44] Hicks, 1978. 379.

[45] Hicks, 1978. 382.

[46] For full technical details see Hughes, Oddy and Werner, 1978. 385 to 393.

[47] Bruce-Mitford, 1978 370.

[48] Bruce-Mitford, 1978 346. We will comment on this below.

He also feels that the stone must have been made for Rædwald in his role as *bretwalda*, which he says means 'ruler of Britain' not 'ruler of the British'.[49] As we saw above, Bruce-Mitford sees Rædwald ruling a mixed population of Anglo-Saxons and Celts and that is the reason for what he sees as a mixed Germanic and Celtic traditions coming together in the form of the stone, that is also why it is buried with Rædwald when he dies - his successor was not a *bretwalda* and, therefore has no need for the stone.

> "There could, then, have been two reasons why the Sutton Hoo sceptre was buried. First, that it was not the sceptre of the East Anglian royal house and so did not require to be handed on, but was personal to Rædwald; and second, if it was the East Anglian dynastic sceptre, that in spite of Roman formal reminiscences, it was an object in its essence thoroughly pagan, and therefore unacceptable in terms of continuing use as a symbol of royal power in a Christian kingdom."[50]

So Bruce-Mitford hedges his bets somewhat and still sees the idea of a 'dynastic sceptre' as a possibility.

We will, just briefly, critically examine some of what Bruce-Mitford says here and also return to his suggestions elsewhere in this volume. Bruce-Mitford doesn't really ever consider that the stone may not be a 'sceptre' and this concept has influenced everything that he says throughout his paper.[51] For instance, if it was not used as a 'sceptre' then it would not need to be held on the knee, as Bruce-Mitford suggests and the saucer shaped bronze fixture at the bottom of the stone may have been for standing the object on. Bruce-Mitford believed that his experiments with the replica conclusively demonstrated that this idea was impractical, and it may well be so with their replica. The replica is made from a light material (hollow plaster, I believe) with bronze fittings.[52] I have handled it at the British Museum and it would be easy to knock it over. However, my replica, made by Brian Ansell and Dave Roper, is made from the same materials as the original and its centre of gravity is much lower than the British Museum replica; it stands very securely on its base and there are reasons to think that this may have been how it was displayed.[53] Perhaps, just perhaps, it was an idol in a sanctuary and was only rarely held – or was held in both hands? As Bruce-Mitford indicates and as practical experience has shown me, it is not an easy object to carry around or to hold for long periods; perhaps it was never designed for this purpose at all? As for whether the stone has ever been used to sharpen anything, well it is not really all that easy to tell, as greywacké is harder than iron and occasional use for honing a knife, that is giving the blade its final edge, would be invisible as it would have little effect on the stone.[54]

Bruce-Mitford is very fond of the idea that Rædwald was the *bretwalda*, ruler of Britain, not ruler of the British. This concept is mentioned really only by Bede, although he never uses the word, and he appears to apply the idea to seven kings, Rædwald being the fourth *bretwalda*, Edwin and Oswald and Oswy of Northumbria came after Rædwald.[55] If the stone was part of the insignia of the *bretwalda*, why was it not passed on to his successor as *bretwalda*?

It may be suggested that it had too much pagan symbolism and that those that came after Rædwald were Christians; however, Ethelbert of Kent, the third *bretwalda*, was a Christian, too, in fact he was supposed to be responsible for Rædwald's temporary conversion. It would appear, then, that the stone is unlikely to be associated with the concept of the *bretwalda*. It is true, too, that we do not really understand what Bede meant by the concept of the *bretwalda*- it certainly didn't include rule over the Mercians and may well just have been a notion of one king being more powerful than some others, rather than as a High King.

---

[49] Bruce-Mitford, 1978 375. See below p.75 for more on the *Bretwalda*.

[50] Bruce-Mitford. 1978, p.377.

[51] Bruce-Mitford, 1978, p.346. Despite saying the object could be an object of veneration earlier, he never really explores this idea.

[52] Bruce-Mitford, 1978. 341.

[53] We will discuss the idea of the stone being vertical elsewhere in this volume.

[54] Brian Ansell, pers. comm..

[55] Sherley-Price, 1990, p. 107-8. We will have more to say about Bede and this idea of the *bretwalda* later.

In addition, if Mound 1 at Sutton Hoo is not the grave of Rædwald but some other important personage, then the *bretwalda* thesis is not valid.

Finally, how secure is the identification of the stone with a 'Celtic' culture? This is important because many subsequent writers have followed Bruce-Mitford's suggestion and at least one has taken it further.[56] For Bruce-Mitford the basis of the identification of the stone being at least partly 'Celtic' is the fact that only in the British Isles are small stones with heads carved on them found. Therefore there must be a tradition of which the Sutton Hoo stone forms a part and that that tradition is 'Celtic'. This may be so, however Bruce-Mitford doesn't define exactly what he means by the term 'Celtic' but his use does appear to be limited to the British Isles and to the influence of the Romano-British, so we will proceed on that basis. It should be noted that the Hough-on-the-Hill and Lochar Moss stones were stray finds, without a context and may not have ever been part of whetstones. As they can't be dated and as they were found in areas eventually settled by Anglians, it is not possible to attach them to a 'Celtic' tradition; it is not improbable that they form part of an Anglian one. However, this may not be so for the two-headed stone from Portsoy in Banffshire. Even if those stones were 'Celtic', the Sutton Hoo stone is such a radical departure from the other designs as Bruce-Mitford recognises[57] that it may well be from a completely different tradition or be an innovation and unique. As far as the stag is concerned, its linkage to the 'Celts' is at least partly based on the supposed, almost complete absence of figures modelled in the round from Anglo-Saxon areas. It is interesting that Carola Hicks uses an example of a boar modelled in the round from an Anglo-Saxon grave at Benty Grange as a comparison. However, you don't have to look far for an indisputably Germanic animal modelled in the round, also with a facetted or carinated aspects; the iron bulls' heads on the stand are in many ways modelled in a similar way to the stag. In addition, many figures of creatures and humans have been found in Anglo-Saxon contexts since the publication of Bruce-Mitford's work, one such is the small figure of a man from a grave at Carlton Colville (Suffolk) (Figure 84), which led to other detector finds being identified as Anglo-Saxon by the Portable Antiquities Service.

It could be that we must consider the origins and the uses of the stone from Mound 1 at Sutton Hoo from a new starting point. However, before we do that we will continue to consider others suggestions regarding the stone.

Gamber (1966)

Dr Ortwin Gamber wrote about the stone in The Arms and Armour Society's journal in 1966[58] and was pretty certain that he knew what it was and what it was for. He was also quite definite about a number of other items in the tomb, even going so far as to make concrete suggestions regarding the colours of the occupant's shoes and stockings.[59] He felt able to explain, at least to his own satisfaction, all the animal symbolism found within the grave.[60] He did this by looking at practices found all over Eurasia during a number of different time periods going as far back as the mesolithic.[61] Nevertheless, his ideas concerning the stone are interesting and we may have to return to them elsewhere in this volume. According to Dr Gamber the 'whetstone' is "the thunderbolt of Sutton Hoo".[62] What he means by this is that the 'whetstone' could be used for sharpening blades and for striking a fire and that the object would be held in the hand of the 'celestial god' and possibly used as a missile. He believes that the evidence includes the bearded countenance of the deity at the top, the red painted balls enclosed by bronze bands and the bronze

---

[56] Enright, 2006.
[57] Bruce-Mitford, 1978. 357 and 362.
[58] Gamber, 1966.
[59] Gamber, 1966. 285.
[60] Gamber, 1966. 271 to 272.
[61] Gamber, 1966. 270.
[62] Gamber, 1966. 272.

dish.[63] The red balls, he suggests, represent the sun, the bronze bands a sun wheel, and the saucer like dish is the 'golden sickle of the moon'. He believed that the 'celestial god' would be Thor.[64]

He reminds us that the iron stand also has four sides and that the bronze stag, which he, and others, believed was at the top of it was,

> "doubtless symbolising landed property and an overlordship founded on the will of god."[65]

He thought that the stag was a proof of the worship of 'Wotan', that it represented a "special creation of God", and represented life and the land in which life existed, because, in the Mesolithic period it constituted the most important source of food.[66]

Cohen (1966)

Sydney L. Cohen, writing during the same year as Gamber, follows his suggestion that the iron stand was associated with Woden, but attributes the concept to Hauck.[67] Cohen tells us that the heads on the stone are surrounded by 'so-called torques'(*sic*) which he thinks has led some to associate the stone with Odin because torcs can be associated with divinity. However, Cohen thinks that

> "It is possible to make a more accurate determination of the significance of the stone, and to identify the deity represented on it, by employing evidence provided by the ground plans of an important group of North-European sanctuaries."[68]

He feels, too, that valid associations with other objects can be made. The objects that he compares the stone to are: a decorated bronze pin from Hagestad, Jutland, Denmark, the stone pillar from Zbruc in Galicia (Figure 75), modern Ukraine and the Gundestrup cauldron.

The Hagestad pin (Figure 72) resembles the stone in that it has four heads, each facing a different direction and they are surmounted by a four legged animal.[69] The animal may be a stag, but it is too worn to be certain. The Zbruc stone pillar (Figure) was found in 1848 and has been dated to the 9th or 10th centuries, it is four sided and has a head at the top of each side. Below each head there are bodies with various attributes which may indicate two females and two males. The heads are surmounted by what appears to be a single tall hat. Cohen suggests that all the sides represent one deity in different 'moods' or disguises'.[70] The Gundestrup cauldron, according to Cohen, is similar to the pillar in that it, too, has faces portrayed on it. In all there are seven remaining, but Cohen thinks that one is missing, four of the heads are of men and three are female.[71]

---

[63] At the time that both Gamber and Cohen (see below) were writing, the thinking was that the stag came from the top of the iron stand, not the whetstone. Gamber also assumes that the saucer and faces with beards were at the top of the whetstone.
[64] Gamber, 1966. 272.
[65] Gamber, 1966. 272.
[66] Gamber, 1966. 270 to 271.
[67] Cohen, 1966. 466.
[68] Cohen, 1966. 466.
[69] Cohen, 1966. 466.
[70] Cohen, 1966. 467.
[71] Cohen, 1966. 467.

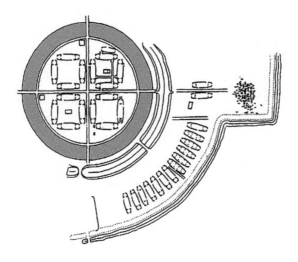

Figure 70 Trelleborg fort diagram

Figure 71 Portsoy stone

Figure 72 Bronze pin from Hagested, Denmark

Cohen then moves on to discuss aspects of the Danish sites of the Trelleborg type. The sites mainly consist of circular earthworks, surrounding sets of longhouses arranged in groups of four. The circular walls have four gates in them, one at each of the four cardinal directions.[72] He says

"My attention was first drawn to the Sutton Hoo whetstone when I was seeking an explanation for the geometric exactitude evident in the ground-plans of four earthworks found in Denmark...."[73]

He thinks that the basic plan was determined by idols positioned in the centre of each circle; his belief is that each idol would have four faces and there would be a face looking out of each gate. The gates provide a 'window for the gods'. He goes on to report on other archaeological sites that appear to have had idols in their centres, the Slavic sanctuary at Rethra, recorded by both Thietmar of Merseburg and Saxo Grammaticus,[74] and another at Kiev, again carefully designed and divided into four sections.[75]

According to Cohen, remains of human and animal sacrifices have been found in three of the four earthworks of the Trelleborg type, including those of four year old children whose bodies were scorched. The remains were swept into pits and at Trelleborg numerous combs were deposited. He notes that many famous men from the Viking period emphasised aspects of their hair in their names, for example, 'Forkbeard' or 'Fairhair' and that at least two gods, Freyr and Thor, had beards and that the goat is sacred to Thor and also has a beard.[76]

Cohen is fascinated by the precise quadratic design of the Trelleborg buildings and suggests that they are reminiscent of the buildings described by Adam of Bremen at Uppsala and the Slavic temple on the island of Rügen. He makes another comparison to the lantern covers on an Anglo-Saxon censer from Pershore, dated to the 10th century.[77] He says that the cover on the censer has a peaked cap, not unlike the hats on miniatures of Thor and Freyr and the hat on the Zbruc pillar (Figure 92).[78]

He comments on the fact that the number four, or two fours, seems to have real significance and is part of the design not just of the Trelleborg type structures but also the Slavic and Baltic ones sacred to Perun, (Russia), Svantovit (Poland) and Perkunas (Lithuania). All of these Cohen equates with Thor on the basis that they were all sky and air gods and have attributes in common, such as goats. He reminds us, too, that the Norwegian king Saint Olaf destroyed an idol of Thor which was fed four loaves every day, presumably in four mouths.[79]

---

[72] There are at least five of these besides Trelleborg, itself: there are others at Fyrkat, Aggersborg and Nonnebaken, all in Denmark and at least one more in southern Sweden, near Lund at Borgeby. (Price, at al, 2011, p. 478)

[73] Cohen, 1966. 467.

[74] Cohen, 1966. 468.

[75] Cohen, 1966. 468 to 469.

[76] Cohen, 1966. 468.

[77] Cohen, 1966. 468.

[78] Cohen is almost certainly referring to the image from Eyrarland, Iceland, for Thor and that from Rällinge, Lunda parish, Södermanland, Sweden for Freyr. These identifications are not absolutely certain. See Perkins, 2001 for details of the images.

[79] Cohen, 1966. 469.

Cohen believes that it is reasonable to identify a four headed stone object, such as the 'whetstone' with Thor (*Thunor* in Old English) and he suggests that the swastika which is associated with the god has four divisions as does the four-spoked wheel, which has been linked to him, too. Finally, he returns to the stone and the arrangements of the heads in fours suggesting that Thor's red beard is echoed in the three bearded faces, that the red knobs may be a reminder of this, too. He thinks that the rings surrounding the faces could be reminiscent of Thor's ring and posits that the 'whetstone' may be used to sharpen a knife with which to make a sacrifice to Thor or start a ritual fire.[80] Sacred fires were dedicated to Thor in Iceland and to Perkunas in Lithuania and Cohen briefly hints at the battle between Thor and the giant where a piece of the whetstone became lodged in Thor's head. Finally he makes it clear that he feels that a whetstone may have been a necessary part of the cult of Thor.[81]

Chaney (1970)

"The standard and whetstone-sceptre could well be symbols of his high office as Bretwalda, an office which on his death left the Wuffinga (sic) family and passed to King Edwin."[82]

Chaney is referring to Rædwald and in this sentence appears to signal his acceptance of the main parts of Bruce-Mitford's thesis. It is interesting, that in the above sentence, the word 'sceptre' is not marked by parenthesis, but elsewhere it is, as we can see here:

"This great sandstone 'sceptre' indicates no trace of use, and its elaborate end-decorations would militate against such employment."[83]

Leaving aside the fact that a better description of the type of stone would be greywacké grit, it seems that Chaney has some reservations concerning the purpose of the object, and indeed he points out that the short sceptre was thought to be unknown amongst Germanic kings until the 9th or 10th century Carolingian kings.[84] It is his understanding, based on art and literary sources, that Teutonic kings used either the spear or long staff, which he suggests represents the weapon of Woden.[85] He feels that the 'whetstone of Sutton Hoo' is part of a Germanic tradition and maybe related to other staffs mentioned in the literature, such as one with a silver knob carried by King Sigurd Sau (*Heimskringla, Saga of Olaf the Holy*)[86] and the gold decorated staff of King Olaf Tryggvason used to smash the idol of Thor (*Heimskringla, Saga of Olaf Tryggvason*).[87] He mentions, too, the "stone-adorned knob used by the Greenland prophetess Thorbjörg." (*Eriks Saga Rauða*). He makes a reference to the staff of Duke Tassilo, that had an incised human face and points out that all the above objects are analogous to the stone but not complete parallels; they are also much later. In a footnote, he refers approvingly to the work of Cohen linking the stone to Thor,[88] but goes on to posit the purpose of the stone may have been

"...to display the king's role as 'giver and master of the swords of his war band' "

---

[80] The sparking abilities of the whetstone, or more precisely the lack of them, are discussed in the *Critique of Enright*, this volume).
[81] Cohen 1966. 470.
[82] Chaney, 1970. 100.
[83] Chaney, 1970. 145.
[84] Chaney, 1970. 145.
[85] Chaney, 1970. 145.
[86] Chaney, 1970. 146.
[87] Chaney, 1970. 147.
[88] Chaney, 1970. 147, fn 133.

This returns him to the ideas of Bruce-Mitford. He continues the sentence,

> "..it may well have drawn also both on the magical properties believed to invest stone in the Germanic North and the supernatural role of the northern smith."[89]

It must be said, though, that Chaney never really proposes any use for the stone other than as a 'sceptre'.

At the time of writing his book, Chaney was not aware that the stag and ring came from the stone and he treats these separately, nevertheless his ideas concerning the ring and stag are worth looking at.[90] He thought that the ring was probably an altar ring, a *stallahringr* (ON), on which oaths were sworn.[91] His references, again, are mainly late and Scandinavian but he also uses the *Anglo-Saxon Chronicle* to show that the Danes swore oaths for King Alfred in 876, *on þaem halgan beage* (OE) something which they had not done for anyone else. He follows this with a brief discussion of the ring oath and points out that it may have changed in later years in Anglo-Saxon England to swearing on Christian religious artefacts.

Chaney says that there is evidence for the stag as a cult animal amongst the Anglo-Saxons and finds the link that some others made to Celtic deity *Kerunnus* (sic) unconvincing.[92] Chaney reminds us that the stag has an association with Freyr, with fertility and the New Year and with dedicated deaths, presumably sacrifices.[93] In support of the stag cult, he does mention *Heorot* (Hart) the name of Hrothgar's hall in *Beowulf*,[94] the four harts that gnaw at the high shoots of *Yggdrasil*, the World Tree of northern mythology.[95] He points out that the hart may have been the divine ancestor of the *Cherusci* and that this animal is associated with the hero *Sigurd*. He also suggests that there are possible connections with various dances and ceremonies that are still performed in England whose origins are obscure and that there are many traces left on the continent, too.[96] He does say that the cult of the stag may have been Christianised into the cult of St Hubert. One final piece of evidence for a stag cult amongst Germanic peoples, according to Chaney, comes from Civezzano, Italy, but is now in the Tiroler Landesmuseum in Innsbruck, Austria. It is a Lombardic sarcophagus which has an iron stag-head with horns (sic) at either end of the sarcophagus.[97] Finally, he makes the remark that the two most prominent stags connected with the Anglo-Saxons, that is the Sutton Hoo stag and *Heorot*, are connected with kings.[98]

Wallace-Hadrill (1975)

In a chapter entitled *The graves of kings: an historical note on some archaeological evidence* within his book of 1975, Wallace-Hadrill discusses his thoughts on the finds from Sutton Hoo.[99] The main purpose of the paper is to explore, using continental comparisons, the idea that Mound 1 is the burial of a king. The paper was originally written circa 1960 - that is before the stone and stag were re-united - but has a postscript to bring it up to date. It must be stated that Wallace-Hadrill wasn't saying that the burial is definitely not royal but felt that the idea of royalty had been too readily accepted and needed to be treated with caution; in any case, he indicated in his postscript that he had rather come round to the royal nature of Sutton Hoo.[100]

---

[89] Chaney, 1970. 147.

[90] Chaney still believed that the stag and ring came from the iron 'standard'.

[91] Chaney, 1970. 148; see also this volume, p.157

[92] Chaney, 1970. 130. Chaney finds little evidence for the idea that Kerunnus (presumably for *Cernunnos*) was known to the Germanic peoples as Freyr.

[93] Chaney, 1970. 132.

[94] Chaney, 1970. 130.

[95] Chaney, 1970. 131.

[96] Chaney, 1970. 131.

[97] Chaney, 1970. 132.

[98] Caney, 1970. 132.

[99] Wallace-Hadrill, 1975. 38 to 59.

[100] Wallace-Hadrill, 1975. 54.

What does he say regarding the stone? He points out that we are pretty uncertain as to what constitutes a kingly symbol as he says that

"*..signa barborum* varied enormously; so it is quite possible to claim almost any item of war-gear or apparel or ornament as royal in a particular group of cases. What is not so easy to prove is that a king wore or bore a particular object because he was a king."[101]

Wallace-Hadrill comments that the stone is not the first to be found in an Anglo-Saxon grave and that they are not uncommon in Sweden, however, he does allow that the one from Sutton Hoo is the biggest and most elaborate. He isn't sure whether it should be called a 'whetstone' or a 'mace'; by this he seems to mean of the 'parliamentary' sort – one that is carried before the significant personage by another.[102] He calls it

"...a symbolic and ceremonial piece.........one that is in the highest degree striking and unusual."

He adds

"It obviously has the character of a whetstone; but it is equally obvious that it is more than a whetstone."[103]

He points out, too, that, as far as he can tell, there is no precedent in the literature of the classical or medieval world of the "symbolic employment of a whetstone." He comments that two German scholars, Wilhelm Berges and Adolf Gauert, believe that it is a symbolic staff and that these are usually made of wood and that it may well have 'magical significance'

"In it would be incapsulated (sic) the special powers that underlay the good fortune of the royal dynasty that owned it, just as Odin's divine power was incapsulated in his spear."[104]

Reasonably, Wallace-Hadrill says that staffs are not whetstones and stone is not wood and goes on to say that if it is

"...symbolic, then we might as properly explore its potential symbolism in some other field, e.g. that of religion, as in kingship;..."[105]

Wallace-Hadrill returns to the subject of the stone in his postscript; by then the stag and ring were firmly on top of the stone, which according to him means that the stone has 'gained in importance'.[106] Wallace-Hadrill says

"I would recognise the whetstone as a symbolic object – though of what I do not know."

He ponders whether it may be, at least in origin, associated with Scandinavian rites; he has read the writings of Sydney Cohen and H. R. Ellis Davidson and wonders whether the answer to the meaning of the stone may lie in the Scandinavian evidence, particularly the tale of Odin and his 'wonderful whetstone' that he used to gain a drink of Suttung's mead. Finally, he asks the question as to whether it belonged to the *Wuffingas* or to someone else.[107]

---

[101] Wallace-Hadrill, 1975. 47.
[102] Wallace-Hadrill, 1975. 47.
[103] Wallace-Hadrill, 1975. 48.
[104] Wallace-Hadrill, 1975. 48.
[105] Wallace-Hadrill, 1975. 48.
[106] Wallace-Hadrill, 1975. 55.
[107] Wallace-Hadrill, 1975. 55.

Evison (1975)

Evison published her well illustrated survey of known pagan Saxon whetstones in 1975.[108] Her paper extrapolates much of its basic material from an earlier work by S. E. Ellis of the British Museum, who shows that the Anglo-Saxons were well disposed to using greywacké stones as honestones.[109] Evison shows that there is a ritual context for this type of stone being included in funerary rites throughout the Anglo-Saxon lands during the early period, often being placed upright in the grave.[110] She also demonstrates that one of the possible source of origin for greywacké proposed by Ellis, is entirely compatible with many of the known finds

> "The suggested source of this rock in southern Scotland is acceptable in view of the fact that the find spots of this group – Yorkshire, Lincolnshire, Bedfordshire and Suffolk – are in Anglian areas which were fairly well placed for contacts in the north of the country."[111]

Evison, it appears, is the first of our scholars who doesn't assume that the stone from Hough-on-the-Hill must be of 'Celtic' origin and seems to think that it is more likely to be Anglian as it was found in an Anglian area[112] – it is also very different stylistically to any of the other headed stones, including the Sutton Hoo. However, if it is of Anglian origin that is of great significance and we shall look at that possibility elsewhere in this volume. She does, briefly, report on the headed stones from British areas but makes little comment about them.[113]

Evison gives the stones from Uncleby quite a bit of her attention, particularly the larger of the two, which she points out is a similar shape to the one from Sutton Hoo and is quite large at 46.3 x 4.8 x 5 cm. She comments on two small and irregular patches of red paint on either end of the stone and in a footnote says that M. Bimson and A.E. Werner of the British Museum found these to be pigments that the Anglo-Saxons would not have had access to. This may need re-investigation, as it is difficult to see why anyone in modern times would add pigments to the ends of the stone.[114]

Storms (1978)

Storms certainly doesn't believe that the main purpose of the stone was as a 'sceptre' and explains very early in his consideration of the stone that it is an idol, 'a hart idol' to be more precise.[115] Storms calls the stone the "most intriguing object among the grave goods",[116] according to him it isn't a practical object but a ceremonial one. Storms is very doubtful, in fact, that it was a 'sceptre' and points to certain difficulties in it performing as such; for instance its weight at more than three kilograms makes it difficult to handle one-armed as a sceptre,[117] he also believed that the circumference and shape of the stone bar added to the problem.[118]

---

[108] Evison, 1975
[109] Ellis, 1969. 135. Of 200 hones that he examined, more than 30 are of greywacké.
[110] Evison, 1975. 83.
[111] Evison, 1975. 79.
[112] Evison, 1975. 77 and 79.
[113] Evison, 1975. 79.
[114] Evison, 1975. 79. The findings were that the pigments were too modern for the Anglo-Saxon period.
[115] Storms, 1978. 323 and 325.
[116] Storms, 1978. 323.
[117] Storms, 1978, p.330
[118] Another factor, which Storms would have been unaware of but practical experience of handling an accurate replica has demonstrated, is that the stag, particularly the antlers, make it quite an awkward burden to manoeuvre when holding as you would a sceptre; this a major problem when walking.

Storms felt that much of what Bruce-Mitford had to say about the purpose of the stone could easily apply to it being an idol, too; for instance he quotes Bruce-Mitford

> "there can be little doubt that this great ceremonial stone is an object of magic and potency, whether in enlisting the aid of the ancestors or warding off evil."[119]

Storms then considers what makes the stone an idol and focuses first on the figure of the stag, which he almost always calls a 'hart'. He tells us that the stag was a sacred animal of the Hittites who left several bronze figurines of them, these figures are often called 'cult standards' or idols. He admits that there is a very large time difference between the Hittite examples and that of Sutton Hoo, but says that we must keep in mind "..early man's innate conservatism in religious matters."[120] He then tells us that Scandinavian rock art often shows the stag prominently displayed, often with ships and sun discs, the latter is important, he feels because it is similar to the figure and ring at Sutton Hoo.[121] He, like Chaney above, calls attention to the Christianised cult of St. Hubert who hunted a deer on Sunday. Apparently, in France Woden's Wild Hunt is called, *La chasse St. Hubert* and there are numerous places on the continent named after the saint.[122] Storms also tells us that Theodore of Tarsus, who was appointed archbishop of Canterbury in 668 AD felt the need to set severe legal punishments for anyone taking part in the Yule practice of *in cervulo vadere*, which involved youths dressed in deer skins running through villages and grabbing women and girls, some of whom did not protest overmuch.[123]

Storms thinks that the annual shedding of antlers was

> "..a good reason for thanking, and consequently worshipping, the hart, for they (the antlers) could be put to all kinds of uses; they could be employed as agricultural tools or as weapons to kill enemies and animals and they were decorative in halls or on the gables of houses."[124]

Storms remind us of the name of *Hrothgar's* hall, *Heorot*, and that this may be because the hart was worshipped.[125] He feels that the stag on the ring is evidence of the cult in East Anglia.

Next Storms mentions that Bruce-Mitford poses four questions that he could not really answer, and they are re-listed for convenience here:[126]

- Why is it made from stone – no other sceptre is made from such material?
- Why is there red paint on the knobs and what does the distinctive treatment of the faces mean?
- Why are there eight faces and why are they placed in this manner?
- Why is the stone of square cross-section?

As far as stone is concerned, Storms's reasoning is that, as it is harder to work than wood, the material would demand more respect for what it represented and, presumably, would be more costly to produce. He points out, too, that the later Anglo-Saxon laws prohibiting the worship of stones may not refer to isolated boulders or stone circles, but to objects like the Sutton Hoo stone. The purpose of the bronze saucer is, he says, to make the object stand on its own. He suggests that as it is probably associated with a fertility cult it may have been important that worshippers touched the stone and this may be why it its surface is so

---

[119] Storms, 1978. 325.
[120] Storms, 1978. 329. Storms is asking a lot here – the Hittites statuettes are dated around 2,000 BC However, there are some quite striking similarities between the way that the stags in the two different cultures are portrayed.
[121] Storms, 1978. 325.
[122] Storms, 1979. 325.
[123] Storms, 1978, 329 Found in *Poenitentiale Theodori, cap. XXVII*.
[124] Storms, 1979. 325.
[125] Storms, 1979. 325.
[126] Storms, 1979. 326. The questions are on page 357 of Bruce-Mitford, 1978. There are also really five, but as Storms has already written about the weight he doesn't mention this aspect again.

smooth. He can only find one place name associated with the stag, and that is some distance from Sutton Hoo - it is Hartest in Suffolk, which may have been *Herthyrst*, 'stag hill'.[127]

His explanation for the colour of the knobs is that red is the colour of blood; blood is powerful as its loss will lead to weakness and death. It is

> "… also the colour of the rising and setting sun, the two moments when man can look at it without being blinded."[128]

He feels that the colour red had magical potency for the Germanic peoples and shows this by referring to an OE word for a red pigment, *teafor*, which is etymologically related to the Dutch word, *tover* and the German word, *zauber*. The latter two words mean 'magic'.[129] To further support his case he quotes from *Leechbook III, I*, "Against headache. Dig up waybread without iron before sunrise. Bind the root about the head by means of a wet red bandage. He will soon be well." And in the *Herbarium X*, "Against a lunatic. Take this herb (clovewort) tie it with a red thread about the man's neck, when the moon is waning, in the month of April or early October."

To explain his answer to the third question (I have listed it as the fourth), Storms draws our attention to the thoughts of Cohen, and repeats the importance of the square ground plans of Scandinavian and Russian sanctuaries and the idol of Svantovit at Arkona discussed in Saxo Grammaticus.[130] He rejects Cohen's arguments that the idols must refer to Thor or Freyr as only they had beards and that the knobs were coloured red to represent the beard of Thor, and reasonably remarks that if this were the case why weren't the beards coloured red? Instead he says that it is Woden who is usually depicted with a beard.

The final question is about the number of heads. He says that this is the hardest question to answer and briefly discusses the idea of Hauck that the heads are linked to the head in the hip of the bird on the Sutton Hoo shield,[131] in this connection, Hauck links the decoration to Odin and mentions one of his bynames, *Elgr*, i.e. 'Elk'.[132] Storms rejects Hauck's identification of the head surrounds on the heads of the stone as being torcs or necklaces on the grounds that the mason could have portrayed these, clearly, had he needed to. Storm believes that these surrounds are cowls (Storms refers to the OE term *grīma*, or 'mask') and that the discs below them are cowl fasteners.[133] For Storms, all eight heads are Woden so there is no need to explain their apparent differences.

---

[127] Storms either did not research this adequately or expressed his findings clumsily. The word *heorot* is far from uncommon in English place-names – *Hertford* is attested as *heorotford* in 673AD, and *heorot* occurs in early forms of many surviving names, e.g. *Hartanger* (Kent), *Hartburn* (Durham), *Hartest* (Suffolk), *Hartfield* (Sussex), *Hartford* (Cheshire, Northumberland and Yorkshire), *Hartham* (Worcestershire), *Harthay* (Huntingdonshire), *Harthill* (Cheshire, Derbyshire), *Hartington* (Derbyshire, Northumberland), *Hartland* (Devonshire), *Hartley* (Berkshire, Dorsetshire, Hampshire, Kent, Northumberland), *Hartlip* (Kent), *Harton* (Durham), *Hartshead* (Lancashire, Yorkshire), *Hartshorne* (Derbyshire), *Hartwell* (Berkshire, Northamptonshire, Staffordshire), *Hartwith* (Yorkshire), *Harty* (Kent). *Harting* (Sussex) is the 'people associated with the stag', *Heorotingas*. (Ekwall, 1960). *Hartest* is spelt *Hertest* in 1050 AD, but in the Domesday survey it is *Herterst* i.e. *heorot hyrst*. The second –r- was lost by dissimilation. A *hyrst* was a low mound or hillock surmounted by a stand of trees. (Pollington, 2011a, p.116)

[128] Storms, 1978. 326. Storms doesn't say this but it could be that the two knobs are representative of the rising and setting sun and we will look at this idea later on in this study.

[129] Storms, 1978. 326.

[130] Storms, 1978. 327.

[131] Storms 1978. 327. He mentions, too, the possibility that a Lombardic shield carried the same device but had been unable to track down the reference. I know of no such Lombardic shield device.

[132] From a 10th or 11th century kenning in the Skaldic poem, *Sonatorrek*. We will have more to say about the shield bird and Woden below.

[133] Storms, 1978. 327.

He does illustrate and refer to two very interesting stone columns in religious buildings. The first is in the church of the former Benedictine monastery of Alpirsbach in the Black Forest in Germany. The carvings are at the top of the column and there are four faces surrounding the column, the capital is in effect four-sided, each face has a beast on either side, rather like one of the motifs on the Sutton Hoo purse.[134] On the other side of the church, there is another column with eight heads.[135] These are the only decorated columns in the church. Storms argues quite convincingly that these heads represent Wotan (Odin) and the reason why they are there is that they represent

> "..the forces that were defeated by the Christian god and that they now have to carry the weight of the church on their backs."[136]

He also reports a similar column in another Benedictine monastery near Andernach in the Eiffel, the church of Maria Laach, built in 1093.

When talking about the meeting of the hart cult and the stone bar, he says

> "The two meet in a mystifying object, consisting of eight sombre-looking faces carved in stone and topped by the image of a hart. That a god had many faces was nothing strange to the Anglo-Saxon mind; werewolves and witch cats retained their credibility for centuries after."[137]

Storms continues his paper with a consideration of other objects from the grave, much of it very interesting but not of direct relevance to this study, except to say that he is certain that the main god celebrated within the tomb and the one referred to in the stone is Woden.[138]

Simpson (1979)

Jacqueline Simpson, who has published English translations of Icelandic sagas and folktales, opens her investigation wondering why the creator of the stone chose 'whetstone' as the material with which to make the piece.[139] She feels that there must have been something of especial significance to the Anglo-Saxons as it is a heavy and not very beautiful material. She believes that a look at Icelandic literature where whetstones are mentioned may provide a clue or two. She does realise that the difference in time separating the Sutton Hoo stone and the writing of the later literature is quite large but does say that the later Germanic material has been found to have some relevance to the earlier period in other matters and that remnants of significance may yet be gleaned which could help us understand the importance of stones during the earlier period.

In her second paragraph she mentions four stories that may hold hints and later on relates a fifth. She begins by looking at a passage written by Snorri Sturluson from the *Prose Edda*. (c 1220 A.D.) This story relates how Óðinn obtained the sacred mead of poetry from the giant Suttung. Óðinn learnt that the mead was hidden in a cave inside a mountain guarded by Suttung's daughter. Óðinn disguised himself as a wandering farmhand called Bölverkr (bale-worker) and approached the land of Suttung's brother, Baugi, where he found nine mowers reaping hay with scythes; he tricked the mowers into slaying each other in a scramble for his wondrous whetstone which allowed him to mow incredibly efficiently. When Baugi heard of this, he was angry but Bölverkr offered to do the work of the nine dead mowers himself in exchange for Baugi's support in his plea to Suttung. (Baugi's appeal to Suttung was unsuccessful and Óðinn had to use magical means to gain the mead.)[140]

---

[134] Storms, 1978. 332.

[135] Storms, 1979. 333.

[136] Storms, 1979. 333.

[137] Storms, 1978. 329.

[138] Storms, 1978. 330 to 343.

[139] Simpson, 1979, p. 96

[140] Simpson, 1979. 96. Enright, 2006, devotes a 14 page appendix to explaining that not one of the saga references mentioned by Simpson is appropriate for comparison with the Sutton Hoo whetstone. We will have more to say on this matter below.

The second story that Simpson mentions is also from Snorri, the tale about a fight between Thor and the giant Hrungnir. Hrungnir uses a hone as a weapon when he fights with Thor. Hrungnir flings his hone at Thor who simultaneously throws his hammer, the two weapons meet and the hone breaks in two. One part falls to the earth, and from it all the hones that have ever been made were created, but the other piece lodges in Thor's skull. However, Hrungnir is killed when the hammer, Mjolnir, continuing on its journey shatters his skull, which was made of stone. Despite attempts, the hone cannot be removed from Thor's skull and when anyone throws a whetstone on earth, the one in Thor's skull moves.[141] It would appear that there were taboos against throwing whetstones in medieval Iceland.

Simpson points out that in Germanic and Nordic culture the thunderbolt is usually represented by a hammer or an axe but that there is ample evidence that stone weapons could fulfil this role and that 'thunderstones' were thought to have magical powers in many areas, including the north. Apparently, the objects most often cast in this role were prehistoric flint arrow heads and stone axes, iron pyrites and types of fossils.[142]

Simpson next draws our attention to *Víga-Glúm's saga* (possibly dating from 983 A.D.) where a whetstone is again used as a weapon.[143] Glúm has a dream in which, using a whetstone, he fought one Thorarin, also armed with a whetstone – the two stones come together and make an almighty crash. Simpson then relates the story in *Gautrek's Saga* in which there is a tale involving a whetstone and a king. In this tale Ref, a feckless youth, is sent to the local Jarl, Neri. Neri sends him on an errand to King Gautrek with a hone that he is to pass to the king. He is told that the king flies his hawk while sitting on his queen's burial mound and that when the hawk tires the king will reach behind him to throw something at the hawk to encourage it. Ref is to put the hone in his hand. The plan goes ahead as Neri had said it would, and the king is so pleased that the bird flew higher that without looking he gives Ref a gold ring. Ref uses the ring to make his fortune and ends up a Jarl himself.

Simpson also relates an episode from *Knytlinga saga* where King Harald Sveinsson of Denmark who died in 1018, was called, *hein* or hone because he was so mild and gentle.[144] The new king, Harald's brother and successor, Knut, told the Danes that he would pay them back for sneering at his brother and that he would be a 'rough whetstone' to them.[145]

Simpson then says that all these tales together show that 'whetstone' and whetstones were important in the Germanic world and proposes that the ancient belief in the thunderbolt of the sky god became attached to whetstones. She suggests that this is because whetstones can spark, however, not all do, so although she may be correct about the connection between thunderbolts and whetstones, her point about sparks is a little weak. She does show that there is a link with whetstones being thrown and with them being used as weapons in fights.[146]

Simpson feels that the stone may have been originally linked to *Tiwaz* (Anglo-Saxon *Tiw* and Norse *Týr*) and only later transferred to Thor. Tiwaz, besides being a sky god, was god of war, of justice, of contracts and of the communal order and the whetstone could

"..symbolise not merely his destructive wrath but also his power and justice." [147]

She says, too, that Adam of Bremen when reporting on the Svear sanctuary at Uppsala (c. 1070) described Thor 'who rules in the sky' and whose image occupied the middle place (between Odin and Freyr) holding a 'sceptre'. This has often been regarded by scholars as a mistake as they think Adam meant 'hammer', but Simpson thinks that he meant what he wrote.

---

[141] Simpson, 1979. 97.
[142] Simpson, 1979. 97.
[143] Simpson,1979. 98.
[144] Simpson, 1979. 99.
[145] Simpson, 1979. 99.
[146] Simpson, 1979. 100.
[147] Simpson, 1979. 100.

She concludes her study with

> "In my view, therefore, the choice of whetstone as material for the Sutton Hoo sceptre finds its explanation in the cluster of ideas expressed in the Icelandic texts. It was a substance which could represent the thunderbolt of the sky-god, and hence could symbolise power, justice, avenging wrath, warfare, and the sacredness of oaths and compacts; if a king carried a bar of whetstone as his sceptre, this indicated his position as the sky-god's earthly representative, as ruler and guardian of justice."[148]

We will return to some of these ideas below.[149]

Mitchell 1985

Stephen A. Mitchell discusses the Sutton Hoo 'whetstone' in his paper, *The Whetstone as Symbol of Authority in Old English and Old Norse* which was published in 1985. Mitchell finds himself in sympathy with the idea of the stone being associated with the king in his role as master and giver of swords.[150] He points out, too, that there are other 'apparently ornamental', 'non-functional' whetstones with religious or symbolic significance found within a Germanic context but that the one from Sutton Hoo is the "grandest example of a 'ceremonial' whetstone". He also accepts the proposition that the whetstone's main function was as a sceptre. Only In a footnote does he describes Cohen's and Storm's suggestions that it may have been an idol as 'imaginitive' and then moves on to mention the more 'sober' explanation provided by Karl Hauck as an *Ahnenstab*.[151] He takes neither of these suggestions any further.

Mitchell believes that Simpson's explanation of the whetstone as 'the thunderbolt of the sky god', with all the connotations that concept would bring, and her references to sagas and mythological literature to be 'inviting'.[152] However, he has some reservations concerning her thesis. First of all, he feels that she left unexplained the exact nature of the connection between whetstones and kings.[153] He thinks, too, that Simpson was unable to demonstrate fully how the 6th/7th century whetstone and the much later literature can be linked together.[154] Mitchell reports that there are few thematic features that bind together the saga stories and the mythological tales, where whetstones are mentioned, and he is also critical of Simpson's ability to interpret the stories in specific terms,[155] he says that, instead she just associates the whetstone with the "proto-Germanic sky god, *Tiwaz and the notion of thunder, with which the whetstone would have been connected because of its 'capacity to emit sparks'".

However, Mitchell does think that Simpson's ideas have some validity and can be greatly strengthened, filling in the gaps in her exploration of the whetstone with certain linguistic evidence as well as that from the literature, archaeology and mythology. The linguistic evidence that he is thinking of are Germanic words connected to the concepts of 'whetting' and 'whetting technology'.[156] He provides a very extensive list of such words within Germanic vocabularies together with their meanings.[157] As a brief example he points out that, "...when an Englishman speaks of something that would *whet* his appetite, or an Icelander of something which would *brýna*, 'whet' his interest, or a Dane of a situation in which he was forced to

---

[148] Simpson 1979. 100.

[149] Although Simpson doesn't mention any actual Icelandic whetstones, Sigrid Cecilie Hansen (2009) provides a good survey and compares them to Norwegian, German and English examples from the Viking period.

[150] Mitchell, 1985. 1. Mitchell is referring to Bruce-Mitford. 1975. 21.

[151] Mitchell, 1985. 23. footnote 2.

[152] Mitchell, 1985. 1.

[153] Mitchell, 1985. 2.

[154] Mitchell, 1985. 2. He mentions that Enright (in his first paper on the subject in 1982) berates Simpson for this failure.

[155] Mitchell, 1985. 5.

[156] Mitchell, 1985. 2.

[157] Mitchell, 1985 see pages 6 to 10 for the full set of examples provided by Mitchell.

ægge, 'egg' someone into activity, all of them are using the modern reflexes of words that originated in activities surrounding weapon and tool technology and which can tell us a great deal about the association of whetstones and kings."[158] He uses the word 'polysemous' to describe the 'sharpening' terms, that is they all have more than one meaning and that in the case of words involving sharpening or whetting technology, one meaning will be connected to 'sharpening', but another may concern the incitement of others or relate to intellectual agility.[159] He, therefore, feels that, "The symbolic value of the whetstone in early Germanic society, and its meaning in the four ON sources, is best understood when viewed in the light of the vocabulary surrounding whetstone technology in the various Germanic languages."[160]

Mitchell goes on to explain that, "The association of whetstones and authority, especially regal authority, probably originated through the metaphoric usages of whetting terminology and the appropriateness of such concepts to leadership, that is, the necessity for a chieftain in early Germanic society to possess a keen intellect and the ability to urge others into action, to speak well at meetings and to have his views incite others, qualities which together must have been regarded as a *sine qua non* for leadership."[161] Mitchell criticises the popular image of the brute barbarian and emphasises the sophisticated skills of rhetoric and other oratorical abilities that would be essential for leading the Germanic peoples. They would need, "..the talent to persuade and incite one's followers and community.." and he reminds us that this talent would not just be limited to kings.[162] Again, he is able to demonstrate very clearly from a profusion of sources that these abilities were highly valued in the north.[163]

He says that it is instructive to look further afield and consider other Indo European languages, some quite ancient, to find that there are a wide variety of words in those languages that use the same word for sky and stone. He provides some examples, and ponders whether this is how the connection between sky and stones began and could be the reason for the symbolic importance of throwing whetstones. He suggests that this supports the part of Simpson's thesis; that the SH whetstone has something to do with the sky god.[164] Mitchell, clearly associates the whetstone with *Tiwaz*, (later OE *Tiw*, ON *Tyr*) because he feels that the linguistic evidence takes the link perhaps as far back as 1700 to 1500 B.C., when the '*Teutons*' started making metal tools that could shape stone.[165] He feels that this ability to manufacture tools and weapons led to the special position that smiths occupied within Germanic society and lists other attributes of the smith's work that would add to his mystique: the '..significance and awe inspiring nature of his work', the sparks produced during the smith's working of metal that could be associated with thunder and the sky and "…the ancient relationships between the concepts of stone and the firmament."[166] Mitchell gives examples, too, of the special regard that smiths were held in within the literature and mentions *Weland* (*Vǫlundr, Velent*), who was able to fly.

Mitchell believes that it is possible to connect the powerful image of the smith to that of the king as 'giver of swords' and quotes Bucholz's noting of the ON tradition of referring to kings and other powerful personages as 'good smiths'.[167] Mitchell retells part of the story of King *Oláf Trygvasson* where *Oláf* gives out sharp swords to his companions to replace their blunt ones during their final battle, as a good example of a king as 'giver of swords'.[168]

---

[158] Mitchell, 1985. 2.

[159] Mitchell, 1985. 5 and 6 to 10.

[160] Mitchell, 1985. 5.

[161] Mitchell, 1985. 11.

[162] Mitchell, 1985. 14.

[163] Mitchell, 1985. 14 to 15. In addition, Mitchell cites a study by James E. Knirk of the Kings' Sagas who found that 24% of speeches in them were 'devoted exclusively to incitation'

[164] Mitchell, 1985. 11.

[165] Mitchell, 1985. 12. This may well be the case, but they did not need metal tools to shape stone as stone tools are quite capable of doing this, too.

[166] Mitchell, 1985. 12.

[167] Mitchell, 1985. 13. This is an idea that Enright also uses. See below.

[168] Mitchell, 1985. 13.

One other concept that Mitchell uses to show the importance of inspiring speech is that of *óðr*, the root of *Óðinn's* name. Mitchell says that it means 'mad' or 'frantic' and reports that it "..provides an interesting testimony to the nature of authority: what more appropriate image for leadership in early Germanic society could there be than that of one who is able to incite his followers into action?"[169] He does emphasise, too, the fact that Germanic leaders would have to persuade their community in other areas besides war.

Mitchell picks up where Simpson left off to explain the connection between whetstones that are thrown in the stories and leadership; he takes us back to the passages from *Gautrek's saga* and *The Prose Edda*, tales where *Óðinn* obtained the sacred mead of poetry from the giant Suttung, and the episode concerning a fight between *Þórr* and the giant *Hrungnir*.[170] In *Gautrek's saga*, the whetstone is passed to the king and, indirectly, Ref becomes a jarl, *Óðinn* uses his authority and incites the thralls to kill each other,[171] Hrungnir, according to Mitchell, was the leader of the giants, as he was the strongest of his race; even in the fight where whetstones were used as weapons in *Víga-Glúm's saga*, Mitchell shows that it was a fight between two protagonists for the leadership of the district.[172]

He discusses the episode from the *Knýtlinga saga* referred to also by Simpson, where *Haraldr* was mocked for being a *hein* (hone). His brother Knútr, (Canute the Great) who succeeded after *Haraldr's* short reign, angry with his people's treatment of his unfortunate sibling, told his new subjects that he would be as a *frekr harðstein* (harsh whetstone) to them.[173] To Mitchell, the main significance of this tale, besides the inclusion of whetstones, is what it says concerning *Haraldr's* speaking abilities, or lack of them; "King Haraldr was a tranquil and reserved man, taciturn, did not speak at meetings, was forced to have others speak for him: he was a man of little importance in those things that require thought, he was no warrior, quiet and gentle with the people and little rule was provided by him."[174] Mitchell feels it is significant that the word *hein* (hone), unlike other, masculine whetting words is a feminine noun in ON.[175]

Mitchell states that he believes that all the evidence combined shows that the physical object of the whetstone would have had a symbolic significance connecting the concept of sharpness, both of weapons and of minds.[176] He says of the Sutton Hoo whetstone, that "…it was the ideal embodiment of an entire complex of ideas associated with authority and leadership: eloquence and rhetorical skill, sharpness of mind, and military prowess."[177] The stone also has 'sacral overtones' as he says that "In all of the cases from the ON literature and mythology, whetstones are affiliated with power and incitement; likewise, all of the Scandinavian texts testify to the association of whetstones with motion." He contrasts this idea with the apparently static whetstones found in Anglo-Saxon England, which according to him and others, show clear signs of being held in the hand.[178] He describes the connection between flying stones, and the sky god moving through his realm as being 'immeasurably old'[179] as it goes back, at least, to the Indo-European stone/heaven concept, and that this concept has a resonance, too, with the later idea of the flying smith. He acknowledges that **Tiwaz* loses some of his attributes to *Óðinn* and *Þórr* as the god's importance fades and so is not surprised that it is *Óðinn* and *Þórr* that are the deities involved in the Icelandic material.

---

[169] Mitchell, 1985. 13.

[170] Mitchell,1985. 5 and 19.

[171] Mitchell, 1985. 20.

[172] Mitchell, 1985. 19. For brief details of the stories, please see our analysis of Simpson's writing above.

[173] Mitchell's discussion of this episode is a comprehensive one. Mitchell, 1985. 16 to 18.

[174] Mitchell, 1985. 17. This is Mitchell's translation of the relevant passage.

[175] Mitchell, 1985. 17.

[176] Mitchell, 1985. 19.

[177] Mitchell, 1985. 20.

[178] Mitchell, 1985. 21. We shall have more to say about the stains on the Sutton Hoo and Uncleby stones elsewhere in this volume. The Uncleby stone shows clear signs of having been knocked about, possibly thrown, before it was interred. See below.

[179] Mitchell. 1985. 21.

Ryan (1979)

Ryan certainly questions the use of the word 'Celtic' in respect of the workmanship - he suggests that more specific terms should have been used such as 'Irish', 'British', or 'Pictish', but continues to use the word 'Celtic' because it has been used so often and it is familiar, and presumably most readers will understand and be aware of the problems when using it.[180]

Ryan is well aware of the importance of the 'whetstone' and says that

"It is difficult to underestimate the importance of the object in influencing the interpretation of the burial as a whole..."[181]

Ryan is aware, too, that there is much debate about the stone, says that several assumptions have been made and that they are,

"..best summed up by the assertion that the whetstone-scepter (sic) represents a survival of Celtic royal practice adopted by the Anglo-Saxons perhaps as part of a legitimation process."[182]

He summarises the findings of Bruce-Mitford and reports that the source of origin for the greywacké-grit was southern Scotland, northwestern England or in Germany - the Harz Mountains or the Rhineland.[183] A little later he mentions the fact that Bruce-Mitford failed to find convincing parallels for the object as a whole in the Germanic world and the great differences that Bruce-Mitford found between the Sutton Hoo stone, as a sceptre, and more classical ones, namely the fact that it is of stone, has red knobs, eight heads and is of square section and heavy.[184] Ryan's own, grudging comment, that

"The scepter (sic) dimly reflects the staffs of office of Late Antique rulers,"[185]

hints at what he really feels.

Ryan mentions, too, Bruce-Mitford's suggestion that the stag was old, possibly an heirloom piece before mounting on the stone and may have been of Celtic manufacture.[186] However he says that the heads on the stone are

"..entirely Germanic in feeling,"

and lists the same parallels that Bruce-Mitford does to support that point - namely, the shield flanges from the Valsgärde 8 and Vendel XII graves in Sweden, and the metal staff adornments from Vimose and Søholdt, both in Denmark. Ryan reminds the reader of Bruce-Mitford's argument about Rædwald being the *bretwalda* and the stone being a badge of that office, but Ryan, himself, doesn't seem too happy with this interpretation and says that,

"Historians must decide on what reality lies behind the title *Bretwalda*."[187]

Here he gives the impression that he is content to say no more on this aspect of the debate.

He carefully considers the other stone evidence, headed or otherwise, that Bruce-Mitford records and points out that some of them - the stones from Hough-on-the-Hill, Lochar Moss, and the 14 cms long piece

---

[180] Ryan, 1992. 83.
[181] Ryan, 1992. 85.
[182] Ryan, 1979. 85.
[183] Ryan, 1992. 85.
[184] Ryan, 1992. 86.
[185] Ryan, 1992. 85.
[186] Ryan, 1992. 86.
[187] Ryan, 1992. 86.

from Portsoy - are all stray finds without a context and may not have been whetstones.[188] Ryan remarks that the Portsoy actually may have been a trial piece.[189] He also says that

> "The earliest firmly-dated whetstone bearing carved heads is that from Sutton Hoo. The parallels quoted from Bruce-Mitford very likely come from various periods and various cultural contexts, and to speak of them as 'known to the Celts' is meaningless."[190]

The last point is aimed at Enright.[191] Again, with Enright in mind, Ryan asks the question: "Did whetstones figure as regalia in the Celtic world?" and reports that the laws of Ireland say nothing on this matter, although a 'grinding stone' is mentioned as a possession of someone in one law. On the Welsh material, Ryan can find only one mention of whetstone as a possession and it was almost certainly a tool.[192]

Figure 73 Carved antler tip
from Ireland, of Viking date

Figure 74 Appliqué mount from
a shield, Vimose, Denmark

---

[188] Ryan, 1992. 86.
[189] Ryan, 1992. 87.
[190] Ryan, 1992. 87.
[191] Ryan, 1992. 87.
[192] Ryan, 1992. 87.

Ryan tells us of a number of whetstones from Ireland which have a resemblance to the one from Mound 1. The first is from Newtownlow, Co. Westmeath (Figure) which is a carefully shaped, square section stone, tapering at each end. It is 20.8 cm long and weighs 309.47 gm. It has a short bronze chain and hook at one end and is attached to the stone via two metal tangs. The metal work is decorated in the Ringerike style, which is Viking, and Ryan dates it to the 11th century.[193] There is another, similarly shaped piece (Figure 68), without provenance, in the National Museum of Ireland, which is a little longer at 22 cm. Ryan discusses some more stones of varying sizes and shapes all without heads from Ireland and says that

> "In the light of recent finds, one can only suggest that metal-mounted, fine whetstones in Ireland belong to the Viking Age and the Dublin ones, in particular, can belong to no other period."[194]

On the subject of 'headed' whetstones, Ryan is equally assertive and is doubtful that they can be claimed, as Bruce-Mitford and Enright have, to be a 'Celtic phenomenon'. Ryan points out that although such things were found in Iron Age Ireland and Britain, they were either two- or three-headed, and that there is no evidence of continuity into the medieval period.[195]

Ryan discusses the heads on the Sutton Hoo stone and, like others before him, is very critical of Hauck's suggestion that the head surrounds portray the insignia worn by the bodyguard of the Emperor Justinian.[196] Ryan says

> "The pear-shaped field defined by a moulding has sufficient antecedents in Germanic metalwork not to require such a specific origin, nor does its disposition over the head particularly suggest the suspension chain of a medallion."[197]

Ryan moves on to consider parallels for the Sutton Hoo iconography from the Migration Period to the Viking Age and finds some:[198]

1 An 11th century bronze stylus from Hagested in Jutland, Denmark; it has four heads at the top surmounted by a quadruped (Figure 72).
2 A 5th century silver pin from an Allemanic girl's grave at Eschborn, Germany; this, too has four heads (Figure 94).
3 A four headed pin from the Viking Age from Praestegaarden, Norway (Figure 118).
4 Two bone objects from Sweden, both with four heads carved in relief (Figures 113 & 115).
5 A small carved antler tip, again from the Viking Age, this time from Ireland, and again with four carved heads (Figure 73).
6 A bronze strap distributor from Bregentved, Denmark (Figure 120) Each of the four links has two distinct opposed heads.
7 The limestone column from Zbruc on the Dniester – with four heads and bodies (Figure 92).
8 A small wooden idol and a whetstone with bronze finial from Wolin, Poland; both have the four-headed iconography (Figure 121)

Ryan finishes his a consideration with a real flourish and no-one is spared. If he seemed a little undecided earlier in his paper, he dispels that impression with:

> "The sceptre is an Anglo-Saxon product; its immediate background is Germanic. Like many Migration Period prestige objects, it represents an adaptation of a Late Antique prototype although, at first sight, this ancestry may not be obvious. There is no discernable Celtic influence in its style and manufacture. Comparisons with the Pfalzfeld pillar, reference to the

---

[193] Ryan, 1992. 87 to 88.
[194] Ryan, 1992. 88.
[195] Ryan, 1992. 88.
[196] Ryan, 1992. 88.
[197] Ryan, 1992. 89.
[198] Ryan, 1992. 89.

practice of headhunting, or appeals to the status of the smith in ancient Ireland do nothing to supply the lack of evidence for a Celtic connection.[199] Petrologically its raw material was easily obtainable within the Anglian kingdom of Northumbria. It follows, therefore, that the sceptre cannot be used to underpin the theory that Sutton Hoo Mound One was the grave of a *Bretwalda* who claimed hegemony over both Celtic and Germanic peoples in Britain and whose claim found its physical embodiment in his regalia."[200]

Thus, Ryan leaves no doubt about where he stands within the debate

Scarfe (1986)

Scarfe is a historian, colleague of Bruce-Mitford and Suffolk enthusiast, his native county. The blurb on the back of his book claims that: "His explanation of the presence of the whetstone-sceptre, printed here, has never been challenged."[201]

According to Scarfe, Rædwald was the *bretwalda* through the exercise of his personal and military power. Whereas Bruce-Mitford believed that much of the regalia was deposited in Mound 1 because, as Rædwald died, so did his *bretwaldaship*, and the regalia went with him to the grave, Scarfe suggests that the regalia was Rædwald's own personal equipment and was placed within the tomb to go on his last journey with him.[202] This is because Scarfe finds it

"..impossible to imagine Rædwald being buried at Sutton Hoo by Christians eager to be discharged of such pagan barbarities."[203]

As Scarfe reasonably shows, Rædwald's successor wasn't converted until some three years after Rædwald's death and then later apostatised. Scarfe also suggests that the two most important items in Mound 1 are the whetstone and the large Celtic hanging bowl.[204]

Scarfe creates an imaginative and entertaining account of the reign of King Rædwald and his queen, King Aethelfrith and King Edwin of Northumbria, all based on the few details that Bede and the *Anglo-Saxon Chronicle* provide, involving the coins and purse from the grave, as well as the whetstone.[205] It's a good story of the gods, honour, greed, power and treachery, it has very little to do with the archaeology, though, as this sentence should demonstrate:

"The sceptre is exactly what I would imagine Aethelfrith holding as he sat alone on the dais at the apex of the wedge-shaped stadium or grand-stand, in a formal open assembly of his chiefs and priests and elders at Yeavering."[206]

Scarfe talks about the 'eight, unblinking totem-heads' each as 'old as time' – displaying

"...all the barbarity of the German ruler who has mastery of his Celtic kingdom by giving them victory and slave-taking in neighbouring British and Pictish territories."

He further describes the whetstone as

"..being crowned with a regally-antlered bronze stag of Celtic craftsmanship.."

and that this

"...was a sound gesture of solidarity with his imaginative people."

---

[199] These refer to claims by Enright.
[200] Ryan, 1992. 90.
[201] Scarfe, 1986.
[202] Scarfe, 1986. 35 to 37.
[203] Scarfe, 1986. 36.
[204] Scarfe, 1986. 36.
[205] Scarfe, 1986. For the full story the reader will have to read the whole chapter, 30 to 37.
[206] Scarfe, 1986. 36.

He then suggests that Rædwald took the 'sceptre' after winning the Battle of the River Idle and slaying Aethelfrith.[207] And the hanging bowl? That was a gift from a grateful Edwin, who was now Rædwald's client king in Northumbria.

It is a lovely story and as it is a work of imagination it is pointless to challenge it. However, what if, and it has never been certain, the Mound 1 grave wasn't Rædwald's?

Wilson (1992)

Wilson was writing at a time when the so-called 'sand bodies' at Sutton Hoo were thought to be contemporary with the mound burials. Martin Carver and his team have to a large extent changed that perception and it is now generally thought that most of these remains are those of executed people from around the 8th to 11th centuries.[208] This means that Wilson assumed that the evidence of hanged men were associated with Woden and human sacrifice.[209] He then goes on to report, following Simpson, that the whetstone has been associated with that god, on the basis of her work with the Prose Edda and sagas. He has nothing further to say on the matter.

Greis and Geselowitz (1992)

Greis and Geselowitz add little to the debate about the stone, and after a brief description of the components, we read that the stone is made from a fine grained sandstone and that the faces are,

"..common to both Celtic and Germanic art."[210]

Greis and Geselowitz repeat what Carola Hicks said about the stag, that it has parallels in Scythian and Romano-Celtic art and that it is not Anglo-Saxon in style

"..especially in the placement of the feet and exaggerated realistic antlers."[211]

They say, too, that the stag was not made for the stone but may have been an heirloom piece and that similar stag figures have been excavated at Pazryk in the Altai. The Pazryk stags apparently came from pole-tops and were used as standards.[212] Unfortunately, they provide no further details and do not illustrate the pieces or tell us what size they are.

Filmer-Sankey (1996)

Filmer-Sankey calls his paper *"The 'Roman Emperor' in the Sutton Hoo Ship Burial"*[213] and that really explains what his thesis is: that many of the items within the tomb are a reflection of the occupant's obsession with what he may have regarded as the trappings of a Roman Emperor, based on images that were available to him on coins, etc. However, we will confine ourselves, mostly, to what he says about the stone.

---

[207] Scarfe, 1986. 36.
[208] Carver, 2005. 315 to 349.
[209] Wilson, 1992. 168.
[210] Gleis and Geselowitz, 1992. 34.
[211] Gleis and Geselowitz, 1992. 34.
[212] Gleis and Geselowitz, 1992. 36.
[213] Filmer-Sankey, 1996.

Filmer-Sankey is very much influenced by a German professor, Joachim Werner, who reviewed the three volume *Sutton Hoo Ship Burial* by Bruce-Mitford and others. Werner suggested that by

> "..defining the practical function of individual objects and then by looking at groups of spatially linked objects, it is possible to gain an overall view of the logic behind the selection of the individual grave goods placed in the grave."[214]

According to Filmer-Sankey, this approach allows for

> ".more firmly based archaeological deductions on the status of the dead man, which are not dependent on shaky connexions (sic) with the sketchy details of East Anglian regnal history given by Bede or on subjective value judgements of the sort of buckle which would have been worthy to support a pair of royal trousers."[215]

This is very interesting, and says a great deal about the way in which he views the objects at Sutton Hoo. He has some interesting things to say about the Byzantine silverware and then remarks that many of the other objects are copies of Late Roman prototypes; this includes the stone.[216]

As far as Filmer-Sankey is concerned, the stone is an attempt to ape the type of sceptre that an Anglian king may have seen in a Late Roman consular diptych.[217] Thus he is able to explain the important differences between the Sutton Hoo 'sceptre' and those of Rome and Byzantium; it's a copy - and a poor copy, too, because the Anglians made it out of stone, it's heavy with too many heads and the knobs are painted red.[218]

North (1997)

Richard North's discussion of the gods of the Anglo-Saxons and his desire to show that the fertility god *Ingui* (later called *Yngvi-Freyr*) was probably the most important of the Anglo-Saxon gods before the conversion to Christianity, seems to have coloured the way that he interprets the Sutton Hoo stone. He doesn't have a great deal to say about the stone except that, while referring to Simpson's idea of connecting the stone to the cult of Thor, he remarks that the stone and stag assembly could show that the ruler interred at Sutton Hoo

> "..divided his attention between his ancestors on one hand and the common people on the other."[219]

Unfortunately it isn't terribly clear what he means by this. Elsewhere, he does suggest that the stone with its stag emblem may refer to royal and popular aspects of paganism and to the god, *Ingui*; it may be a thunder numen, or a reference to the ancestors and to laws. Curiously, he follows Wallace-Hadrill's suggestion that it could be seen as neither Christian nor pagan.[220]

---

[214] Filmer-Sankey, 1996. 1. Which, of course, is fine provided you are absolutely correct about what those functions are.

[215] Filmer-Sankey, 1996. 1 to 2.

[216] Filmer-Sankey, 1996. 4.

[217] Filmer-Sankey, 1996. 6.

[218] The latter comments are mine, I am afraid, however, they are implied by Filmer-Sankey.

[219] North, 1997. 234.

[220] North, 1997. 322 to 323.

Carver (1998)

Carver, in his 1998 book, makes some rather unexpected comments about the design of the stone ensemble although in most respects he follows Bruce-Mitford; he thinks the position of *bretwalda* was 'more imaginary than real'.[221] Carver says

> "One can imagine it as the product of a seventh-century 'regalia working party' which was instructed to come up with something that would impress a Byzantine emperor and a British potentate, but without alarming the champions of pagan independence."[222]

He also suggests that it may have been placed in the tomb because it was, 'a ridiculous conceit' but that we will never know for sure.

Discussion

This examination has been a very long and quite detailed one and there is yet further to go with the ideas of Enright and his belief in the 'Celtic' origins of the piece. However, I feel that we should spend a short period reflecting on some of the suggestions that we have met with on our journey. Is the stone a sceptre, a mace, an idol, an ancestor staff, a dynastic symbol, a judgement sceptre, a magic staff, a phallic symbol, a fertility symbol , a thunderbolt, a missile, a weapon, a symbol of the mastery over weapons, an altar ring, an oath ring, a firelighter, a badge of office, a symbol of an agile mind and rhetorical ability, or just a whetstone? All these ideas have been suggested in the texts that we have considered. Is it pagan? Does it symbolise Thunor, Tiw, Woden or Ing? Is it of religious significance at all? Can it be any or all of these at once? Are any of the suggestions mutually exclusive?

Hopefully, there are one or two ideas that won't survive this discussion, which will narrow our search for an answer. For example, I am not convinced that it could be a missile as it is so finely made and the stag and ring would easily be damaged, but it certainly could represent one - perhaps a mythical one?

Whatever it is, someone went to a lot of time, trouble and effort to make it and it was considered important enough to be placed in a position of honour, upright in Mound 1.[223]

To some extent Rupert Bruce-Mitford has been the 'market leader' in all things Sutton Hoo justifiably in many ways because he was responsible for the massive three-volume publication on the finds and he has had great influence over the way that many scholars and the public have interpreted the objects. His descriptions of the finds are definitive and unlikely ever to need to have to be re-written, except in matters of detail. However, his interpretation is a different matter, particularly when it comes to the stone.

Bretwalda

One of the things Bruce-Mitford said that has influenced several other commentators and has been repeated in various media fairly frequently, is the suggestion that the stone was a badge of office for Rædwald as *bretwalda*.[224] It would seem that Bruce-Mitford is on very shaky ground here. I briefly criticised this idea earlier but I would like to take that line of thought a little further to see how much validity there is in the whole concept of the *bretwalda*.

In some ways the idea of the *bretwalda* rests with Bede who lists seven kings (mentioned above in our discussion of Bruce-Mitford's work).[225] Bede, however, does not use the word and it isn't written down until a century later, it is mentioned in the *Anglo-Saxon Chronicle*, the Parker manuscript (MS A).[226] This

---

[221] Carver, 1998. 170.

[222] Carver, 1998,p.170.

[223] Carver, 2006, p.185-97

[224] Bruce-Mitford, 1978 376 and 377.

[225] Sherley-Price, 1990, p.107-8

[226] Fanning, 1991. 4. Keynes, 1992, p. 110. Swanton, 1996. 61, also fn 10.

appears to be the earliest use of the word during the Anglo-Saxon period. Variations of the word are used in other manuscripts and at other times; *brytenwalda* (MS B), *bretananwealda* (MS C), *brytenwealda* MSS D, E) and *brytenwealda* (MS F).[227] The problem is that the last four versions of the word do not appear to mean what Bruce-Mitford claimed that *bretwalda* meant, 'ruler of Britain' not 'ruler of the British'[228] According to Fanning *bryten* and its variations mean 'wide' or 'broad' or 'great' as in *bridun giwald* (great ruler) *brytengrunde* (wide earth) *bryten rice* (wide kingdom) *brytencunning* (great king) so that *brytenwalda* should mean 'wide-ruler' or emperor.[229] Keynes comments

> "...the Parker manuscript may be the oldest surviving manuscript, but it is not the original, and its readings are not always the best."[230]

adding

> "...the draftsman of a charter purportedly issued by King Æthelstan used it in a way that can only mean 'wide ruler'.[231]

Perhaps it would be useful to look at the word that Bede actually used. Bede was writing in Latin and doesn't actually give the seven kings a particular title at all, he does use the word, *imperium* and variations of it, in order to describe the type of rule credited to the seven powerful kings. Apparently, the word means 'sovereignty'.[232] Incidentally, Bede tells us almost nothing about the first two kings on his list. Fanning explains that Bede's usage of imperial language throughout his histories is entirely consistent with Late Roman usage and remarks,

> "...*imperium* did not require anything more than domination of another people or kingdom."[233]

The words, *imperium* or *bretwalda* did not mean 'ruler of the British' or 'ruler of the Britons'; the early English kingdoms were more than capable of squabbling among themselves and trying to dominate each other - of course they wouldn't have missed an opportunity to do the same to the Picts, Scots or Britons either.

After saying that, there certainly were overlords (and presumably underlords) of various kinds. Keynes says of Bede's list of *Bretwaldas*

> "...there was no such thing, and the assumption that the overlords had a collective identity as successive holders of a status or office that was recognized as such by their contemporaries, that existed independently of themselves ...... should be resisted."[234]

Fanning, is a little more explicit

> "Thus there is no evidence that there was a *bretwaldaship* or that there was the office or status of *bretwalda* in Anglo-Saxon England. The entire concept ought to be abandoned."[235]

It would appear, then, that Bruce-Miford's claim that the 'whetstone' is the "symbol of the *bretwaldaship*" and was buried with Rædwald as it represented his personal achievement, is no longer a viable one.[236]

---

[227] Fanning, 1991, p.2; Keynes, 1992, p.111; Swanton, 1996, p.61. All spellings of Old English are as given in Fanning, 1991. Keynes, 1992, has slightly different versions.

[228] Bruce-Mitford, 1978, p.375

[229] Fanning, 1991, p.22-3. Swanton also takes this interpretation, whereas Keynes is less sure. Keynes, 1992, p.111

[230] Keynes, 1992, p.111.

[231] Keynes, 1992, p.111.

[232] Keynes, 1992, p.105.

[233] Fanning, 1991.15.

[234] Keynes, 1992, p.116.

[235] Fanning, 1991. 26.

[236] Bruce-Mitford, 1978. 375 to 376.

Ahnenstab

One other idea that it is possible to dispense with here is the concept of the *Ahnenstab* or 'ancestor staff' first mentioned by Karl Hauck as it would seem that this is an original idea of Hauck and has no precedent in literature or in history. It is perhaps not surprising that it has caught the imagination as it is a romantic idea, but that is all it is. Besides, it would seem a little odd to just list eight ancestors when the surviving king lists always list more than that, and the real possibility that some of the heads are female would be a problem for this proposal. I am not quite sure where this would leave the possibility of the stone being a dynastic symbol, as the same criticisms probably apply to that concept too.

Rhetoric

The symbolic connection that the stone may have to the ability to speak well, and to sharpness of mind, both of which seem to have been prerequisites for a successful king, is certainly something to be taken further. We know that kings and leaders were expected to speak at assemblies and elsewhere, sometimes in a highly ritualised manner[237] and many times not. They would certainly have to command attention and ensure that they were listened to. The fact that words associated with sharpening weapons and tools have meanings that relate to favourable intellectual capacity is important and may well have a bearing on how the stone was both used and viewed.

Firelighter

Another possibility that would appear unworkable is that of the stone as a firelighter. It seems that the greywacké will not spark; we have tried, very hard, with all types of metals and with other forms of stone and not once could we get a glimmer. If it symbolises a thunderbolt, then it isn't because this type of stone is capable of making fire. However, if the thunderbolt or thunderstone is seen as the result of a strike, rather than the initiator of it through sparking, then that is a different matter.

That still leaves us with much to explore.

---

[237] Sundqvist, 2002. 209. Beowulf, lines 1214 – 1231. Mortimer, 2011. 211. See also Pollington, 2009 for a full exploration of the environment of the hall and speaking within it.

5. Michael J. Enright's "The Sutton Hoo Sceptre and the Roots of Celtic Kingship Theory": a Critique

Paul Mortimer

Introduction.

Michael J. Enright is the only academic to have devoted a whole book to the subject of the stone from Mound 1 at Sutton Hoo.[238] As Enright is a scholar with a respected body of work, it is important to critically examine his ideas in order to see whether they can help us unravel the significance and meaning of the stone.

Enright's Thesis.

Enright, in 1982, originally wrote a paper on the same subject which appeared in the journal *Anglo-Saxon England* volume 11.[239] His thesis was heavily criticised by Michael Ryan[240] who felt that Enright had not been able to adequately support his ideas and suggested that the Celtic connection promoted by Enright was non-existent. Perhaps that was why Enright felt the need to publish his book-length treatment, which appeared in 2006.

Enright's thesis is that the whetstone-sceptre was made by Celtic craftsmen and that it can only be interpreted in the light of Celtic traditions, and Celtic ideas of kingship; therefore it had little or nothing to do with Germanic traditions. He says that, "it is rooted in a belief system that links a solar/fire cult to metallurgical practices and then to the 'craft' of royal rule."[241] He believes that the stone was created in southern Scotland.[242]

A Selection of Enright's Evidence.

It would not be possible in so short a treatment as this to deal with all of Enright's ideas, however most are based on a few key themes and it is to some of those that we will now turn to see whether or not Enright's thesis has the capacity to explain the stone.

It must be said that he does set himself a formidable task: "The most basic requirement is that one sets out to examine all of the sceptre symbols and not just selected examples: i.e. the stag, the ring, pedestal, heads, surrounds and knobs must all be discussed and cogently related to each other."[243]

---

[238] Enright, 2006

[239] Michael J. Enright, *The Sutton Hoo Whetstone Sceptre: a Study in Iconography and Cultural Milieu* in, *Anglo-Saxon England* (1982), 11 : pp 119-134. Cambridge

[240] Michael Ryan, *The Sutton Hoo Ship Burial and Ireland: Some Celtic Perspectives*, in Farrell and Neuman de Vegvar (eds) 1992.

[241] Enright, 2006, p 10

[242] Enright, 2006, po. 58, 76, 244

[243] Enright, 2006, p. 9

Figure 75   Pfalzfeld pillar

The main object that Enright compares to the stone is the Pfalzfeld Pillar, found in Hunsrück in Germany during the 17th century. It has been dated to the 5th or 4th century La Tène culture. Over the years it has been reduced in height, probably from around 2.8 metres but it is still an impressive object standing around 1.48 metres tall,[244] and is made of sandstone; it dwarfs the Sutton Hoo stone but according to Enright "The similarities between the pillar and sceptre are manifest and remarkable."[245] Later, on the same page, he says, "...the correspondences between the two objects are so striking and impressive that a strong artistic relationship cannot be doubted." Indeed, he goes further, "....it is already plain that the two monuments cannot be separated."[246]

We will consider some aspects of similarity and difference below, but first we will have a brief look at some of the other claims that Enright makes. Just one thing that we must mention here regarding both objects is that Enright considers them to represent, amongst other things, an iron smelting furnace. He does realise that both are roughly square in section and that shaft furnaces are usually circular, but that, he feels, is a minor problem and it may even be that the La Tène people had square-section shaft furnaces.[247]

Enright tells us that sparks are able to be struck from the stone,[248] the smoke from which will reach up to the sun; this is a very important component of his thesis and he refers many times throughout his book to the ability that the stone has to make fire, especially in conjunction with iron. He goes on to remark that the ring above the sceptre is a sun-wheel and this amplifies the message that the stone and iron (ring) together can create fire.[249]

He tell us that, in Celtic religiosity, the god of the sun is the god of poetry and truthful speech and that the smoky coloured bar represents smoke (messages) rising to the gods. According to him, the stone's two red knobs represent fire reduction furnaces which, he believes, are powerful symbols for the separation of true speech from untrue speech. Iron was refined in such furnaces, so the true speech can be called 'iron speech'. The top knob represents a divine furnace and the bottom one a furnace on earth.

Enright says that the stag is an animal peculiarly associated with the sun and fertility, and is shown as the smith's creature on Jupiter's pillars from the early Roman Empire and elsewhere. The stag, he asserts, can only have been created by Celts. His reasoning is that this animal does not appear often in the art or literature of the Germanic people, at least, as far as concepts of authority are concerned.[250]

He claims, too, that the heads on the stone are severed heads[251] (among other things) and that those without beards have been rested on beds of hair to contain the drips. The surrounds around the heads and the discs are chains with 'penannular' rings[252] which show binding to an oath.[253] The circles or discs under the heads containing a slight dimple are symbolic apples.[254]

---

[244] Enright, 2006, p. 34

[245] Enright, 2006, p 35

[246] Enright, 2006, p. 36

[247] Enright, 2006. P 252

[248] Enright, 2006, p.14. He picks up on the suggestion that Cohen makes in passing in his paper. It becomes a major part of his thesis. See Enright, 2006 p 36, p 176, p 182, p 123, p 201, p209, p 226, p 333 and page 338. Even though on page 24, he chides Simpson for suggesting that the whetstone could generate large quantities of sparks. Simpson (1979) was being criticised for introducing Icelandic evidence to explain aspects of the whetstone.

[249] Enright, 2006, p. 48 and p 242

[250] Enright, 2006, p. 75, p 48-9. See Pollington (this volume, p.94) for contrary views.

[251] Enright, 2006, p. 56, p 65, p.93 and elsewhere.

[252] Enright, 2006, p. 58, p 77

[253] Enright, 2006, p. 58

[254] Enright, 2006., p70, p.78 and p.83.Enright sometimes uses the term, 'stops' to refer to these circular formations.

He believes that the image on the hip of the bird is related to the stone heads, and that the 'sceptre' and shield must be considered together. Transforming birds as seen on the shield are divine messengers of the sun god, who communicates with kings to maintain cosmic truth. He suggests that the shield ornament - in fact all the Sutton Hoo jewellery and the stone - could have been made by the same man and that all these objects are 'Celtic'.[255] He says "Nor, of course, is it clear that any design pre-existed for the jewellery. What emerges instead is the appearance of Celtic artisans who seem to have had a particular responsibility for work on the more personal royal regalia.",[256] Another reason that the jewellery must be of Celtic origin, according to Enright, is the inclusion of pieces of millefiori in some of the designs.[257]

Figure 76 Bronze plate-brooch from Lejre, Denmark, with a human face on the hip.

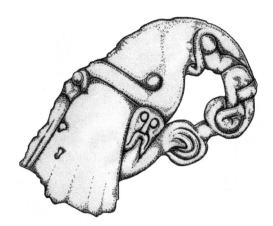

Figure 77 Bronze shield-mount from Skorping, Denmark, in the form of a bird with a human face incised into the hip.

He also suggest that the stone must be Celtic as Germanic peoples didn't carve stone or make representations of things in the round but the Celts did.[258]

To conclude this section, and so that we can be absolutely clear concerning Enright's ideas about the origin of the craftsmen involved with the Sutton Hoo materials, while refuting Bruce-Mitford's suggestion of a Germanic origin for the stone, Enright remarks, "There is no longer any reason to suppose that a Scandinavian or Scandinavia-trained Anglo-Saxon artist fashioned the heads on the sceptre."[259] He goes on to say, "…the notion that a non-Celt carved the sceptre is inherently improbable."[260]

---

[255] Enright, 2006, p. 66, p 74-8. On page 66 he says that "it simply seems most likely that the sceptre craftsman worked on the shield bird." On page 75 he suggests that there was at least one Celtic craftsman working at Sutton Hoo, but by page 76 he has broadened the possibilities to 'Celtic artisans'. Enright never makes it completely clear which elements of the jewellery he considers to have a 'Celtic' origin – he is certainly including the shield bird, the shoulder clasps and the purse lid.

[256] Enright, 2006, p. 76

[257] Enright, 2006, p. 75

[258] Enright, 2006, p. 75-6

[259] Enright, 2006, p. 74

[260] Enright, 2006 p 75

Some of the Problems with Enright's Ideas.

As already mentioned, there are many other ideas and concepts contained within the book, but it should be sufficient to look at some of the above claims in order to begin to unravel the validity of parts of his main thesis and to decide whether or not his idea of the stone being made by a Celt, and presumably for Celts, is one which can be sustained.[261] I should mention before we begin our closer look at Enright's ideas that I have benefitted greatly from the work of Brian Ansell (see p.19) and Dave Roper (see p. 14). Brian Ansell has made two replicas, one for the Sutton Hoo Visitors' Centre and one for me. Dave Roper reproduced the metal work for the stone replicas and much else from the Mound 1 regalia. Both craftsmen have been able to provide insights from their practical experiments that other writers, including Enright, could not have been aware of.

First, does the Sutton Hoo stone and the Pfalzfeld pillar bear as close a resemblance as Enright claims? To some extent, it depends on how you look at them, they are both vaguely square in section and have heads on each face. The four faces on the pillar are all more or less identical; the eight faces on the stone have all been carved to be deliberately different; some may be female and others male - certainly some have beards and others do not. The heads on the top of the pillar are the right way up when it is positioned vertically whereas those on the bottom of the stone are not. The carving of the detail on the pillar is crude in comparison to that on the stone. There is a precision in the planning, layout and design of the stone that is absent from the pillar.[262]

Another difference is that the stone has an equal number of heads at both ends; the pillar probably never did, and certainly doesn't in Enright's reconstruction.[263] The heads on the stone, at either end, are in opposition to each other; i.e. not the same way up.[264] There is the fact, too, that the two objects are basically quite different in shape: the pillar is broad near the base but tapers inwards as each face is trapezoidal. The stone design is more complex and has globular bulbs at each end, then the heads; the narrowest parts of the bar are where the heads join the bar which then gently curves outwards towards the centre.[265] Overall, the bar maintains a uniform thickness of about two inches. Then there is the complete difference in scale between the two objects.

Enright attempts to explain away these problems by stating that the Pfalzfeld pillar represents the start of the development of Celtic kingship theory and the SuttonHoo stone is its culmination.[266] The difference in time between the making of the two objects is considerable; if we take the pillar to have been constructed in the 4th century BC and the stone in the 6th century A.D., then it is over a thousand years! Enright is well aware of this and uses it to explain the significant design and constructional differences between the two objects when he writes, "Over a millennia span, one can easily imagine considerable artistic variation. Indeed, one should expect it."[267] Is this explanation sufficient to allow for the very real differences? Is he correct when he says, "…the correspondences between the two objects are so striking and impressive that a strong artistic relationship cannot be doubted."?[268] I would suggest not, the two objects are quite different in so many ways that it is hard to understand how he could make such a statement with

---

[261] Enright, 2006, p.76 even rejects the possibility of a 'Celto-Germanic' collaboration.

[262] See the description of the construction of the replica stones by Brian Ansell (p.19) and the discussion at the end of this essay.

[263] Enright, 2006. fig. 8. He suggests that the top of the pillar was surmounted by a 'probable Janus' type head, which, presumably would have had two faces. p 35.

[264] Brian Ansell (pers comm.) remarked that the 'classical proportions' of the head being one seventh of the total length of a human being would actually mean that if complete bodies had been carved the feet would meet in the middle of the stone bar.

[265] See Brian Ansell and Paul Mortimer's paper (this volume) for a full discussion of the whetstone's geometry.

[266] Enright, 2006, p. 36

[267] Enright, 2006, p. 69

[268] Enright, 2006, p. 35

conviction. He seems to change his mind later: when he wants us to be convinced about the 'Celtic' origins of the jewellery, he tells us that "A more correct interpretation of the sceptre then, beginning with its thousand year-old-design that had not evolved greatly by AD 600, means that other objects at Sutton Hoo must be viewed in a new light."[269] Is Enright trying to have it both ways here?

Although both objects are made from types of sandstone, the Sutton Hoo stone is made from the harder greywacké grit; which is capable of taking a much more detailed finish when carved. It is odd that throughout his book, Enright never mentions the more precise description of the type of stone the Sutton Hoo stone is made from. Only once does he even use the word 'grit'[270] and most of the time he refers to the material as 'sandstone' or 'whetstone'.[271] This is a little peculiar because he must be aware of the material the whetstone is made from, as he used the word 'greywacké' in his original paper.

Incidentally, 'whetstone' is not a type of stone of itself; it is a class of object made from stone. The petrological properties of the two types of stone would appear to be very important to Enright's thesis as he refers to their ability to produce sparks and light a fire. Unfortunately, greywacké, being a fine grit, will not give a spark when struck with iron and neither for that matter will most types of sandstone. This would be of little importance if Enright hadn't repeatedly used the idea of sparking throughout his work in many contexts in order to link the stones to all sorts of ideas, including solar cults, smiths, smoke, sun gods, etc.

Enright is mistaken, too, in his notion that the stag does not appear in Germanic art and literature; he is aware that in *Beowulf*, *Hrothgar's* hall is called *Heorot* (Hart) but just dismisses it. In fact Enright, says "....nor in the name *Heorot* for the Danish royal hall in *Beowulf*, however, can one find a clear link between stags and kingship as such."[272] Now when a king's hall is named after a stag – *Heorot* is actually Old English for 'hart, stag' - it seems that the animal could easily be associated with concepts of authority![273] Is it possible that Enright just wants to get rid of any possible Germanic connections as soon as he can? He is quick, too, to put aside any reference to the many depictions of stags and sun-wheels in Bronze Age Scandinavian rock art, where, according to him, "...they undoubtedly indicate sun worship." He goes on to say, "But it is difficult to move from this sphere to the Middle Ages. On these stones the stag is only an 'optional' alternative to the more prominent horse."[274] His use of the term, 'Middle Ages' is interesting; why didn't he use the more usual, 'Early Middle Ages'? Some of the rock art was created during the Bronze Age but some of it is more recent and therefore may be relevant;[275] in any case Enright is not above using quite ancient evidence when he feels that it suits his case. He uses Homer's *Illiad*, for example, to show a connection with royalty, smiths and a sceptre;[276] the Old Testament is recruited to show the connection between 'sparking speech', fire and smiths where Enright refers to Daniel, Elijah, Nebuchadnezzar and Herod to make his points.[277] He is ready, too, to enlist the aid of various stages of the Halstatt Culture[278] in order to link aspects of Celtic kingship to his conception of the whetstone. He even uses the 'Bronze Age' to show the longevity of the 'bird man' in

---

[269] Enright, 2006, p.77

[270] Enright, 2006, p.338

[271] Enright, 2006, p.29. "It is universally recognised that the most striking and crucial fact about the sceptre is its whetstone substance." and "Carved from sandstone, a common material for whetstones,...." when referring to the pillar, p.35.

[272] Enright, 2006, p.48

[273] Carola Hicks agrees that the name, *Heorot*, must be associated with kingly authority. (See Hicks in Bruce-Mitford, 1978. p 382.) It is odd that Enright misses this point and doesn't try to explain it away as he is very happy to cite her when she is stating that the stag is of probable Celtic origin. Enright, 2006, p.18

[274] Enright, 2006, p. 48. See Pollington, this volume, p.109 for a discussion of the stag in Germanic culture.

[275] See for instance, Kaul, 1998

[276] Enright, 2006, p. 90, 116 and p 332

[277] Enright, 2006, p. 183

[278] Enright, 2006, p. 116, p 312, 313 and p 318

Celtic thought.[279] To return to Germanic stags for a moment, it should be pointed out that there are numerous depictions of deer on Anglo-Saxon pots[280] (Figure 84) and examples of stags on the Gallehus horn[281] (Figure 95) and on fibulæ from Germanic areas that were designed to display status.[282]

It is not impossible that the heads on the stone do represent severed heads, but there are serious problems with some of the other claims Enright makes regarding aspects of the features that are close to them. Firstly there is the idea of the 'chain' surround. If Enright had looked closely at the design of the so-called 'surround', he would have realised that the surround is not quite what it may at first glance appear to be: it is just a device that allows the curves above the top of the heads to transfer down and conform to the shape of the bar around and below the heads. In fact, there is no flat surround at all, the edge of the 'surround' is angled down towards the sides of the heads.[283] Besides, if the artist who carved the stone had wanted to show chains, especially annular[284] or penannular ones, he was certainly more than capable of doing so judging by the skill he has displayed elsewhere on the stone, as Enright observes "The sceptre craftsman was exceptionally skilled…"[285]

This brings us to the suggestion of the discs below each head and the possibility that, as Enright says, they are 'apples' and that the indentations are 'dimples'. Firstly, it must be said that not all the discs are 'dimpled' but some are – Enright puzzles over this, but he still insists on the fruit being present; unfortunately, he is simply wrong. We know this from the work of Brian Ansell, who has been able to explain all the mysterious marks on the original stone and demonstrate on the replicas what they are; in the case of the 'dimples' they are the original centre marks of the discs scribed by the mason when marking the stones out. All other marks are the result of tooling and sometimes show the limitations of the equipment that the mason was using. Once again, the mason had the skill to carve apples if that is what he wanted to show but the discs are quite plainly that, perfectly circular discs and not at all apple shaped! Once again, this wouldn't matter much if Enright hadn't made so much of his 'discovery' of 'apples', but they do play quite a part in his thesis where he is able to connect the presence of 'apples' to various 'Celtic' legends.

That brings us to the shield bird and its 'Celtic' origins. According to Enright, transforming birds as seen on the shield are divine messengers of the sun god, who communicate with kings to maintain cosmic truth.[286] Well they maybe, but is the design on the shield 'Celtic' or not? Enright certainly thinks so, when discussing Bruce-Mitford's attempts to link the piriform design of the head to Germanic parallels he says "Although some Vendel head-shaped contours exist on birds they are not the same as that on Sutton Hoo. (sic) There is 'a point of difference'. What we see at Sutton Hoo is 'not merely a face, but one within a border, 'stopped' below the chin by a semi-circular opaque yellow inlay."[287] He goes on to claim "In addition, when that piriform shape appears on the thighs of Gotlandic birds it is a form alone and contains no face within."[288] So, Enright just dismisses empty piriforms in Gotland, a Germanic land, as of no consequence on page 66, that is unless they appear in a 'Celtic' area like Ireland; on page 67 he says "Empty piriforms suggesting human heads exist in Ireland on a whetstone

---

[279] Enright, 2006, p. 223. Enright even refers to Vedic and Iranian texts p 212

[280] See Pollington, Kerr and Hammond, 2010. fig 4.26 and 4.28

[281] Pollington, Kerr and Hammond, 2010. fig 13.60

[282] See for example, Herzog and Koller; 2001. p 80

[283] To see this in detail, look at Brian Ansell's photos showing how the stone was made.

[284] Enright, 2006, p. 58, 82, 83, 95, 225 Enright repeatedly refers to the surrounds as chains. The pages listed here are just a sample.

[285] Enright, 2006, p. 30

[286] Enright, 2006, p. 339

[287] Enright, 2006, p. 64

[288] Enright, 2006, p. 66. Enright also says that the "exact form" (of head in bird's, presumable) design does appear on an Irish whetstone that he has mentioned earlier. Unfortunately, on this page he does not tell us which whetstone that he is talking about, nor does he provide a picture.

around 700 AD…" He may be correct about the birds from the Gotlandic material but Bruce-Mitford only mentions shield-birds from the Vendel and Valsgärde graves, and does not refer to material from Gotland in the context of the shield at all.[289] Perhaps Enright is unaware of Swedish geography? In any case, Enright does need to explain why this self-same image – the bird with a man's face on its hip - appears in other Germanic areas and is dated to about the same period as the Sutton Hoo shield bird - see for example Figure 77, an image of a bird on a shield mount from Skørping, Denmark, and Figure 76, a brooch from Ljere, also in Denmark.[290] Then there are the piriform heads that appear on shield flanges from Sweden (Figure 78 & 79) and the recently discovered pressbleche from the Staffordshire Hoard, England, Figure 80. It should be noted that in all these the face of a human appears on the hips of the zoomorphic animal, according to the conventions of Salin Style II. One bird that contains a man's face on the back, but still within a piriform, and again from the 6th or 7th century, is a bird brooch from Uppåkra in southern Sweden, (Figure 81). Whatever Enright claims for this design, it is a Germanic one. Perhaps Germanic culture had transforming birds, too?[291]

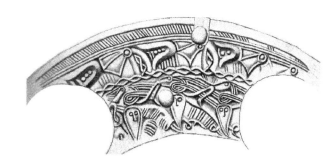

Figure 78 Gilt-bronze flange from the boss of a shield, found in Mound 7 at Valsgärde, Sweden.

Figure 79 Gilt-bronze flange from the boss of a shield, found in Mound 8 at Valsgärde, Sweden.

Figure 80 Reconstruction of a pressblech foil design from the Staffordshire Hoard. (Courtesy of D. Roper)

---

[289] Bruce-Mitford, 1978. p 91-9

[290] The shield bird from Skorping, Denmark, is found in Headeger, 2011. fig 4.16 p 72 and the brooch from Ljere, Denmark, is in Niles, 2007, plate XIII. In addition, there are very similar faces within piriform shapes on the hips of quadrupeds found on at least three sword pommels from the Baltic area. (Marek, 2005, plate 21)

[291] There is evidence for human-bird transformation in Germanic culture, including the story of Óðinn's transformation into an eagle (see p.143) and Freyja's *fjaðrhama*. Loki could become various animals. See the discussions in Mortimer, 2011, for specific reference to transforming birds with relevance to the regalia from Sutton Hoo. See also Tolley, 2007 and Price, (ed), 2001 for discussions on shamanism and transformation in a Germanic context. Avian transformation is shown in much Iron Age Germanic art.

As for the rest of the jewellery, despite Enright's claims, very few serious scholars of the period would agree that the designs are anything but Germanic as many analogues appear, from the 6th and 7th centuries in Germanic areas.[292] He may be right when he says that Celts made the millefiori[293] but that does not mean they made anything else in the jewellery - craftsmen, or more likely kings, may have had access to a supply, as they certainly did with garnets and gold. The jewels and metals would have been passed to their craftsmen who would then incorporate them into the jewellery, utilising traditional designs that would have carried clear messages to any person familiar with 7th c. Northern European Germanic culture able to observe them.[294]

Incidentally, Enright provides no evidence that the 'Celts' made millefiori - in fact during the early medieval period much glass manufacture took place along the banks of the Rhine.[295]

Before we leave the bird, much has been made of the shape appearing below the face on the thigh of the bird, and not just by Enright;[296] however, that shape is definitely not a circle - it is actually very similar in both size and shape to the man's mouth above it. The discs on the stone are, as mentioned before, perfect circles; whether this difference is significant or not, it must be pointed out that the craftsmen involved could have added whatever shapes they wanted. It should be noted, too, that the shape is situated wholly within the surround and not at its nadir, as on the stone heads.

Figure 81 Bird brooch with a male head on the back, from Uppakra, Sweden.

The design of the heads on the stone, as mentioned before, does not stylistically resemble those on the pillar nor do they resemble any carved heads on any Celtic piece that Enright mentions, nor any other definitively 'Celtic' artefact that I have seen. Enright picks up on Bruce-Mitford's suggestion that the eyes on the faces "are bulging in a tradition that seems to be Celtic but finds a counterpart in the faces of the Sutton Hoo sceptre."[297] He goes on to say that 'bulging eyes' are, "fairly widespread in Celtic art." I think the implication is that they are not in Germanic art. If that is this the case, Enright is not correct, Thor is almost always portrayed with bulging eyes, for

---

[292] See for example, Pollington, Kerr and Hammond, 2009. Bruce-Mitford 1972. Explorations of Style I and Style II art can be found in Salin's *Die Altgermanische Thierornamentik* (1904) and Webster's recent *Anglo-Saxon Art: A New History* (2012). Hines's *A Corpus of Great Square-Headed Brooches* (1997) shows many examples of human-bird hybrids, also seen in Hedeager's *Iron Age Myth and Materiality: An Archaeology of Scandinavia AD 400-1000* (2011); Aarni Erä-*Esko Germanic Animal Art of Salin's Style I in Finland* (1965); .Birger Nerman *Die Vendelzeit Gotlands* (1969-1975); Seichi Suzuki *Anglo-Saxon Button Brooches: Typology, Genealogy, Chronology* (2008) and George Speake *Anglo-Saxon Animal Art and Its Germanic Background* (1980). Mortimer, 2011, deals with the subject of Enright's claims about the rest of the jewellery.

[293] Enright, 2006, p. 75

[294] Despite Enright's claim (p 77) that the bird of prey seizing a duck is a 'Celtic' design, he fails to show any Celtic analogues. However, there are Germanic depictions of birds of prey seizing other creatures.

[295] Pollington, Kerr and Hammond, 2010. p 313

[296] Bruce-Mitford, 1978. p 358

[297] Enright, 2006 p 65 – the quote is Bruce-Mitford's.

example.[298] However, when looked at closely, it seems to me that the eyes on the stone, although portrayed carefully, are not unnatural and not particularly prominent; in fact, all the eyes are quite small in comparison to their faces.

Figure 82 (left) Gilded, moustachioed, man's face with bulging eyes in a copper alloy, piriform surround. A recent detector find from England. Portable Antiquities Scheme Unique ID: BUC-D33162. Dated to 500 A.D. to 700 A.D. Reference: finds.org.uk/database/artefacts/record/id/59846

Figure 83 (right) Another man's head with moustache and bulging eyes with a piriform surround. Again a recent detector find, this time from Lincolnshire (2012) and dated to the 7th century. Made from copper alloy. 13 mms x 10 mms. It can be seen at: www.ukdfd.co.uk/ukdfddata/showrecords.php?product=40094&cat=114

As for the style of the heads, they do resemble other Germanic ones. Bruce-Mitford[299] provides several examples but there are more.[300] The shape of the heads on the stone and those in much of Germanic art, though not all, are similar in a number of ways. Firstly the very careful treatment of the hair does seem to have had particular meaning to Germanic peoples of the time, although quite what this meaning may have been is not entirely clear. Secondly, the piriform shape of the head is repeated elsewhere in examples of shield ornaments and fibula within the canon of Germanic art. Then there is the careful placement of the eyes; on the stone they are halfway down the head from the top and this tends to be the case with heads in Germanic art frequently - and not so often in Celtic art where they are more usually situated in the top half of the head.

---

[298] Perkins 2001. There is a very interesting and ongoing discussion in this book regarding 'bulging eyes'.
[299] Bruce-Mitford, 1978. See the discussion on the human faces, p 358 to 360
[300] Enright objects to Bruce-Mitfords identification of the heads as Germanic. Enright, 2006, p. 65

Figure 84
A silver-gilt amuletic
figurine from Carlton
Colville, Norfolk.

Incidentally, Enright claims that the portrayal of heads in Germanic art was rare; he is most certainly wrong on this point, as far as the 5th to 7th centuries are concerned. The portrayal of heads on their own, or in combination with other themes, is actually very common on the ornament of the time. See, for example, the button brooches where a man's face is frequently portrayed,[301] then there are the great square headed brooches where heads usually form a significant part of the design.[302]

As for severed heads lying on beds of hair to collect the drips; it is an interesting idea but there is absolutely no evidence for it, apart from Enright's suggestion. It is true that the texture under the unbearded heads is carefully moulded and, like Enright, I find it difficult to accept Bruce-Mitford's and Ryan's suggestion of 'throat beards'.[303] Brian Ansell feels that the design under the heads has just been included as an artistic device to finish off the unbearded heads and to balance them with their more hirsute companions.

Enright, in mentioning oaths and binding in connection with his idea of 'chains' around the heads, doesn't seem to realise how important those concepts were to Germanic peoples in the 5th to 7th centuries, where it is a very frequent theme in many pieces of artwork and, of course, in the later literature. It tends to form the basis of much of Style II artwork, in England, the Continent and in Scandinavia. One example on a sword scabbard from the grave at Valsgärde 7 in Sweden, for instance, shows a man entwined in fetters. [304] Then there are the later stories of the Fenriswulf and of Loki being bound. Apart from this, it is clear that oaths made at *symbel* or in a sanctuary were binding on those who made them.[305]

Enright is encouraged by the British context for the whetstone mentioned by Bruce-Mitford.[306] In his report on the whetstone, Bruce-Mitford does cite a number of other stones from the British Isles that have carvings of heads on them. All are crude in comparison to the one from Sutton Hoo, some are fragmentary, three are unprovenanced river finds,[307] which are extremely difficult to date and may well not be 'Celtic', as they were found in areas that became Anglian. However, Enright emphatically claims them all to be 'Celtic' without reservation.[308]

---

[301] Suzuki, 2008

[302] Hines, 1997

[303] Bruce-Mitford, 1978. p 358. Ryan, 1992.p 88. One reason is that when looked at carefully the design is carefully delineated from the face, it doesn't actually touch it. Observation by Brian Ansell. Curiously, Enright doesn't seem to notice that Bruce-Mitford's writes of throat beards but heavily criticises Ryan for doing so. Enright, 2006 p. 30

[304] See Mortimer, 2011, p. 106 for a good illustration of this scabbard.

[305] Pollington, 2003 and Enright 1995, both contain discussion on this subject.

[306] Bruce-Mitford, 1978 pp. 369, 375

[307] The examples from Lochar Moss, Hough-on-the-Hill, Lincolnshire and Portsoy, Banffshire.

[308] Enright, 2006, p. .17

Enright does attempt to explain why an Anglian king would want such a 'Celtic' object as the Sutton Hoo stone: he tells us that he may have seen Celtic rulers who had imposing stones , so he may have wanted one too. Enright calls this "sceptre envy".[309] However, if it had no real significance to the King of the East Angles or his people, why go to the bother of having it fabricated? Enright never attempts to tell us why an Anglian king would want Celtic symbolism on his shield or belt, though.

Were the Germanic peoples capable of making objects in the round, or did they want to? Well the answer to both questions must be 'yes'. There remain many objects that are representations of creatures and people in the round, from the Carlton Colville man[310] to wooden idols and ship figure heads; from the bulls' heads on the so called Sutton Hoo standard to the pin head from Dover Buckland grave 161,[311] there are numerous figures modelled in three dimensions.

Several times in his writings, Enright tries to connect the manufacture of the Sutton Hoo stone with southern Scotland.[312] I am not entirely sure why Enright has fixed on this particular region as he doesn't make his thought processes on this matter terribly clear; perhaps it is because he feels that this area remained truly 'Celtic' for longer than other parts of the mainland and that this area has been suggested as one from which the greywacké for the Sutton Hoo stone may have come.[313] However, greywacké grit is more common than Bruce-Mitford realised at the time of writing and, in fact, the stone for the replicas came from Yorkshire.

In his writings, Enright refers to the ability of the stag to be removed from the stone. He says "The feature of removability, therefore, is a traditional one where stags are concerned. But on the sceptre the antlers are not removed but rather the stag as a whole."[314] He is talking about representing the seasonal removal of the antlers from the stag. He goes on to say that, with the Sutton Hoo stag, making just the antlers demountable with such a small model would be impractical, but that, "..removability was perceived to be indispensable." Through the work of Dave Roper we now know that the stag was permanently fixed to the stone, although the stag could revolve.[315] Where does this leave Enright?

General Problems with Enright's Approach.

Enright's book has nearly 400 pages and many of the items, such as the Farley Heath Sceptre and the many Irish and British whetstones that he refers to are not illustrated which presents a difficulty for the reader who is unfamiliar with those items. If Enright were not relying so much on the details of these objects to support his theories it might not matter, but in a book such as this, where he discusses the nuance and subtleties of design, it surely does. The only objects shown are the whetstone, some of the Sutton Hoo jewellery, the Pfalzfeld Pillar and a reconstruction of the Weiskirchen ornament.

He also casts his net very widely indeed and includes evidence from before 600 BC to 1200 A.D. and covers many civilisations including Greece, Rome, the Etruscans and the Hebrews. He enlists the help of many characters from history for instance Ptolemy, Adam of Thebes, Pythagoras, Posidonius of Aparniea, Homer, Alexander the Great, St Jerome, some Old Testament prophets and Jesus to name just a few. Then there are the mythic figures: Agamemnon, Zeus, Hermes, Pandora, Heiphastos and many more. Rarely does he mention anyone or anything of Germanic origins, unless it is to find a way of dismissing them and explaining that they are not significant; for instance, regarding the story of Thor who had a whetstone lodged in his head, Enright explains that this could not possibly be relevant to the Sutton Hoo 'whetstone' in any way.[316]

---

[309] Enright, 2006, p. 76. To be fair, he does also suggest that the 'sceptre would have had an importance for the Anglian kings' 'Celtic' subjects.
[310] *Treasure Annual Report*, 2000 p.45 (Portable Antiquities Scheme)
[311] Evison, 1987
[312] Enright, 2006, p. 58, p.76 and p.244
[313] Bruce-Mitford, 1978, p. 384
[314] Enright, 2006. P. 207-8
[315] See Roper's contribution to this volume, p.14
[316] Despite what Frances Magoun and Sydney L Cohen may say. Enright, 2006., p. 14

Enright has provided such a vast panoramic background to his ideas that he was certain to come up with something that could help him, no matter how tenuous the connection. Without calling on such a broad spectrum of sources Enright would have great trouble in making a connection with whetstones and concepts of authority in the 'Celtic' sphere and even then the connections need tortuous reasoning and complex explanations. There is nothing simple or direct about the way Enright goes about his task.

In his original paper Enright says

"For instance, if identification of the whetstone as a sceptre now seems almost certain (were there ever doubts)..."[317]

For him the stone is a 'sceptre', he never entertains any other possibilities - but, of course, they exist and must be considered.[318] If the stone's major function were something other than a sceptre, then almost everything that Enright has written would be irrelevant.

Then there is the problem that Enright doesn't often define his terms: for instance what does he mean by 'Celt' and 'Celtic'? His interpretation seems to be of the broadest kind possible and he gives the impression that he sees continuity from the earliest times, more or less to the very recent.[319] He does say that this is not the case, but it is difficult to trust him on this when reading his book, because of the way that he is prepared to take his evidence from such a large compass, almost, without qualification.[320] According to him, 'Celts' seem to include, amongst others, the peoples of the Halstatt and La Tène cultures, the Gauls, the Picts, the Irish, the Britons, the Scots, the Welsh and possibly even almost all the English.[321] He gives the impression, too, (at least to this reader) that he sees real and continuing connections between the Celts, the Greeks and the Etruscans[322] and to some extent the Romans. It should be mentioned that Enright is very unhappy with recent scholars, mainly English, he claims "..who have become existentially concerned with a verification of past 'identities,'" and who, it seems have questioned the notion of the 'Celt'.[323] He doesn't really define what he means by the word 'sceptre' either.

Another problem with the way that Enright builds his argument is that a 'suggestion' on one page can become a 'fact' later in the book. For example, on page 58 Enright suggests that the "torc-like frames" around the heads may be 'chains'. He rejects the notion of a 'ribbon', suggested by Bruce-Mitford, because "..it is too narrow and slight to suit the depiction. The sceptre frames are rounded ridges deliberately made quite thick in proportion. It seems right to think of a chain….." By page 71, "At Sutton Hoo the original plant motif (*on some Celtic depictions*)[324] became a head frame with a large terminal stud. It was meant to indicate a neck ornament……". On page 75 it is definitely a "chain-with-ring surround". This is reinforced on page 77 when he says that, "since these peculiar chain surrounds appear on both objects, …" (he means the shield bird's thigh and the stone's heads). From then on, no hint of a doubt is entertained about the function of the head surrounds. As mentioned elsewhere in my paper, this identification of the head surrounds cannot be established with any certainty and it would appear that they are not true 'surrounds' in any case. Now, I have picked out just one example of a 'suggestion' becoming a

---

[317] Enright, 1982, p. 134.
[318] See the discussion on the functions of the whetstone in this volume.
[319] At the time of writing this, Enright's personal page on the University of East Carolina proclaims that he is preparing a course on *The Celtic World from 700bc to1603ad* which may be telling.
[320] Incidentally, in this book, the word 'Germanic' refers to people who spoke a Germanic language at the time in question, which is identical to the definition of 'Germanic' that Enright uses in his original paper. Although he doesn't define 'Celtic' in that paper either. Enright, 1982.
[321] Enright doesn't believe there were ever many Germanic 'invaders' in Britain; he believes in the idea of élite dominance – something which, when considering the movement of Celtic culture, he seems to be very much against. Enright, 2006, p. 11.
[322] There is a discussion on Etruscans adopting Celtic identity in Enright, 2006, page 249
[323] Enright, 2006, p. 248
[324] My words in italics and brackets.

'fact' later on and it is a very important one, but there are many more to be found; many, are perhaps minor details, but however important they are Enright tends to repeats them again and again, as if to hammer them home and by doing this, they will become lodged in the reader's mind as 'facts'.

Michael Ryan, Enright's critic, said that

> "The scepter (sic) is an Anglo-Saxon product; its immediate background is Germanic."

> "There is no discernable Celtic influence in its style and manufacture. Comparisons with the Pfalzfeld pillar, references to the Celtic practice of headhunting, or appeals to the status of the smith in ancient Ireland do nothing to supply the lack of evidence for a Celtic connection."[325]

Ryan also asks the question, "Did whetstones figure as royal regalia in the Celtic world?" and answers it, at least as far as the Irish are concerned, by saying that "The ancient laws of Ireland are completely silent on this question."[326] He does find a whetstone listed as being in the possession of a king but points out that as he also had a sword and knives, this was probably of no more significance than that of being a tool.[327] Enright is very unhappy with Ryan's criticisms and discusses some, but not all, of Ryan's comments.[328] He dismisses all of the Germanic and Baltic parallels that Ryan uses - we will examine one of those later - but he doesn't directly take Ryan to task over the lack of evidence connecting the 'Celtic' aristocracy with whetstones. As mentioned before, Enright's book contains many references from many cultures and time-periods in order to try to address this lack. Enright seems to own up to the lack of written evidence concerning the whetstone when he says that, "It must be admitted however, that no text specifically refers to the actual employment of a whetstone despite its documented existence as a symbolic artefact."[329]

Is Enright successful in showing that the Celtic aristocracy had a tradition of demonstrating authority through the use of whetstones? I have to agree with Michael Ryan's original criticism and suggest that, even with this book length treatment he is not.

Germanic Parallels?

We will consider other possible Germanic and northern European parallels to the Sutton Hoo stone in another essay in this volume (p.124) but let's just consider one for now in order to see how Enright can so easily dismiss anything that may get in the way of his 'Celtic' thesis.

Ryan mentions the horse harness mount from Bregentved, Denmark (Figure 120) as an object that has much in common with the stone, and it must be said that stylistically and from a point of design, it is similar to the stone. Both have eight heads, both have four heads at each end and the heads at the bottom of the design are upside down when compared to the heads at the top, unlike on the Pfalzfeld pillar which only has right way up heads and these are at the bottom. Both the stone and the horse harness have a faceted bar separating the heads. All the heads on both objects have carefully described hair. Both objects would appear to have been made in 6th or 7th centuries. Of course there are differences, too: the Bregentved harness mount doesn't have different faces on each end and the object is made from copper alloy and not stone, but it could be said that

> "...the correspondences between the two objects are so striking and impressive that a strong artistic relationship cannot be doubted."

to use Enright's own words. What does Enright say about this object?

---

[325] Ryan, 1992, p. 90
[326] Ryan, 1992, p. 87
[327] Ryan, 1992, p. 87
[328] Enright, 2006, p. 29 to 32
[329] Enright, 2006, p. 183

"Not only are they looser parallels, they lack (*he is referring to the pins and remains of staffs that Ryan also mentions as well as the Bregentved horse harness, which he doesn't deign to name*)[330] the necessary direct connection to authority."[331]

The pillar, when compared to the stone, could be dismissed in similar terms - after all, we only have Enright's word for it that the pillar is about concepts of authority and stylistically it has little in common with the Sutton Hoo stone.

Celtic Connections?

It would seem, then, that Enright has not proven that the Sutton Hoo stone is of Celtic manufacture as his work contains many assumptions and links that are not valid, and some, like the shield bird, are just wrong. Others, such as the supposed southern Scottish origin, cannot be proven. He has been unable to show that the stone represents a tradition of Celtic concepts of kingship or authority without incorporating many non-Celtic connections.

This is particularly a problem because he has never really explained to us what he means by 'Celtic' or even told us who the 'Celts' were – he just assumes that we know and implies that there was continuity of thought and ideas over very long periods of time involving many different peoples. For much of the book, 'Celt' seems to refer to the peoples of Ireland and parts of Britain; 'British', Pictish', 'Irish' and 'Welsh', at times, seem to be synonyms for 'Celtic'. However, he refuses to be limited by geographical or temporal constraints when it suits him

He has not been able to demonstrate that the object is definitively a sceptre because he has not considered any alternative functions.[332] It may well have performed the functions of a sceptre but it certainly doesn't resemble any known one and, therefore, other possibilities should have been considered and, if shown to be unworkable, dismissed.

Enright has tried very hard, perhaps too hard, to explain all the parameters of the Sutton Hoo stone that he set out in his original declaration of intent: "The most basic requirement is that one sets out to examine all of the sceptre symbols and not just selected examples: i.e. the stag, the ring, pedestal, heads, surrounds and knobs must all be discussed and cogently related to each other."[333] However, in order to try to achieve his goal he has had to incorporate an extremely broad spectrum of ideas from a huge time period, and he has not been able to demonstrate that many of these ideas were necessarily a part of Celtic culture.[334] It certainly wasn't possible to do as Enright suggested without using a great deal of imagination.

There are other parameters that he didn't consider: for instance, the geometry of the design which is, it would seem, of paramount importance to understanding what the stone is for, is contained within its dimensions and their relationships with each other. He did not consider the artistic parallels in an unbiased way. He had made his mind up from the outset that the 'sceptre' was 'Celtic' and far too easily dismisses objects that do have a resemblance to the stone and may provide clues as to its function. This is particularly true of anything Germanic, although he will use and absorb other sources, including ones from India, Iran and Israel.

It would be just as possible to use many of the connections in the way that he does and adjust them to the Germanic sphere and come up with similar results concerning Germanic kingship theory.

It must be said that there are several notions he discusses that there may be some profit in pursuing, for instance the possible connection of the stone with the position of the smith and the possibility of the

---

[330] My words in brackets and italics.
[331] Enright, 2006, p. 61
[332] We shall examine other possibilities in the essay on *The Functions of the Whetstone* in this volume.
[333] Enright, 2006, p. 9
[334] For instance, those from the Old Testament.

whetstone being involved in a solar cult. The latter point is of just as much relevance to the Germanic peoples as it was to any other northern European heathens. There is, too, the choice and combination of materials; this may well have some deeper meaning and it may well be that some of Enright's suggestions are useful lines of enquiry.

The Roots of Anglian Kingship?

In preparation for some of the work that will follow this essay, we should briefly consider whether the Sutton Hoo stone may have an origin other than a 'Celtic' one and there are a number of qualities that the stone has which does seem to point to an Anglian origin, apart from the Germanic style of the heads and that the stag can be associated with kingship.

The first is the fact that it has been carefully planned and designed and that the man who made it was at the top of his profession, a master mason; he had served his apprenticeship and probably made his own tools. Incidentally, the likelihood that the mason also made the jewellery is very slim indeed owing to the level of training and the differing skills required for each profession. The idea that the stone was made with great and rare skill and is of exceptional quality accords with almost all of the other personal items found within Mound 1. As discussed above, artistically, most of the personal items from Mound 1 would seem to be of Germanic origin.

Another reason for thinking that the stone is closely connected to the Anglians is that there is the Anglo-Saxon measurement called the 'rod'. This is around 16 feet 6 inches (4.65 metres) and is a measurement used to base the size of houses and other important structures on. The actual measurement varies from area to area, but in Suffolk, judging by the houses from West Stow, it would appear to be, usually slightly over 16 feet.[335] This is important because, when Brian Ansell was measuring the original Mound 1 stone, he found that the curves that give the bar its shape have a diameter of 16 feet 4 inches, or just about a rod.

Finally, we must remind ourselves that Enright's suggested theory of Celtic kingship involves, among other things, making right judgements, speaking the truth, poetry, ritual speech, contractual speech, the swearing of oaths, land claims, combat, the king acting as intercessor between the divine and the people and the king ensuring fertility and protecting his folk. All of these concepts are found within the Germanic context, too,[336] and probably in other parts of Europe during the first millennia – there is little specifically 'Celtic' about them.

---

[335] Pollington, 2003; Pollington, this volume, *The Anglo-Saxon Rod and the Sceaftmund.*
[336] For a full discussion in Germanic contexts, see Chaney, 1971; Sundqvist, 2002. There are also the ideas of Mitchell, (1985) which are discussed at length above and clearly provide evidence regarding the importance of rhetoric, etc, to the Germanic peoples.

6. The Vocabulary of Rule

Stephen Pollington

In considering the nature of kingship in Anglo-Saxon society, it occurred to me that there has not been a recent survey of the main elements of vocabulary relating to the office of the king. The following paper includes a brief discussion of a selection of words for 'ruler, leader' found in Old English (OE) texts, followed by some OE names for the accoutrements of rulership.

Citations are taken in the first instance from Bosworth & Toller. In Proto-Germanic forms, 'x' stands for the voiceless guttural continuant heard in German 'ach' and '3' for the voiced equivalent in German 'sagen'. Proto-Germanic forms, being hypothetical, are marked with a preceding asterisk, e.g. *kuningaz* but citations from Orel's *Handbook of Germanic Etymology* do not repeat this feature.

Anglo-Saxon Leaders and Rulers

There is a great variety of terms for 'leader', 'chieftain', 'headman', 'warlord' and the like known from the OE corpus. With the emphasis of the prose records on legal matters (laws, property exchange, etc.) and on political history (*Anglo-Saxon Chronicle*, Bede's *Historia*, etc.), we are fortunate to have a good many words for 'leader' to set beside the greater wealth of terms found in the poetry.

Æðeling

The term *æðeling* is found in both prose and verse with the meaning 'nobleman, man of noble birth', derived from the adjective *æðele* 'noble, eminent' with associated noun *æðelu* 'nobility, birth' and 'family, race, kindred'.[337] The *–ing* suffix is considered below (see *Cyning*) denoting 'association'. The technical sense of the term in West Saxon documents appears to be 'prince, male member of the royal family other than the one(s) called *cyning*'. It is cognate with Tocharian A *ātäl* 'man' and Greek ἀταλός 'tender, delicate'.

Bealdor

This word occurs in verse such as *Beowulf* (l.2567) where it evidently means 'lord, prince'; the variant *baldor* is in line 2428 *sinca baldor* 'lord of treasures'. It may be cognate with the ON *Baldr* (OIc *Baldur*), the name of one of Óðinn's sons whose untimely death foreshadows the end of the world.[338] Curiously, out of the eight instances of the word in OE, nearly all refer to a man who dies in his youth, so it may have had nuances of 'tragic hero'.[339]

Bora

This term, meaning 'one who bears', is used in the phrase *rices bora* 'he who holds rule' in the poem *Christ and Saturn* (l.500). This may be the only instance of the word used as a simplex, but there are many examples of compounds in which it forms the second element, such as *mundbora* 'protector', *rædbora* 'counsellor, consul'.

The word is derived from the verb *beran* 'bear, carry', a weak noun based on the zero-grade of the verb, used as an agent 'he who/that which bears'.[340] Holthausen links it to the cognate Greek *-phoros* 'carrier' among other words.[341]

---

[337] Orel, 2003, *aþalan, aþaljaz, aþalingaz, aþaljan*
[338] Holthausen, 1974, *bealdor*; Orel, 2003, *balþaz*
[339] Pollington, 2011a, p.221
[340] Campbell, 1987, p.249

Brega, Brego

This word occurs chiefly in poetry, with the meaning 'leader' as in *Judith* l.12 *beorna brego* 'leader of men'. It is cognate with OIc *bragr* '*vir primarius, princeps*' (leading man, prince) according to Bosworth. Holthausen links the words to a sense of MHG *brogen* 'rise up, be prominent'.[342] A possible connection to Bragi, the Norse god of poetry, has also been posited.

Bregoweard

In the poem *Genesis*, *bregoweard* is used to mean a 'royal guard, powerful keeper'. It is a compound with the sense of a *weard* 'keeper' who is also a *brego* 'prince'.

Bretwalda

See Paul Mortimer's discussion of this term on p.75.

The early spellings suggest that the compound was originally *bryten* 'broad, wide' and *wealda* '(he) who rules', later confused with *Brytene* 'Britain', *Brytenlond* 'the land of Britain'.

Cyning, Cyng

Cyning, and its later form *cyng*, are the standard OE terms for 'king' in all the political and spiritual senses. The word's derivation is *cynn* 'kindred', family + '-ing', an associative suffix.[343] The sense is evidently 'scion of the family line' and derives from the tradition of leadership residing within specific lineages – as Tacitus says of the 1st c. Germanic tribes *Reges ex nobilitate, duces ex virtute sumunt* 'they take their kings for their noble birth, their warlords for their ability'.[344]

The morpheme *cyne-* occurs in some OE words relating to royalty and kingship, such as *cynehelm* 'kingly headgear' and the cognate ON form *konr* means 'nobleman'.[345]

There are many compounds with *cyning* as the second element (deuterotheme): *æðelcyning* 'noble king', *beorncyning* 'king of heroes', *brytencyning* 'king of a broad realm', *eorðcyning* 'king of the land', *eþelcyning* 'king of the land', *folccyning* 'king of a nation', *gastcyning* 'king of the soul', *gearcyning* 'consul, leader for a year', *guþcyning* 'warrior king', *hæðencyning* 'heathen king', *heahcyning* 'high king, supreme ruler', *heofoncyning* 'king of heaven', *leodcyning* 'king over a people', *mægencyning* 'mighty king', *rodorcyning* 'king of heaven', *sæcyning* 'sea-king', *segncyning* 'king with a banner', *sigecyning* 'victorious king', *soþcyning* 'true king', *sweglcyning* 'king of heaven', *þeodcyning* 'king of a nation', *þrymcyning* 'king of glory', *þryþcyning* 'king of glory', *woroldcyning* 'earthly king', *wuldorcyning* 'king of glory'.

Drihten, Dryhten

The term *drihten* (and variants) is long-lasting as an OE word for 'lord', in religious verse. It appears in what may be the oldest example of English poetry, *Cædmon's Hymn*, where the epithet *ece dryhten* 'eternal lord' occurs in the West Saxon version, and *eci dryctin* in the Old Northumbrian.[346] The same half-line occurs in *Beowulf* (l.108) and elsewhere.

The word derives from Proto-Germanic **druxtinaz*, from **druxt-* 'warband, band of young men' and the suffix **-inaz* denoting 'master of', which was very productive in the formation of OE words for 'leader, lord'.[347] The term 'warlord, leader of a band of youths' may have suggested itself to the early Anglo-Saxons as a positive epithet to apply to Jesus and his disciples, but it remained a popular poetic term for a

---

[341] Holthausen, 1974 s,v. *bora*

[342] Holthausen, 1974 s,v. *brego*

[343] Holthausen, 1974 s,v. *cyning*; Orel, 2003, *kuningaz, kunungaz, kuniz*

[344] Rives, 1999 *Germania*, ch.7

[345] Orel, 2003, *kuniz*

[346] Both the Moore and Leningrad Versions agree as to the spelling of the phrase. Sweet, 1967, pp.181-2

[347] Kershaw, 2000; Orel, 2003, *druxtinaz;* Pollington, 2003, appendix 3

secular 'lord, ruler' e.g. *Beowulf* l.1050 *eorla drihten* 'lord of heroes'. It is also used to translate Latin *Dominus* e.g. *ego sum dominus deus tuus – ic eom drihten ðin god* 'I am the Lord thy God'.

Drihtealdor

Transparently a compound of *driht* 'warband, band of young men' (see *drihten*) and *ealdor* 'elder, person in authority'; the term occurs in one of the *Homilies* with the meaning 'lord of a feast'.

Ealdor, Ealdormann

Ealdor is the comparative of the adjective *eald* 'old' and like its modern cognate 'elder' it can mean both 'one who is older' and 'one who is in charge'.[348] It can be used in OE to mean a 'parent' or 'forefather', and doubtless from this sense arose the meaning a 'senior' and 'overseer, governor'. *Ealdormann* is a formal title in later OE, meaning 'regional or provincial governor' from which the modern *alderman* derives. An *ealdormann* was always a deputised official invoking a higher kingly authority, rather than a ruler in his own right.[349]

Ealdorwisa

Ealdorwisa means 'chief ruler' and occurs in *Genesis* l.1237, probably in the sense of a *wisa* 'leader, director' who is also an *ealdor*.

Eodor

This is a common word for a 'fence, hedge, boundary' and means 'leader, protector' with transference of the sense of someone or something keeping undesirable things out.[350] King Hroþgar is called *eodor Scyldinga* 'protector of the Scyldings' in *Beowulf*, l.428.

Eorl

In OE verse, *eorl* appears to mean primarily 'brave man, warrior, hero' but its meaning in the later prose approximates rather more closely to a title or rank.[351] The phrase *eard ond eorlscipe* 'land and noble rank' occurs in *Beowulf* (l.1727) and *eahtodan eorlscipe ond his ellenweorc* 'they valued his heroism and his deeds of courage' (l.3173). The influence of the cognate Norse *jarl* 'leader, man of rank' may be responsible for the word's narrowing towards the meaning 'leader', equivalent in some senses to OE *ealdormann*.

Folcfrea

A compound of *frea* (see below) and the word *folc* which has the sense 'nation, people' but often with a military nuance as in *folctoga*.

Folcgesiþ

The plural form *folcgesiþas* occurs with the meaning 'the leading men of the country, the princes of the nation'.

Folctoga

The meaning 'leader of a people' is deduced from the constituent elements *folc* 'nation, people' and *toga*, an agent noun derived from *teon* 'draw, pull, lead'. It occurs in the plural in *Beowulf*, l.839 in the phrase *ferdon folctogan feorran ond nean* 'folk-leaders travelled from far and near'. See also *Heretoga*.

---

[348] Orel, 2003, *alðran* cites Celtic cognates Old Irish *altru* foster-father and Welsh *athraw* 'teacher'.
[349] Loyn, 1953
[350] Orel, 2003, *eðaraz*
[351] Orel, 2003, *erlaz*

Frea

Another term from *Cædmon's Hymn*, *frea almihtig* evidently means 'almighty lord', referring to the act of creation.[352] Holthausen derives it from a root meaning 'in front' which gives Gothic *frauja* 'lord', Slavonic *pruvu* 'first' and Greek *prora* 'prow of a ship'.[353] An alternative derivation links it to OE *freogan* 'love' and implies a meaning 'beloved (one)'. In OE texts such as *Ælfric's Colloquy on the Occupations*, social superiors are addressed with the epithet *leof* 'dear, beloved', so this idea may have some merit. (See also *Wine* below.) A link to the Norse god Freyr is also plausible, although the god's name is a strong a-stem noun while OE *frea* is weak: in *Beowulf* l.1166 we hear of the court official, Unferþ, who *æt fotum sæt frean Scyldinga* 'sat at the feet of the lord of the Scyldings'.

Frea- occurs as the first element in poetic compounds meaning 'lord' such as *freadrihten*, *freareccere*, *freawine*.

Fruma

The word *fruma* has three distinct senses: (i) a beginning; (ii) an originator, author, inventor, creator; (iii) a prince, lord, ruler. All three derive from the adjective *frum* 'original, first' in distinct senses: (i) what is first, a beginning; (ii) who is first, an originator; (iii) who stands in front, a leader. Holthausen cites a parallel in the Gothic word *frums* 'forefront' and a wider cognate in Greek *prámos* 'leader'.[354] A link in sense to *frea* and *pruvu,* discussed above, seems likely.

Geræswa

This is an unusual term, which appears to be an agent noun based on the verb *geræswian* 'consider, think through'. However, it is more likely that the verb derives from the noun, and that *geræswa* denotes 'leader' in the sense of 'planner, tactician'. Holthausen derives the noun from *ræs* which has two senses (i) an onset, attack, swift running (ii) deliberation. The noun *ræs* varies with *ræd* 'counsel, advice' in compounds: OE *ræsbora* 'bearer of counsel' denotes an 'adviser' and *ræsele* 'solution to a riddle'; these may be compared with *rædbora* 'counsellor' and *rædels* (m) *rædelse* (f) which mean (i) consideration (ii) debate, discussion, speech (iii) conjecture, imagination (iv) a riddle.[355] Holthausen distinguishes *rædan* and *ræsan* 'rush, attack, run towards' cognate with Greek **erosein* 'flow, well up', but clearly there are two senses of *ræs(an)*, with separate etymologies, one denoting 'running' and the other 'planning'.[356]

The planning senses are based on or derived from the verb *rædan* which has two conjugational classes – strong class VII (preterite *reord*)[357] and weak class I (preterite *rædde*). The strong verb is rare, and gives rise to the deverbal noun *reord* 'speech, voice'. The weak verb means 'advise' or more rarely 'ask advice', derived from the older sense 'speak with, consult, exchange ideas'; it has extended meanings such as 'debate', 'decide', 'solve a riddle', 'rule, control, govern', 'read, decipher', 'read out loud'.

The balance of probabilities is that the word indicates the role of the leader as 'planner, tactician'.

Heafodwisa

In the poem *Genesis*, l.1619, we read that *Chus wæs æðelum heafodwisa* 'Chus was (the) chief lord to the nobles'. The element *heafod-* here has the sense 'first, chief, most important, principal' which it shares with other terms such as *heafodbotl* 'chief dwelling', *heafodburh* 'capital, chief town', *heafodcwide* 'chief saying', *heafodcirice* 'main church, cathedral', *heafodfæder* 'patriarch', *heafodgetel* 'cardinal number',

---

[352] Pollington, 2011, p.30, 242ff

[353] Holthausen, 1974 s,v. *frea*; Orel, 2003, *frawjon*

[354] Holthausen, 1974 s,v. *fruma*; Orel, 2003, *frumaz*

[355] [355] Lass, 1994, p.201

[356] Holthausen, 1974 s,v. *ræsan, rædan*; Orel, 2003, *raiðaz, raiðjanan, reðan*

[357] Lass, 1994, p.160 cf. OE *rædan / reord* with Gothic *radan / rairoþ*.

heafodgylt 'capital crime',[358] *heafodleahter* 'deadly sin', *heafodmæg/ heafodmaga* 'close kinsman', *heafodmann* 'chief, leader, prince, headman', *heafodmynster* 'chief church', *heafodport* 'chief market town', *heafodrice* 'empire', *heafodstede/heafodstol* 'main place', *heafodweard* 'chief guardian', *heafodwyrhta* 'chief workman, foreman'. As a *heafodwisa*, he was therefore the principal 'director' and leader of his folk.

Heahealdor

This term means a 'high elder' or 'chief leader', combining the prefix *heah-* denoting excellence or extremity with the word *ealdor* (see above).

Helm

The principal meaning of *helm* is 'covering, headgear, helmet' but it is used figuratively to mean 'protector' as with *healdend* below.[359] In *Beowulf*, l.1321, King Hroðgar is called *helm scyldinga* 'protector of the Scylding [people]'.

Heorra

In *The Battle of Maldon*, the East Saxon troops learn of the fall of Ealdormann Byrhtnoð and in line 204-5 *ealle gesawon heorðgeneatas þæt hyra heorra læg* 'all the hearth-companions saw that their leader lay [dead]'. This is the only certain occurrence of the word in OE; a homonym *heorra* 'hinge' is found occasionally. It is possible that the word is based on ON *hjarri* 'warlord', or that it is a unique example of an OE cognate of the German word *Herr* 'master, gentleman'. If the poem does reflect the local East Saxon dialect of the 10th century, then the latter is the more likely.[360]

Heretoga

This word glosses *dux* 'duke, warleader' in Ælfric's glossaries and *comes* 'count' elsewhere. In *Numbers*14:4 we read *uton us gesettan heretogan* 'let us set a leader [over us]'. Clearly, the word comprises *here-* 'aggressive army, raiding force' and *–toga* 'one who draws, pulls, leads', an agent noun based on the verb *teon*.

Hierde, Hirde, Hyrde

The word *hierde* normally means 'keeper, herdsman' and is used figuratively for 'one who watches over others' (cf. *Healdend* above).[361] In *Beowulf* l.610 the hero is called *folces hyrde* 'watchman of his people'.

Hofding

The word *hofding* appears only in late OE, and is probably borrowed from the ON *höfðingi* 'leader, inciter'. In the *ASC*, manuscript 'E', we read under the year 1076 that *Rawulf eorl 7 Rogcer eorl wæron hofdingas æt þisan unræde* 'Earl Ralf and Earl Roger were leaders in this bad advice', meaning that they were ringleaders in a disastrous plot.

Latteow

Etymologically *latteow* and its variant *ladteow* are derived from *lad-þeow* 'a servant who leads'.[362] The OE Bede describes Hengest as *se ðe wæs ærest ladteow ond heretoga angelcynnes on Breotene* 'who was first the guide and army-leader of the English nation in Britain'. It is one of the many OE words used to render Latin *dux*, alongside *ealdorman*, *cyning* and *heretoga*.

---

[358] Here the sense may be ambiguous - both 'chief crime, deadly sin' and 'crime for which one pays with one's head'.
[359] Orel, 2003, *xelmaz*
[360] Scragg, 1981
[361] Orel, 2003, *xerðjaz*
[362] Loyn, 1953, p.514

Mundbora

A *bora* 'bearer' of *mund* 'protection', a person who guarantees the safety of another. The narrow meaning of *mund* is 'hand', but the figurative meaning includes the protection afforded to a supporter, legal guardianship and the 'king's peace'.[363]

Onwealda

A person who has *onweald* 'power, might, authority'; although the verb *onwealdan* is not recorded, this agent noun is regularly formed. See *Wealdend* below.

Rædend

A 'ruler' in the senses discussed above under *Geræswa*. This agent noun is an active participle from *rædan* 'advise, set in order, etc.'.

Ræsbora

A word used to describe a 'bearer of good advice', a person who takes thought for the good of those who follow him, and therefore a wise leader. In *Genesis* (l.1810-1) we read that *Þær ræsbora þrage siððan wicum wunode and wilna breac* 'there a wise leader for some time after dwelt in mansions and enjoyed pleasure'.

Reccend

There are two verbs spelt *reccan* in OE, one meaning 'reach, stretch out, tend towards' and the other 'reckon, consider, tell a story'. They are derived from homonymous nouns *racu* meaning (i) running, a river bed (where water runs) and (ii) a story, comment, report.[364] The original idea may have been 'grounds, foundation' giving rise to both senses. The agent noun, an active participle, means 'one who reckons, one who judges wisely' and thus 'one who decides for others, judge, governor'.

Regolweard

A *regolweard* is a 'guardian of rule, keeper of order' and thus an 'authority'. For *weard* see below. The noun *regol* (from Latin *regula* 'a rule') is used for both the ecclesiastical rule of a monastic house, and for 'custom, standard, norm'. It is often used of authorities within the church who interpret the will of God, and of provosts who ensure proper observance of house rules. It does not appear to have any secular applications.

Rica

This is an example of the adjective *rice* 'powerful, noble, important' used substantively 'he who is powerful'.[365] The word *rice* only developed the sense 'powerful in wealth, having many possessions, rich' with the monetisation of the Anglo-Saxon economy in the 10th c.

Ricsiend, Ricsere

Two agent nouns derived from the verb *ricsian* 'rule, exercise power, govern, reign'. It belongs to a group of denominal and deadjectival Class II verbs with the standard *–ian* infinitive and *–s-* formative: examples include *clænsian* 'cleanse' from *clæne* 'clean' and *miltsian* 'take pity on' from *mild* 'mild, kindly'.[366] The ending *–ere* denotes agent nouns derived from verbs (cf. modern drive/driver, learn/learner).[367]

[363] Orel, 2003, *munðo*
[364] Holthausen, 1974, *reccan, racu*; Orel, 2003, *rakan, rako*
[365] Orel, 2003, *rikjaz*
[366] Orel, 2003, *rikjanan* Lass, 1994, p.203. The source of this *–s-* has been linked to the *s*-aorist in Latin, e.g. *dico* 'I say' versus *dixi* 'I said'.
[367] Campbell, 1987, no.337

Rihtend, Rihtere

Two agent nouns derived from the verb *rihtan* 'set right, correct, restore to a proper position, amend' meaning 'he who sets things right, regulator, judge'.[368] The form *rihtere* and its OHG counterpart *rihtari*, is possibly a calque on Latin *rector* 'he who corrects'.

Scildend, Scildere

Two agent nouns, *scildend* formed as the active participle of the verb *scildan*, (*sceoldan, scyldan, sceldan*) 'shield, protect, defend' and *scildere* with the *–ere* agent ending.[369] The meaning is 'one who protects' with a sense similar to *helm* above.

Strengel

The word *strengel* appears in *Beowulf* (l.3115) *wigena strengel* where it means 'one who gives strength to warriors, a man of fortitude, a leader'.[370] For the formation, see *fengel* below.

Wealdend

This word is another agent noun formed from the active participle of a verb (cf. *scildend, rihtend, ricsiend*).[371] The verb *wealdan* means 'wield, exercise power over, control' and the noun 'ruler, governer' as in *Beowulf* (l.17) *wuldres wealdend* 'the governor of glory' and the *Anglo-Saxon Chronicle* MS 'C' s.a. 1065 where the phrases *freolic wealdend* 'bounteous ruler' and *hæleða wealdend* 'ruler of heroes' occur in the verse epitome of the annal.

Wine

This is a very common word for 'friend, loved one' which can refer to people of equal or superior status, although as noted under *frea* above, terms of endearment could be used as a respectful form of address.[372]

Compounds with *wine* as the second element include *freawine* 'lordly friend, leader', *goldwine* 'gold-friend, generous lord', *guðwine* 'battle-friend, weapon', *iuwine* 'friend from the old days', *mægwine* 'friendly kinsman', *sundorwine* 'close friend', *unwine* 'not-friend, enemy'. Others with *wine* as the first element include *winedrihten* 'friendly lord, beneficial leader', *winemæg* (=*mægwine*) 'friendly kinsman', *winetreow* 'trust between friends'.

Þengel

This poetic word refers to a nobleman or prince. In *Beowulf* (l.1507) the hero is described as *hringa þengel* 'lord of rings', i.e. the wealth which he distributes to his companions. The word *þengel* is derived from the Proto-Germanic **þangilaz* from the verb **þenghanan* 'thrive, succeed' found in OE as *þeon* 'thrive', and the passive participle *geþungen* with the meaning 'excellent'.[373] For the formation, see *fengel* below.

Þeoden

This poetic term means 'lord of a tribe', based on the word *þeod* 'tribe, folk, nation'.[374] For the formation, see *drihten* above.

---

[368] Orel, 2003, *rextaz*

[369] Orel, 2003, *skelðuz*

[370] Orel, 2003, *stranȝaz*

[371] Orel, 2003, *walðaz, walðiȝaz, walðjan*

[372] Orel, 2003, *weniz*

[373] Holthausen, 1974, *þengel*; Orel, 2003, *þangilaz*

[374] Holthausen, 1974, *þeoden*; Orel, 2003, *þeuðo-*; Pollington, 2011a, p.184

Taking, Holding, Giving, Sharing as Lordly Deeds

The gathering and distribution of resources was one of the key functions of a leader from the Neolithic period onwards. The vocabulary of such acts is, in the poetry at least, expressed in terms of high-status and symbolically powerful objects which add lustre and renown to the giver and to the recipient.[375] The performance of tribute-taking and reward-giving in public ceremonies underscored the power of the leader who performed them, and enhanced the reputation of those who received such public acclaim.

Beahgifa

This term means 'ring-giver', evidently referring to the 'lord' as the donor of gifts of treasure. The noun *beah/beag* means 'curved thing' from the verb *bugan* 'bow, bend' and *gi(e)fa* is an agent noun from *giefan* 'give'.[376]

In the setting of the meadhall, the leader sits in the position of power (*giefstol* 'gift-seat')[377] from which valuables are distributed; these are generally objects with high display values, such as wargear, feasting equipment, tableware and jewellery – all objects which can be used to display status and *weorþ* 'honour, standing, value' to other members of the group.

The awarding of a ring (*beahðegu* 'ring-taking', *Beowulf*, l.2176; *hringðegu* 'ring-taking', *The Seafarer*, l.44; *hringweorþung* 'ring-honouring', *Beowulf*, l.3017) is not the equivalent of a pay-day parade in the modern army, but perhaps closer to a ceremony at which medals are awarded, these medals serving as obvious tokens of participation in community events (campaigns, acts of valour, etc.)

The rings (*hringas, beagas*) themselves are symbolic of personal worth and honour, and are given to males and females: Hroþgar's queen is described as *beaghroden* 'adorned with rings' (*Beowulf*, l.623), an expression of female beauty in costume and appearance expressing both personal virtue and the wealth of the community to which she belongs. (*Hring* is also used of the iron links of a mailshirt: *hringiren* 'ring-iron', *hringloca* 'rings locked together', *hringnett* 'net of rings', etc.)

Other compounds ending in –*gi(e)fa* with similar meanings include: *argifa* 'benefit-giver', *blædgifa* 'wealth-giver', *eadgifa* 'blessing-giver', *feorhgifa* 'life-giver', *goldgifa* 'gold-giver', *hyhtgifa* 'hope-giver', *lacgifa* 'gift-giver', *maððumgiefa* 'treasure-giver' (see *Maððumgiefa* below), *rædgifa* 'advice-giver, adviser', *sincgifa* 'jewel-giver' (see *Sincgiefa* below), *symbelgifa* 'feast-giver', *wilgifa* 'desire-giver'.

Brytta

This agent noun linked to the verbs *breotan* 'break up, cut up', *brytnian* 'divide, share out', *bryttian* 'break up, divide' has the meaning 'sharer, divider, dispenser'. Also derived from this verbal group is *brytsen* 'fragment, piece broken off'.[378]

In *Beowulf*, leaders may be called *beaga brytta(n)* 'sharer of rings' (l.35, 352, 1485), *sinces brytta* (l.605, 1170, 1920. 2070) 'sharer of treasure'.

Fengel

The poetic term *fengel* appears in *Beowulf* (l.1400-1) where *wisa fengel geatolic gende* 'the wise prince travelled in splendour'. (The adjective *wisa* here is declined weak despite the absence of an article.) The word is derived from the Proto-Germanic root **fang* 'hold, catch, seize' with associative suffix **-ilaz*; the sense appears to be 'one who is involved in seizing, taking or acquiring'.[379] The OE cognate of the verb **fanxanan* is *fon* 'take, grasp, seize' most often seen in the phrase *feng to rice* 'he seized power' appearing in the *Anglo-Saxon Chronicle* e.g. for the year 488 *Her Æsc feng to rice* 'Here Æsc came to power'.

---

[375] Pollington, 2003; Pollington, 2011a

[376] Holthausen, 1974, *beag;* Orel, 2003, *baugaz, ȝebon*

[377] Orel, 2003, *ȝebostolaz*

[378] Holthausen, 1974, *brytta, gebrot, breatan, brytsen;* Orel, 2003, *brutan, brutjojanan, brutjon*

[379] Holthausen, 1974 s,v. *fengel;* Lass, 1994, p.201; Orel, 2003, *fanȝan, fanxanan*

Healdend

The active participle of the verb *healdan* 'hold, keep, watch over, protect, guard', this noun denotes 'one who keeps, protects'.[380]

Hlaford

The modern word 'lord' derives via Middle English *lavard* from OE *hlaford*, a compound of *hlaf* 'loaf, bread' and *weard* 'keeper, watchman, warden' (see *weard* below). The name relates to the trio of roles in the Anglo-Saxon meadhall –*hlafweard*, *hlafdige* (lady) and *hlafæta* – as 'loaf-keeper', 'loaf-maker' and 'loaf-eater' respectively. The term *hlafæta* refers to an undifferentiated member of the community, known in Gothic as a *gahlaiba* 'with-loaf (man)', one who shares food and eats alongside; the same sense is given in Latin *companio* 'messmate, companion' from *panem* 'bread'.[381]

The dominant male and female roles are characterised as relating to the production of food as the female *hlafdige* and the control and protection of food as the male *hlafweard*.[382] The *hlaford* was responsible for the management of the food resources in terms of husbandry and supply management. Perhaps more important was his management of consumption – using food resources to create and maintain networks of alliance with which the community's security and prosperity could be safeguarded.

Maððumgiefa

This is a compound of *maððum* and the agent noun *giefa* 'giver' discussed in *Beahgiefa*. The word *maððum* is also spelt *maðum*, *maðm* and the plural may be *maðmas* or *madmas*.[383] Its basic meaning is 'a precious thing, a treasure, an ornament'. Its Gothic cognate *maiðms* glosses the Greek *doron* 'gift' implying that it refers to an item of value held with a view to use as a reward. A wider link to its cognates Latin *mutuus* 'common (property), reciprocal (gift)' and *mutare* 'move, change' suggests that the word relates specifically to the economy of prestige exchange.

Sincgiefa

A term used in verse to denote 'jewel-giver', a magnanimous lord, a leader who distributes treasures. The second element *giefa* has been discussed above (see *Beahgiefa*) while the word *sinc* evidently meant 'jewel, precious stone' and may be related to the practice of decorating high-status items with cloisonné and cabochons, especially in the polychrome jewellery of the 6th-7th c. seen at Sutton Hoo Mound 1 and elsewhere.[384]

Sinc- alternates with *beah*- and *hring*- in gift-giving compounds. The term *sincgiefa* is used in the poem *Christ*, in *The Metres of Boethius* in *Beowulf* and *The Battle of Maldon*. *Sincþegu* 'jewel-taking' (*Beowulf*, 1.2884) mirrors *beahðegu* 'ring-taking' and *hringðegu* 'ring-taking' discussed above under *Beahgiefa*. *Sincweorðung* 'honouring with a jewel' occurs twice in *Andreas* (1.272, 477). *Sinchroden* 'decorated with jewels' occurs in *Andreas* (1.1673).

---

[380] Orel, 2003, *xalðanan*

[381] Orel, 2003, *xlaibon*

[382] Holthausen, 1974, *hlaf*; Pollington, 2003; Pollington, 2011b

[383] Holthausen, 1974, *maðum;* Orel, 2003, *maiþmaz*. Orel cites a further link to PGmc **maiðjanan* (Gothic *maidjan*) 'alter, change, falsify', the causative of **miþanan* (OE *miþan* 'hide, conceal') meaning 'make hidden' – perhaps 'put into hiding, put away from sight' with reference to placing valuables into safe storage until they are to be handed on(?).

[384] Holthausen, 1974, *sinc* declares the word to be of unknown origin. Pollington, Kerr & Hammond, 2010, p.123 relate the term to the verb *sincan* 'sink, impress into a surface' and to the technique of producing jewelled surfaces in which the stones and glasses are flush with the surrounding cells, the cloisonné technique.

Weard

The base meaning of *weard* is 'watchman, guardian' with extended meaning of 'one who keeps watch over, protector' with senses similar to those of *helm* above.[385]

The Gothic cognate in the compound *daurawards* 'door-ward, doorman' shows the sense of vigilance and responsibility. The word is very productive in compounds, some rather mundane or low-status such as *carcernweard*, *cwearternweard* 'jailer', *ediscweard* 'parkland watchman', *hægweard* 'cattle watchman', *leacweard* 'gardener', *leactunweard* 'garden watchman', *mylenweard* 'mill-keeper', *wyrtweard* 'tender of plants, gardener'. There is also a military or maritime dimension to some of the names, such as *batweard* 'boat watchman', *brycgweard* 'bridge-keeper', *burhweard* 'defender of the town walls', *heafodweard* 'chief guard', *hyþweard* 'harbour watchman', *landweard* 'coastguard', *lidweard* 'ship's master, captain', *mereweard* 'sea warden', *nihtweard* 'night watchman', *scipweard* 'ship's master', *stocweard* 'townsman'. The term *mearcweard* 'one who watches the boundaries' refers to a wolf who seeks to find a way into the settlement.

The word seems most appropriate in the context of the meadhall where officers with special responsibility were appointed: examples would include *botlweard* 'steward', *duruweard* 'door watchman', *healfweard* 'partner, co-owner', *heargweard* 'temple watchman', *hofweard* 'public official, ædile', *renweard* 'house watchman', *seleweard* 'hall watchman', *stigweard* 'steward, house warden', *wuduweard* 'woodward, forester'. The office of headman is also included in the 'keeper, watchman' role: *bregoweard* 'princely guardian', *drihtenweard* 'lordly warden', *freoðuweard* 'keeper of peace', *goldweard* 'keeper of gold', *guþweard* 'watchman in war', *hordweard* 'keeper of wealth', *irfeweard* 'keeper of inheritance, heir', *lastweard* 'successor, follower', *regolweard* 'provost, keeper of monastic rule'.

The 'Sceptre' and the 'Whetstone'

The notion that the stone bar with its copper-alloy fittings is a symbol of office has become generally accepted. Enright based his entire book[386] on this idea, and sought confirmation for it in some very unlikely places. That said, the imposing faces and sheer bulk of the stone and its fittings clearly had great importance for the commissioner of the work – it would have been perfectly possible to make a 'sceptre' out of wood, walrus ivory, antler or bone at a fraction of the cost in labour. (We return below, p.166, to some other ideas which require investigation.)

The vocabulary of such 'badges of office' is not clearly defined in OE, although a number of terms beginning with the element *cyne-* 'kingly' indicate that a class of items could be marked out by royal associations: *cynebotl* 'kingly dwelling', *cynecynn* 'kingly descent', *cynedom* 'kingly rule, kingdom', *cynegewædu* 'kingly clothing', *cynegierela* 'kingly robe', *cynegild* 'king's compensation', *cyneham* 'king's manor', *cynehof* 'king's palace', *cynemann* 'royal personage', *cynereaf* 'kingly garment', *cynerice* 'kingly authority', *cyneriht* 'king's right', *cynescipe* 'kingship', *cynesetl* 'kingly seat, throne', *cynestol* 'king's seat, palace', *cynestræt* 'king's highway, public road', *cyneþrymm* 'kingly wonder, majesty', *cynewise* 'kingly state'.

Most interesting is the term *cynegeard/cynegyrd* 'kingly staff', which appears in the writings of Ælfric and in glosses, translating Latin *sceptrum* 'a sceptre' meaning 'mark of authority' e.g. *hi to ðæs caseres cynegyrde bugon* 'they submitted to Caesar's sceptre'. The word comprises *cyne-* kingly and the noun *geard* which can mean 'staff, rod, stick, stake, pole' and is the origin of the modern word 'yard' as a measure of length. *Cynegyrd* glosses Latin *baculum* 'staff, cudgel', *virga* 'rod', *palus* 'stake, pole', *fascis* 'bundle of sticks'. In the mind of the glossator a *sceptrum* was a king's staff, while in the *Corpus* glosses, *sceptra* is rendered *onwald* 'great rule, authority' (see *Onwealda* above).[387]

---

[385] Orel, 2003, *warðaz, warðjanan*
[386] Enright, 2006
[387] Sweet, 1979, p.83

Promising at first sight is the compound *cynningstan* which appears to be 'king-stone' but further investigation reveals that the term glosses Latin *turricula* 'little tower' and Greek *pyrgos*, referring to a small wooden structure on the side of a gaming board into which dice were thrown at the top to issue at the bottom onto the board without human interference. The compound's first element is thus *cenning* 'trying, making trial, proving' and the item is part of the equipment for board games.

As a description of the stone rod in terms of 'sacred power' and authority, the expression *eorcnanstan* might be invoked. The word has variants *eorclanstan*, *earcnanstan*, glossing *lapis pretiosus* 'precious stone', *gemma* 'pearl', *topazion* 'topaz'. In *Beowulf* (l.1208) the plural *eorclanstanas* describes the treasures Beowulf carried off over the waves from the Frisian raid. Interestingly, the first element of the compound, *eorcen-*, is not elsewhere recorded in OE, but OHG has *erchan* glossing *egregius* 'exceptional' and the Gothic cognate *airknis* means 'holy, filled with power'. Orel gives *erknastainaz* as a Proto-Germanic word meaning 'jewel', perhaps from a root meaning 'bright, shining'.[388]

The compound *halstan* appears promising, because *hal* 'wholeness, health, wellbeing' is the source of the word 'holy', yet the OE word is difficult to locate in the corpus. Orel cites OE *halstan* as a term for 'crystal' in his discussion of the Proto-Germanic root *xelaz* meaning 'slippery, icy'.[389] However, Clark-Hall gives *halstan* as a variant spelling of *heallstan* 'small cake' (i.e. a 'hall-stone, dumpling').[390] Likewise, the compound *weohstan* 'holy stone' appears as a personal name – as discussed below, p. 122.

The OE word *stæf* 'staff, rod' has many extended meanings including 'written sign, letter', 'collection of written signs, text', 'letters, literature'.[391] Its Gothic cognate *stafs* can mean 'element, rudiment'. It glosses *baculus* and may be used for 'staff of office'. However, it does not appear to have been used with royal associations in Anglo-Saxon England, and its role may derive from the use of the symbolic staff in the form of a bishop's crook.

The curious term *wælgim* occurs in Riddle 20 of the *Exeter Book* in characteristically ambiguous language:[392]

> *Byrne is min bleofag, swylce beorht seomað*
> *wir ymb þone wælgim þe me waldend geaf*
> My warcoat is colourful, thus brightly hangs
> A wire about the 'slaughter-stone' which the ruler gave to me.

The term *wælgim* evidently refers to part of the sword's scabbard (described as a *byrne* 'mailcoat,' meaning the sword's covering used in war) or its suspension straps, and recalls the use of glass and amber beads on early swords of the 6th and 7th century.[393] The element *wæl* means both 'slaughter' and 'results of slaughter, dead body' while *gim(m)* means 'precious stone' (from Latin *gemma* 'pearl') and figuratively anything gem-like such as the eye, e.g. *Guthlac* (l.1302-3) *swylce he his eagan ontynde, halige heafdes gimmas* 'thus he opened his eyes, the holy gems of the head'. The similarity between the bosses used on the straps supporting swords and eyes has been noted elsewhere.[394]

[388] Orel, 2003, *erknastainaz*
[389] Orel, 2003, *xelaz*
[390] Clark-Hall, 1984, *halstan*.
[391] Orel, 2003, *stabiz ~ stabaz*
[392] With thanks to Dr. Sam Newton for bringing this word and its context to my attention.
[393] Meaney, 1981; Menghin, 1983
[394] Mortimer, 2011, p.112ff and references there.

Figure 85 Whetstone from a heathen Anglian burial ground at Uncleby, Yorkshire, found placed upright in the chalk at the foot of grave 11. It is dated to the 6th or early 7th century. Length: 46.2 cm, maximum width: 5.1 cm. Reference: Bruce-Mitford, vol.2, pp.362

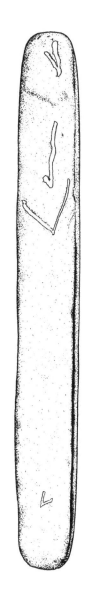

The OE name for a whetstone is *hwetstan*, which appears in glosses and in one of the leechdoms. The first element *hwet-* derives from the verb *hwettan* 'whet, sharpen', from the adjective *hwæt* 'sharp, keen'. The underlying notion is of a very sharp angle, seen in the Latin cognate **quet-* in *triquetrus* 'three-cornered, three-angled'.[395]

The word 'hone' is from OE *han*, from Proto-Germanic **xaino-* . Holthausen links this to Avestan *saeni* 'spit, spike, point' and Orel to Greek *ko(i)nos* 'pine-cone'.[396] A hone is used for putting the final edge to a blade which has been whetted.

Crowns and Symbols of Rule

The following OE words are used to denote either a 'crown' or a symbol of rulership.

Byge

This noun, based on the verb *bugan* 'bend, curve', refers to the cone or skull of a helmet.[397] See *Cynehelm* below. It is related to the noun *beah, beag* 'ring, circlet' which may also refer to a diadem or crown.

Corenbeg

The noun *corona* 'crown' with explanatory extension *–beag* 'ring'.

Corona

The Latin word *corona* 'crown' used unmodified in OE, from which a derived verb *gecoronian* 'to crown' is formed.[398] An alternative is *beagian*, 'to set a circlet (on someone)'.

Cynebænd

A compound of *cyne-* 'kingly, royal' and *bænd, bend* 'band, fastening, ribbon, circlet'.[399] It evidently refers to a ribbon or diadem indicating royal authority. Interestingly, the iconography of many C-type bracteates features a stylised male head with an impressive plait of hair at the rear; this is believed to derive from Roman medallions with an imperial bust shown with a laurel wreath tied at the rear. The wreath thus serves as a *cynebend* 'kingly fastening'.

---

[395] Holthausen, 1974, *hwæt;* Orel, 2003, *xwataz, xwatjanan*

[396] Holthausen, 1974, *han;* Orel, 2003, *xaino*

[397] Clark-Hall, 1984, *byge;* the same verb gives *beag* 'circlet, ring'.

[398] Clark-Hall, 1984, *corona, +coronian*

[399] Clark-Hall, 1984, *cynebænd;* Orel, 2003, *bandan, banðan, banðjanan*. It is possible that echoes of the separate word **banðwo* 'visible sign' (Gothic *bandwa* 'sign, marker') are present within the semantic field of OE *bænd*. The sign in question may have been a knotted cloth or cord.

Figure 86 B-type bracteate from Skrydstrup, Denmark, showing the prominent headdress.

Figure 87 C-type bracteate from Lolland, Denmark, showing a head with plaited hair above a horse.

Cynegold

This term is used in the poem *The Phoenix* (l.605) *ðeodnes cynegold soðfæstra gehwone sellic glengeð* 'the lord's golden crown excellently adorns each of the righteous'.

Cynehelm

In the biblical book of Matthew we read that the tormentors *wundon cynehelm of þornum 7 asetton ofer hys heafod* '[they] wound a crown from thorns and set [it] over his head'. *Cynehelm* here glosses Latin *corona (de spinis)*. The word is composed from the elements *cyne* 'kingly' and *helm* which means (i) a helmet or headcovering, (ii) the cover afforded by trees, (iii) any kind of covering, (iv) a lordly protector (see p.98 above). The noun derives from the verb *helan* 'hide, cover up' which also provides *heolstor* 'darkness', *heall* 'hall, covered place', *hell* 'hell, the grave, the covered place' and other words relating to concealment.[400]

There are no certain references to Anglo-Saxon kings being crowned or wearing a crown before the 10th century; the present coronation ceremony was devised by St. Dunstan and first enacted in 973 AD for King Eadgar. In or after 924 King Æðelstan issued a series of coins in which he is shown wearing a crown, with the legend *Rex Totius Britanniae* 'king of all Britain', but the imagery appears to have been drawn from Carolingian models.[401] Before then, the mark of a king or leader appears to have been the wearing of a helmet. This was probably not an economic restriction: later Anglo-Saxon laws stipulate that every soldier presenting himself for duty must have a helmet, shield, spear, etc.

It seems likely that donning a helmet marked certain men out as 'extraordinary', perhaps imbued them with specific powers or attributes and, given that the earlier styles of helmet were very enclosed, it is likely that the *cynehelm* was conceived as a helmet with a faceplate, otherwise known as a *grimhelm* 'mask-helmet'.[402] The examples from Sutton Hoo Mound 1, and the contemporary mounds at Vendel and Valsgärde in Sweden, are good examples of this type.[403] See *Freawrasn* below.

---

[400] Holthausen, 1974, *helan, helm;* Orel, 2003, *xelmaz*
[401] Livingston, 2011, p.6
[402] Pollington (forthcoming)
[403] Mortimer, 2011

Cynewiþþe

This term glosses *redimiculum*, a royal diadem. It is a compound of *cyne-* (see above) and *–wiþþe* 'withy, thong, cord'.[404]

Freawrasn

This expression occurs in *Beowulf* (l.1451) in a description of a helmet: *ac se hwita helm hafelan werede ....since geweorðad, befongen freawrasnum* 'yet the bright helm warded the head … made worthy with gems, surrounded with lordly chains'. The word is a compound of *frea* 'lord' and *wrasn, wrasen* 'band, chain'.[405] It may refer to the kind of helmet with a mail aventail or curtain suspended from the rim and face-plate, e.g. the examples from Valsgärde mounds 7 and 8.[406]

Gyldenbeah, Gyldenbend

Two compounds with the first element *gylden* 'golden' and the second *beah* 'ring' (see *Corenbeg*) and *bend* 'band, ribbon' (see *Cynebænd*).

Heafodbeag, Heafodbend

Two compounds with the first element *heafod* 'head' and the second *beah* 'ring' (see *Corenbeg*) and *bend* 'band, ribbon' (see *Cynebænd*).

Heafodgold

This term occurs in Psalm 8: *þu hine gewuldrast and geweorðast, and him sylst heafodgold to mærðe* 'you marvel at and honour him, and give him a golden headband for his glory'.

Hroðgirela

The *Regius Psalter* uses the compound *hroðgirela* for 'crown'.[407] The first element is an archaic word for 'glory' found in personal names such as Hroþgar, Hroðmund, etc. The second element is *(ge)gierela* 'dress, adornment'. The sense would appear to be an item of apparel with associations with glory, especially martial glory.

Mind

This word occurs once in the sense 'diadem' in the *Durham Ritual*.[408] Holthausen indicates that it is a loanword from Old Irish.[409]

Sigebeag

The phrase *onfeng sigebeah* 'he received the ring of victory' occurs in the OE Bede, with a reference to the laurel-leaf crown worn by a victor at Roman games. The element *sige* refers to military victory and feats of arms.[410]

The compound *Sigebeah* also occurs as the name of a moneyer operating under King Beorhtwulf (839-53 AD). [411]

---

[404] Clark-Hall, 1984, *cynewiþþe, wiþþe;* Orel, 2003, *wiþiz*
[405] Clark-Hall, 1984, *wrasen*
[406] Newton, 1993, p.41; Mortimer, 2011
[407] Clark-Hall, 1984, *hroðgirela;* Orel, 2003, *xroþaz*
[408] Clark-Hall, 1984, *mind*
[409] Holthausen, 1974, *mind*
[410] Orel, 2003, *se3ez ~ se3az*
[411] Keary, 1887, p.43

Discussion

The words denoting 'lord, leader, king' fall naturally into groups denoting social, military and economic leadership, e.g. *ðeoden* 'leader of a tribe', *cyning* 'scion of a family line', *folcfrea* 'lord of a folk', indicate the social function; *drihten* 'leader of a warband', *heretoga* 'army leader', *guðwine* 'battle-friend' indicate the military function; *hierde* 'herdsman, guardian', *hlaford* 'food-protector', *weard* 'watchman' denote the economic function. That said, the terms show considerable variation in both status (e.g. *weard* and *hierde* are also lowly if important occupations, 'watchman' and 'herdsman') and popularity (*drihten* is a very common word in the surviving literature, due mainly to its extension to mean 'our Lord (Jesus)' imitating the Latin *dominus* while *strengel* and some other words are found only once in the corpus of OE.

The wide variation in the terms used may be due to the requirements of alliterative verse and the technique of apposition used by Anglo-Saxon poets;[412] this incremental release of information is used in all types of poetic composition from the epic verse of *Beowulf* to the humbler *Exeter Book Riddles*. The requirements of alliterative verse make it useful for the poet to have at his command a wide variety of terms for the same person, thing or idea – hence a 'lord' may be a simple *helm* (one long syllable, alliterating on h-), a *rica* (two short syllables, alliterating on r-), a *wealdend* (two long syllables, alliterating on w-) or a *winedrihten* (four syllables, alliterating on w-). The choices of other words in the line, the placement of the word to be chosen and the metrical pattern would all affect the range of words for 'lord' the poet might use.

These same constraints apply no less to the terms for 'sceptre' and 'crown', which find their place in the settings of meadhall and royal palace – the natural environment of poets working to please wealthy patrons.

The use of such florid language in a meadhall or palace for routine communication may seem to us unlikely. But we should not forget that one of the purposes of verse was to supply information in a memorable form – a use which did not die out with the introduction of stylus and vellum. It is perfectly possible that the king's spokesman was chosen for his ability to frame formal speech in ways which were consistent with some of the customary practices of poets.

---

[412] Robinson, 1985

7. The Stag in Anglo-Saxon Tradition

Stephen Pollington

This section is adapted from material published in Pollington, Kerr & Hammond, *Wayland's Work: Anglo-Saxon Art, Myth and Material Culture from the 4th to the 7th Century*.

Background

The Sutton Hoo stag figurine has been viewed as an exceptional item without close parallels in early mediaeval art. While this is to some extent true – examples of stags modelled in the round are rare in mediaeval northern Europe – there are in fact many instances of stags in Germanic art of the 4th-7th centuries, and Anglo-Saxon art of the same period. Cervids generally had great cultural importance for certain societies, Germanic and others.

Stags (and other hunted animals, such as boars) appear regularly in European art during the last millennium BC.[413] Stag figurines feature prominently in the Kurgan culture of the Eurasian steppe and examples made in gold and silver occur at some splendid Kurgan burial sites.[414] Stag-horned warriors are depicted on the Arch of Constantine in Rome, where they may represent Germanic troops called *Cornuti* 'horned ones'.[415]

The Germanic tribe called *Cherusci* may have been the 'stag-people', if their name is based on the root **xerut-* 'hart';[416] the spelling *Cherusci* is the Roman interpretation of the name which may have appeared as **xerutisk-* in the 1st century BC, in Caesar's *De Bello Gallico*. This tribe spawned the leader Arminius (probably **Erminiaz* 'great one'), who famously tricked Varus into leading three Roman legions to annihilation in the Teutoburgerwald in 9 AD. The *Cherusci* remained a political force into the mid-1st century AD and are then heard of no more. They may have formed one of the components of the emergent tribal associations later known as *Saxones* or *Franci*.

The stag may reasonably be inferred to have formed part of their cult, perhaps being regarded as a totem for them. Another antlered beast, the elk, may have featured in Germanic cult, if the name of the deities called *Alcis* (Tacitus, *Germania*, ch.43.3) is indeed related to the name of this animal.[417] Caesar records the word *alces* used by the Germani for the elk, in his *De Bellum Gallicum*, 6.27.1. The *Alcis* were regarded as divine twins like the Greek *Dioskouri*.[418]

The use of stag imagery and cult processions did not fade away with the advent of Christianity to England. Indeed, the stag seems to have remained an important animal in the symbolic repertoire of the Anglo-Saxons, possibly connected to the god Woden and to the phenomenon of the Wild Hunt; links to Christian tradition, especially the psalms, have also been adduced in connection with both hart imagery and King Hroðgar's hall.[419] Tales of this cavalcade of departed souls are found across Germanic-speaking areas of Europe and appear to be of some antiquity. The hunt itself has been linked to forms of religious observance quite distinct from the round of the agricultural year.

---

[413] László, 1970, p.94-103; Greis & Geselowitz, 1992; Wells, 2001.

[414] Mallory & Mair, 2000

[415] Alföldi & Ross, 1959; Speidel, 2004, ch.3. Almgren, 1983, links these horned warriors to the horn-adorned helmets worn by the dancing warriors on the Sutton Hoo helmet plates.

[416] Orel, 2003, *xerutuz ~ xerutaz*. The word is linked etymologically to PIE **ker(u)-* 'horn'.

[417] Rives, 1999, p.307

[418] Pollington, 2011a, p.254

[419] Schichler, 1996

Hofler suggested that the early accounts of the Wild Hunt, which are often quite explicit about the nature of the phenomenon, refer in reality to bands of warriors who formed cult groups for the worship of their war-god, performing nocturnal rituals and frenzied activity afterwards. [420] This in turn gave rise to the reputation of one tribe, the Harii, for unstoppable night attacks in which the men, their equipment, clothes and armour were all painted black so that their enemies were entirely unnerved by the sight of them. [421]

It may have been such a warrior band that was seen in England in 1127 AD, according to the Laud Manuscript of the *Anglo-Saxon Chronicle* in a much-cited passage: [422]

> *Ne þince man na sellice þ we soð seggen for hit wæs ful cuð ofer eall land þ swa radlice swa he þær com þ wæs þes Sunendæies þ man singað "Exurge quare O.D." þa son þær æfter þa segon 7 herdon fela men feole huntes hunten. Ða huntes wæron swarte 7 micele 7 ladlice 7 here hundes ealle swarte 7 bradegede 7 ladlice 7 hi ridone on swarte hors 7 on swarte bucces. Þis wæs segon on þe selue derfald in þa tune on Burch on ealle þa wudes ða wæron fram þa selua tune ta Stanforde 7 þa muneces herdon ða horn blawen þ hi blewen on nihtes. Soðfæstemen heom kepten on nihtes sæiden þes þe heom þuhte þ þær mihte wel ben abuton twenti oðer þritti horn blaweres. Þis wæs sægen 7 herd fram þ he þider com eall þ lented tid on an to eastron. Þis was his ingang; of his utgang ne cunne we iett noht seggon. God scawe fore.*

> *Let no man think it strange which we truly tell, since it was well known through all the land that as soon as he [Abbot Henry] came there – that was the Sunday when one sings "Exurge quare O.D." – then soon thereafter many men saw and heard many hunters hunting. The hunters were black and large and ugly, and their hounds all black and big-eyed and ugly and they rode on black horses and on black bucks. This was seen on the deer-park itself in the estate at Peterborough and in all the woods which extended from that same estate to Stamford, and the monks heard the horns blowing which they blew at night. Truthful men [who] kept watch at night said this: that it seemed to them that there might well be around twenty or thirty horn-blowers. This was seen and heard from the time he came there all through Lent, on up to Easter. This was his arrival; of his departure we cannot yet speak. May God provide!*

The horse- and buck-riding huntsmen here are clearly practising some nightly activity designed to frighten and disquiet the local populace, aimed it seems against an unpopular Norman cleric. While the circumstances of their objection are possibly of no great significance, the form that their display of opposition took has strong overtones of Woden-worship and the terrifying spectacle of the nocturnal attacks of the *Harii*.

The early church disapproved of stag imagery and cult activity. Storms notes that Theodore of Tarsus, a North African ecclesiastic who was appointed archbishop of Canterbury in 668 AD, set severe legal punishments for anyone taking part in the Yuletide custom of *in cervulo vadere* 'going about in deerskins', which involved youths dressed in deerskins running through settlements and grabbing females. [423] This description recalls the customs of many early European societies in which – at certain liminal times – normally inappropriate behaviour was sanctioned.

---

[420] Cited in Simek, 1993.

[421] Kershaw, 2000; Pollington, 2003; Pollington, Kerr & Hammond, 2010. Their name, if the same as the Germanic root of OE *here,* means 'raiders'.

[422] Pollington, 2011a, p.448

[423] Storms, 1978, 329 citing the *Poenitentiale Theodori, cap. XXVII.*

Hart and Stag Images

Figure 88 Sutton Hoo (left) stag figurine and image (right) from the Gallehus horn.

Naked figures with bucks' horns on their heads appear on the 4th-5th c. Gallehus horns where they appear to be gods, supernatural figures or legendary heroes. A doe suckling her young also appears on one of the horns.[424] They were found in the old Anglian homeland in Jutland, at spots about 15 metres (50') apart but the discoveries were separated by 95 years (1639 and 1734 AD).

Aside from such high-status imagery, there are far humbler examples in early Germanic art. The figure of a stag was carved into the handle of an early triangular comb from a cremation in the Alemannic cemetery of Altendorf; the mode of depiction strongly recalls the south-eastern Sintana de Mures culture which is associated with the Goths.[425]

A footstool from the coastal site at Fallward, abandoned in the 5th century, bore a carved scene involving a stag and hound.[426] An undated, possibly mediaeval or earlier, bronze stag figurine modelled in the round was found at Høyland, Denmark; it is similar in its stance and proportions to the example from Sutton Hoo.[427]

The thin gold-foil discs called bracteates, found in Anglo-Saxon England, northern Germany and southern Scandinavia often bear scenes with supposed mythological content, particularly types B (one to three figures, sometimes with animals) and C (a large male head above a quadruped). An example of type B from (Denmark) (Figure 86) shows a complex scene with probable mythic content:[428] a central male figure is

[424] Ellis Davidson, 1988, p.43; Gunnell, 1995, p.49-53; Vang Petersen, 2003, p.293, fig.13

[425] Menghin, 1990, pl.12; Noble, 2006, p.15

[426] Schön, 1999

[427] Franceschi, Jorn, & Magnus, 2005 plate 11

[428] Pesch, 2007, p.124. The bracteate, no. IK166, is classified as a B6a, a hybrid or variant (*Bastardstück*) on the standard B6 theme of a swordsman with two wolves.

shown in profile with arms raised, wearing trousers and a belt, with a large headdress from the rear of which develops a bird's head; before him is a bird with its beak touching the figure's face, and a rosette of pellets between; beneath the bird is an advancing quadruped, a stag with antlers; beneath the stag is a pair of entwined snakes forming a guilloche pattern; behind the figure is a canine with open jaws and aggressive teeth, grasped in the right hand of the figure; between the figure's waist and the neck of the stag, the word **lau<u>ka</u>z** appears in runes facing left to right;[429] before the stag, the word **alu** appears in runes, facing right to left; a series of pellets in square and triangle formations are placed in the scene. The text *laukaz* is an early form of the OE *leac* meaning 'leek, onion' and is used for a number of medicinal plants;[430] the word *alu* may be the mundane OE word *ealu* 'ale', although it is often a magical or sacred word used to empower objects.

Bolin notes that horned animals – identified with the elk in his paper, but clearly representing a range of antlered beasts – are the most frequently depicted motif in Swedish rock art.[431] These carvings are often dismissed from considerations of the Germanic Iron Age since they appear to date from Neolithic (or even late Mesolithic) times, around 4000-5000 BC. However, recent re-evaluations in the light of carvings of boats found at Padjelanta (Swedish Lapland) strongly suggest that the custom of rock-carving was still a living tradition into the Late Iron Age (i.e. what in England we would call the Viking Age) and into the early Middle Ages.[432] Indeed, Bolin is quite clear in his assertion that 'rock art' is of wide social and mythical significance:[433]

> "Earlier theories about the northern rock art tradition have usually interpreted the rock carvings and rock paintings as a means to bring hunting luck. Various rock art studies that adhere to this interpretative tradition have claimed that the elk motifs provided clear evidence of the elk as one of the principal quarries within the hunting and trapping culture (e.g. Forsberg, 1993; Jensen, 1989; Hallström, 1960; Lindqvist, 1994; Malmer, 1992; Ramqvist, 1989). This line of argument is primarily based on the assumption that elk is depicted because of its dietary importance. I am sceptical of this kind of postulation that primarily connects rock art and subsistence. However I can accept the assumption that the elk in the northern areas was and still is one of the principal quarries from an economic point of view. In a general sense one can argue that it is completely misleading to treat prehistoric rock art as if it had a single purpose, because rock art has probably possessed more than one level of significance (e.g. Bradley and Fábregas Valcarce, 1998; Tilley, 1991). In my opinion rock art is not just a direct reflection of a well-defined economic subsistence system. It should rather be explained according to the ancient cosmological world-view and religious beliefs (e.g. Tilley, 1991; Helskog, 1995), and one important task of rock art research is to sift out the images from the panels and interpret their mythological messages."

Noting the 'shamanic' nature of some rock-art, he continues:[434]

> "Shamanism is really applied animism, or animism in practice, which involves the attribution of conscious life to souls and spirits and to nature and natural phenomena. However, it is interesting to note that shamanism also seems to have played a central role in the so called 'Germanic' religious traditions in the southern and middle part of Scandinavia during the mid-Iron Age. Lotte Hedeager (1997) has, for instance, suggested that the worship of Odin, from around AD 400–500, was to a large extent based on shamanic traditions and ideas (Hedeager, 1997: 115–18)."

---

[429] Conventionally, runic texts are transliterated into bold type. Underscore indicates a bind-rune (here **k** and **a** share a common staff).

[430] The spelling is identical with the reconstructed Proto-Germanic form (Orel, 2003, *laukaz*) but the text probably dates from the 6th century. Bracteates were not a long-lived phenomenon.

[431] Bolin, 2000, p.153

[432] Bolin, 2000, p.154 citing research by Mulk.

[433] Bolin, 2000, p.155

[434] Bolin, 2000, p.157

The stag may then have had an importance for the heathen Angles in Suffolk which dates back millennia, based not solely on primitive hunting rituals but rather on an understanding of animals as mediators between the worlds of gods and men.

Stag motifs were not confined to the continent and Scandinavia. The images of a stag and a snake apparently had some place in the iconography of West Saxon pre-Christian temples.[435] In the late 7th or early 8th century, Aldhelm of Sherborne wrote a letter praising the fact that Christian learning was now being conducted in buildings which were built on the sites of heathen shrines, where previously pillars stood bearing the images of the "foul stag and the snake".[436] He may have been thinking of a temple to the fertility gods, perhaps Ingwe, since the stag was associated with his Norse counterpart Freyr.[437] The snake may have been a reference to many serpentine creatures which characterise Style II art, and which developed into the Insular Style popularised by the 8th c. Christian establishment.[438]

In the verbal arts, references to stags and other antlered beasts are not common. One puzzling allusion in the Icelandic poem *Sonatorrek*, composed by Egil Skallagrimmson, is to a being called *Elgr* 'elk' in the phrase *alþjóð elgjar galga* (see p.63). This is a dense form of word-play, typical of the Norse skaldic art, meaning 'all-folk of elk's gallows'; the presumed reference is to a tree (gallows) of a being called Elgr 'elk' with which a large number of people are associated, and the assumption is that Elgr is a by-name for Óðinn and the 'gallows of Óðinn' is Yggdrasill, the World Tree, thus 'all folk of the World Tree' means 'all mankind'.[439] What the name 'elk' means in reference to Óðinn is never explained.

The Hall *Heorot*

In *Beowulf*, the great hall of the ageing King Hroþgar is called 'hart' (*heorot*). It may be linked thematically to the mythical hall *Breiðablik* owned by Balder in later Norse tradition. Both are noted for being free of contention - *facenstafas/feicnstafi* or 'baleful runes':[440]

……*nalles facenstafas*
Þeod-Scyldingas þenden fremedon

… no baleful runes
did the Folk-Shieldings work at that time   *Beowulf*, l.1018-9

er ec liggia veit
fœsta feicnstafi

where I know lie
few baleful runes   *Grimnismál*, l.125-6

Furthermore, the cult of the goddess Nerthus, the traditional patron of the Angles, was also associated with a prohibition on weapons, according to Tacitus, which may have extended to both the god's precinct and

---

[435] Pollington, 2011a, p108

[436] North, 1997, p.51 citing archaeological research by Blair; Pluskowski, 2007

[437] Pollington, 2011a, p.242, 260. Freyr is sometimes given the title *Yngvi-Freyr* 'Lord Yngvi', hence the name Freyr is a shorthand reference to the god known to the English as *Ing* or *Ingwe*, and to the Norsemen as *Yngvi*. Simek, 1993, s.v. *Heorot* resists the idea that the stag could be associated with any particular Nordic god.

[438] Pollington, Kerr & Hammond, 2010, p.489

[439] Einarsson, 2003

[440] Simek, 1993, s.v. *Heorot*; Liebermann, 2004, p.40

the king's hall.[441] Nerthus has a later counterpart in the god Njörðr who, with Freyr and Freyja, forms a separate clan in the Norse pantheon, the Vanir.[442]

In *Beowulf*, we learn that the stag was proud but could be frightened by an uncanny place:

> ðeah þe hæðstapa hundum geswenced,
> heorot hornum trum, holtwudu sece,   *Beowulf*, l.1368-9

> *The heath-treader, though hard pressed by hounds –*
> *the hart with firm horns – may seek the woods*

but he will not enter the dark pool where Grendel's Mother dwells.

If a stag's antlers were prominently displayed in both the god's shrine and the king's hall, this would link King Hroþgar, the hall's owner, to the cult of the Vanir gods and especially to Freyr, who was said to have killed his opponent, Beli, with a hart's horn as he had lent his sword to his servant, Skirnir.[443] That Hroþgar may have been a worshipper of the Vanir gods is made plain by the epithets used of him in *Beowulf*: *eodor Ingwina* 'shelter of the friends of Ing' (l.1044) and *frean Ingwina* 'lord of the friends of Ing' (l.1319). (For *Eodor* and *Frea*, see *6. The Vocabulary of* Rule, this volume.)

There is the further consideration that, although weapons were to be locked away in the presence of the goddess Nerthus, the numerous bog sacrifices from Denmark show evidence of violent death through strangulation: probably the indiction was against the spilling of blood in the holy places, and alternative means of sacrifice were employed. If so, the Gundestrup cauldron figure with the snake and the stag's antlers, holding up a coil or torc in his hand, may indeed have been part of the sacrificial rite, with this neck-ring as the device by which his victims were claimed.[444]

Scenes of Predation

Hunting scenes were a common artistic motif in the late Roman world, and they were also popular with early mediaeval nobles. Predation was part of the ideology and worldview of the early mediaeval establishment. Stags were evidently prized as prey, and their antlers were taken as trophies.

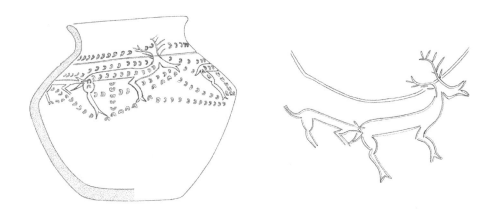

Figure 89 Urn from Grave 2594 at Spong Hill, Norfolk.

---

[441] Pollington, 2011a, p.267ff
[442] Pollington, 2011a, p.90
[443] North, 1997, p.51-2; Grigsby, 2005, p.90
[444] Glob, 1969; Grigsby, 2005, p.103-5, 130 *Ynglingatal* mentions several Swedish kings who were strangled with their neck-rings.

The decoration of Anglian funerary urns with freehand rather than stamped decoration is quite rare, almost confined to one corner of East Anglia. However, there are two examples of freehand friezes where the artists have managed to convey the sense of the scenes as stag-hunts.[445] Urn 2594 from Spong Hill (Norfolk) (Figure 89) shows an antlered stag being bitten in the rear by a prick-eared dog, followed by another. The next scene shows two dogs opposed, joined at the mouth as if fighting or possibly tearing at a piece of meat, while another looks on from behind. Another urn (unprovenanced, pictured in Myers's *Corpus*, no.1966) shows a procession of five fleeing deer – a stag, two hinds and two more stags – followed by a smaller animal with carefully marked shaggy hair biting at the last stag's heels; this looks like a deerhound in pursuit of its prey. It is possible that the cremated Anglian in the urn was fond of the hunt – as so many Anglo-Saxon nobles were – and that the urn was decorated in a fitting manner for this commemoration. It is even possible that the deceased met his end while out hunting. Remains of stags inside funerary urns are not common: mainly portions of unworked antler from large, early cemeteries such as Sancton and Spong Hill.[446]

The Sutton Hoo Stag

The stone from Sutton Hoo Mound 1 is surmounted by an iron plaited wire ring, on top of which stands a unique three-dimensional stag. The overall design of the piece suggests Scythian and eastern European parallels and the placement of the hooves as well as the exaggerated antlers support this.[447] The Sutton Hoo stag has been considered as an existing artefact – perhaps an heirloom of the Wuffings – re-used by the Anglo-Saxon maker of the whetstone; however, recent re-evaluation by Brian Ansell (p.42ff) indicates that the geometry of the stag and ring are congruent in many respects with the overall design of the stone, indicating that it was conceived as a single unit.[448] Three-dimensional cast quadrupeds used as mounts or finials are known from Saxony in the 3rd c., and these may be less impressive examples of the artefact type.[449]

There are occasional examples of antlered beasts shown on bracteates, e.g. the fragmentary example from Skrydstrup (Denmark, Figure 86) which features a male god with avian headdress gripping a wolf's jaw while a bird pecks at his eye, a stag walks away from him and a pair of intertwined snakes are trampled by the god and the stag.[450]

A remarkable decorated bowl from Lullingstone (Kent) features circular escutcheons (common on Romano-British metal vessels) filled with Germanic-style interlace panels.[451] Attached to the panels are T-shaped plates forming a cross, between which there is a procession of eight metal plaques in the form of stags. Between the T-shaped plaques, there are pairs of confronted birds standing on a decorated strip, below which another bird clutches a fish. The style of the decoration has been ascribed to the British northwest, with moulds for similar plaques having been found at the Mote of Mark (Kirkcudbrightshire, Scotland). This bowl seems to be part of the English fashion for British metalwork in the late 6th to early 7th c. but the details of the

---

[445] Hicks, 1993, p.22 fig. 1.6
[446] Hills, 1977; Myres, 1989, p.82; Timby, 1993, p.307. It is noted that the Sancton cemetery contained early Germanic pottery of a southern Germanic type, which was connected by Myres to the nearby Iron Age stronghold of *Almondbury*, possibly to be interpreted as 'stronghold of the *Alamanni*'.
[447] Bruce-Mitford, 1978, p.333-43, 347; Greis & Geselowitz, 1992; Coutts, 1993 (ed.). There are parallels in the archaeology of Bronze Age Luristan and elsewhere
[448] Bruce-Mitford, 1978, p.339-43; Hicks, 1993, p.73ff. The association with the whetstone is not totally secure, but no better candidate has been suggested for what it may have been mounted on, and the works of Ansell and Roper (both this volume) seem to strengthen the case.
[449] Coblenz, 1975, p.40, fig.48, an example from Lützschena-Hänischen, Leipzig. Snyder, 1998, suggests a parallel arefact found at Gateholm (Pembrokeshire) and subsequently lost.
[450] Pollington, 2000, p.484
[451] Kitchingham, 1993

design suggest a local, Anglo-Saxon smith had copied elements of the British hanging-bowl tradition.[452] The procession of stags may have been influenced by those on the shoulders of Anglian funerary urns, such as those discussed above.

After the introduction of Christianity, the stag symbol appears to have fallen completely out of use, possibly due to some irremediable association with the old ways and beliefs.[453] This is surprising if only for the fact that the stag – and its counterpart the boar, which also fell from favour – were game animals and it should have been possible to convert them to symbols of high status through the association with hunting, as happened with the bird of prey. However, falconry came late to Germanic Europe (perhaps in the 7th c.?) [454] and it is possible that the hunting of stag and boar involved some rather un-Christian rites and superstitions which had no place in mainstream Christian culture, while the recently-introduced sport of hunting with birds had not evolved any corresponding body of ritual. Even into modern times, English huntsmen marked their first kill by daubing their faces with the fresh blood of the animal; if similar but more explicitly non-Christian rites were observed in the 7th c., the church might well have taken exception to the whole practice.

The OE words *stagga* 'stag' and *bucca* 'buck' are not found in personal names, but *Deor* 'deer' is so used in the *Exeter Book* poem which is now known by that name, as well as in some place-names such as Desborough (Northamptonshire) which was *Deresburc* at the time of the Domesday survey, 'Deor's stronghold'.[455]

Conclusion

The stag or hart was an important animal in northern Europe, both economically and symbolically, from the Bronze Age onwards. Elements of cult were associated with it, and especially with the magnificent spread of antlers which the older males display.

The stag figurine from Sutton Hoo Mound 1 captures something of the majesty of the beast and it forms an appropriate badge for kingship, perhaps linked with the god Ing and the cult of fertility.

---

[452] Laing, 1975; Hicks, 1993, fig. 1.7; Pollington, 2003, p.162ff
[453] Hinton, 2005, p.103
[454] Owen-Crocker, 1991
[455] Anderson, 2003, p.427-8 The poet's name may have been based on the adjective *deor* 'dear' or even its homonym meaning 'brave, bold'.

8. The Anglo-Saxon Rod and the *Sceaftmund*

Stephen Pollington

The system for designing and laying out Anglo-Saxon buildings, especially in the early period (400-650 AD), has been discussed by a number of scholars. The opinion of the Council for British Archaeology, published in 1948, typifies the point from which modern research began:[456]

> The invaders were for the most part in a culturally primitive condition ... their habitations were so wretchedly flimsy-a rectangular scraping in the ground with wattle walls and thatched roof seems to have been the limit of their known architectural competence--that traces of them have been recognized at only about a dozen places in the whole country.'

While conceding that:

> It is impossible to imagine a man of the type buried in the Taplow barrow having no more adequate domestic amenities in life than those provided by a wattled hut of the Sutton Courtenay model

the disparity between the literary evidence and the archaeologically detected remains appeared irreconcilable. Further research was undertaken with a view to closing the gap between the squalid huts found in the earth and the gilded halls described in *Beowulf* and elsewhere. Excavated sites such as Yeavering and Cheddar have done much to save the reputation of the Anglo-Saxon builder.

The scarcity of published excavation reports has been a major limiting factor to detailed research, although this situation has improved in the last 10-15 years. The increased awareness of the fugitive nature of postholes and pits has also assisted in determining where such buildings may be found.

Rod, Pole or Perch

Anglo-Saxon buildings were generally laid out to a plan, whose origins lie in the traditions of the cultures that erected them. The buildings were planned as rectangles with right-angled corners, although in the course of execution the final results vary somewhat from perfect geometry. The proportions may be 1:2 or a variant thereof, meaning that the width was about half the length. Subdivisions of the rod were 1/6, 1/3 and ½ - all detectable in ground-plans according to research carried out by Huggins in the 1980s and 1990s.

It was established by Petrie[457] that the footings of buildings were marked out on the ground using a standard measuring device, probably a kind of surveying pole and perhaps similar to the Roman military device called a *groma* – a pole with a crosspiece at the upper end from which are suspended four weights. The device was a practical solution to the problem of ensuring true angles and measurements, within acceptable tolerances. Many Anglo-Saxon sites show evidence for having been laid out according to a specific predetermined measurement, or a set of these.[458]

One of the high-status Anglian graves at Yeavering (Northumberland) held an adult male buried in a slightly flexed position, as well as a pig's skull and a bronze-bound wooden staff topped with the image of

---

[456] Cited in Raleigh Radford, 1957

[457] Petrie, 1934

[458] Bettess, 1991 is doubtful about the validity of such studies, although his computer-based analysis seems over-exact in dealing with measurements which are difficult to extract from excavation data and which may not have been applied exactly when they were used.

the sceptre's lateral curvature was laid out using a circle with a 16'4" circumference. The stone would therefore have a height equal to 1/27 of the circumference – in other words, twenty seven sceptre-lengths would form a complete circle.

The significance of the number twenty seven may be that it is 3^3 or (3x3)x3 – an important number in Germanic cosmological systems, where triads and groups of nine are so prominent.[463] It equates, for example, to the moonlit nights in a single lunation of 28 days, i.e. the period between one new moon and the next is 27 nights plus the night without a moon.

Meotod, the Measurer

One of the concepts which the Christian church happily adopted from pre-Christian thought was that of God the creator as *Meotod* 'the measurer'. The term appears in the earliest OE verse, *Cædmon's Hymn*, where the poet uses a number of words and phrases to characterise 'the creator' e.g. *wuldorfæder* 'father of glory', *ece dryhten* 'everlasting lord', etc.[464] The term *metod* (or *meotod*, *meotud*) in this context – the creation of the world – refers most naturally to the setting out of the visible environment. This is the West Saxon version of the poem:

> "Nu sculon herigean heofonrices Weard,
> Meotodes meahte 7 his modgeþanc,
> weorc Wuldorfæder, swa he wundra gehwæs,
> ece Drihten, or onstealde.
> He ærest sceop eorðan bearnum
> heofon to hrofe halig Scyppend;
> þa middangeard monncynnes Weard,
> ece Drihten, æfter teode
> firum foldan, Frea ælmihtig."

> "Now we must praise the Keeper of heaven,
> the Measurer's might and his mind's thought,
> the Glory-father's work as for each wonder he,
> the everlasting Lord, set the beginning.
> He first made the earth for men,
> heaven as a roof – the holy shaper –
> then Middle-earth mankind's keeper,
> the everlasting Lord made thereafter,
> the world for men – the almighty Lord."   *Cædmon's Hymn*

While it is possible to relate this notion of 'measurement' to the ancient view of life as a skein of threads which are spun, measured out and at some point cut (as with the Greek *Moira*, Latin *Parcae*, Scandinavian *Nornir*), the verse certainly evokes the Measurer as present at the beginning of creation, and *heofon to hrofe* 'heaven as a roof' above men's heads. This can hardly be accidental in view of our knowledge of Anglo-Saxon practice in setting out the ground-plan of a building on the earth before construction. Measuring precedes building.

Meotod is perhaps to be classed with *Wyrd* as an impersonal universal power. However, the fact that Cædmon felt able to attribute to Meotod *mict end modgidanc* 'power and purpose' implies that there is some guiding intelligence behind the 'measurer' and that this concept could therefore be adapted to Christian purposes.

---

[463] Pollington, Kerr & Hammond, 2010, p.362
[464] Pollington, 2011a, p.264ff

Conclusion

Regardless of whether we think it possible that the Anglo-Saxons could have had any practical application for a distance exceeding three miles but expressed down to three barleycorns (=1 inch), the fact is that highly symbolic and formally ritualised language was used to create and express the measurement.

With the increase of kingly power in the later 6th and 7th centuries, and the conversion of Anglo-Saxon societies from Iron Age chiefdoms into literate, western European kingdoms, the need for a standardised and closely-defined set of measurements became paramount. It is likely that similar processes accompanied the adoption of a monetised economy in the 7th and 8th centuries.

9. A Note on Weohstan

Stephen Pollington

The male personal name *Weohstan* appears in the Anglo-Saxon epic poem *Beowulf*. In lines 2612-4 *þam æt sæccé wearð, wræccan wineleasum, Weohstan bana meces ecgum* "In battle Weohstan became the killer of those friendless exiles with his sword's edges". Later, in line 2862 the poet tells us that *Wiglaf maðelode, Weohstanes sunu* "Wiglaf spoke, the son of Weohstan".

Weohstan was a member of the *Wægmundingas* folk, to whom Ecgþeow also belonged; Ecgþeow was the father of Beowulf. Wiglaf, son of Weohstan, the last loyal warrior who stood by Beowulf to face the dragon, was thus his kinsman. Weohstan took no active part in the story, although he was a loyal supporter of King Onela who slew the rebel prince, Eanmund, and received the latter's weapons and armour as a reward. (This story is also referred to in Snorri Sturluson's story in the *Skáldskaparmál* where *Weohstan* is called *Vésteinn* and Onela is *Áli*.)

The name is not confined to legend, as we read in the *Anglo-Saxon Chronicle* MS 'D' for the year 800:

> *Her wæs se mona aþystrad on þære oðre tid on niht on .xvii. Kalendas Februarii. 7 Beorhtric cyning forðferde 7 Worr ealdorman, 7 Ecgbryht feng to Westseaxna rice. 7 þy ilcan dæge rad æþelmund ealdorman of Hwiccum ofer æt Cynemæresforda, þa mette hine Weohstan ealdorman mid Wilsætum, 7 þær wearð mycel gefeoht 7 þær begen ofslægene wæron þa ealdormæn, 7 Wilsæte namon sige.*

> *Here the moon darkened at the second hour of the night on the 17th calends of February. And King Beorhtic fared forth, and Worr the ealdorman, and Ecgbryht took rule of the West Saxons. And the same day that Ealdormann Æþelmund rode from the Hwicce to Cynemær's ford, Weohstan ealdorman met him with the men of Wiltshire, and a great fight broke out there, and both the ealdormen were slain there and the Wiltshire men took the victory.*

The relevance of this to the sceptre-whetstone lies in the name, *Weohstan*, which is derived from two elements: *weoh* 'holy, sacred' and *stan* 'a stone'. If the object in Mound 1 was really an object of veneration, then it might well have been called 'a holy stone'. That a man bearing just this name played a part in early East Anglian history is an interesting hypothesis, backed up by some historically attested examples of the name in use.

Old English masculine personal names ending in *–stan* are not rare: *Æþelstan*, *Wulfstan* and many others are attested in the sources. But the prototheme *weoh-* is unusual, confined to various spellings of *Weohstan* (*Weoxtan*, *Wihstan*) in some land-grants and the equally resounding name *Wehhelm* (holy helmet) in similar documents.[465] Saint Wihstan was a 9th c. Mercian royal saint who was buried at Repton (Derbyshire).[466] The *weoh-* element is only found in OE records with *–stan* 'stone' and *helm* 'helmet'; that Mound I contained highly significant finds of two such 'holy' items is a tantalising coincidence!

---

[465] Redin, 1919, s.v. *Wehha*
[466] Newton, 1993, p.80

A shortened form, *Wehha Wilhelming,* occurs in the East Anglian royal king-list in *Textus Roffensis*; this *Wehha* is a hypocoristic form of a name in *Weoh-*, such as *Weohhelm* or *Weohstan*.[467] Wehha, according to the controversial *Historia Brittonum*, was the founder of the East Anglian line, although in the Anglian collection of royal geneaologies he is the son of Wilhelm and father of Wuffa.[468]

In other words, the name *Wehha* in the East Anglian pedigree conceals a possible link to *Beowulf*'s *Weohstan* and strengthens the case for the epic (in whole or in part) having been composed under the auspices of an East Anglian patron.[469]

---

[467] Newton, 1993, p.112. The assumption that Wehha = Weohstan is very attractive, but the second element of the name is not known for certain.

[468] Newton, 1993, p.62, 77

[469] See Newton, 1993, for a good summary of the case for the identity of Hroðmund in *Beowulf* with the man of the same name in the East Anglian royal line.

10. The Stone of Destiny

Stephen Pollington

This section is adapted from material published in *Elder Gods: The Otherworld in Early England.*

A wider perspective on the role of a symbolic stone in ancient Europe can be gleaned by extending the search for comparanda beyond the Germanic field. Comparative studies can often clarify obscure points by providing a little more information, or a slightly different interpretation of familiar material. A fruitful approach is the so-called 'ideology of three parts' (*idéologie tripartie*) of the French scholar Georges Dumézil for the older myths, often still traceable in the later tales among peoples speaking languages of Indo-European origin.

From a wide-ranging study of vocabulary and storylines, Dumézil deduced that a common structure underlay the traditions of many different peoples: Greek and Roman, Celtic, Baltic, Germanic, Iranian and Indian among others. As a young man in the 1920s, he held an academic post in the newly secularized Turkey and took the opportunity to familiarize himself with many of the languages and cultures of Asia Minor and the Caucasus. In the early 1930s he was appointed to a post at Uppsala (Sweden) and continued his researches into the Baltic, Slavic and Germanic cultures. He was therefore well placed to approach the customs, languages and cultures of a variety of peoples – ancient and modern – from a position of close familiarity. He promoted comparative studies in mythology and language and became one of the foremost mythologists of the 20th c.

One of the many valuable insights which Dumézil promoted was that gods within a polytheistic tradition should not be studied in isolation, but rather must be seen as part of a larger system. The particular specialism of any god must therefore be contrasted with those of his colleagues. Only by looking at the pantheon – the overall system – would it be possible to understand the place of any individual within it. Dumézil's ability to see connections between widely separated traditions and to validate the data, enabled him to make many valuable studies of mythology in general, backed up by sound philological argument.

The insight with which Dumézil's name is most closely linked is the *idéologie tripartie*, which has changed the way many ancient myths are viewed.[470] The essential idea behind this threefold division is one of opposed pairs, divided into social 'functions' (*fonctions*). The first function (F1) comprises leadership, in the opposed pairing of religious (sacral, the priest) and secular (regulatory, the king) command. The second function (F2) comprises the military activities of competition for resources and protection from aggression. These two 'lordly' groups are paired against the more lowly grouping of the artisan-farmer classes: this third function (F3) comprises the providers and producers, both the food-producers (farmers, fishers, hunters) and creators (merchants and craftsmen). In this way, the whole of society can be slotted into predefined positions connected with rule, warfare and production. (Subsequent scholarship has added a fourth function to Dumézil's original proposal, being that of the 'outsider', either the foreign slave at the bottom of the hierarchy, or the foreign overlord at the top.)

In Germanic terms, one might offer as examples of the socio-mythic functions the three divine brothers Óðinn, Vili and Vé: Vé means 'sanctity' and refers to the F1 priestly function, Óðinn refers to 'fury' and the F2 military function and Vili means 'will, lust, pleasure' and refers to the F3 'fertility' function.[471] Dumézil further determined a characteristic mythic theme which he dubbed *les trois péchés du guerrier* 'the three sins of the warrior' which are (i) regicide, killing of the (F1) king; (ii) cowardice, violation of the (F2) warrior function; (iii) adultery or rape, a violation of the (F3) sexual tabu.[472] The central position of the warrior in some communities, interacting with the rest of society, might account for the later Germanic prominence of warriors and military cults.

---

[470] Russell, 1994, p.113-5
[471] Bek-Pedersen, 2006
[472] Russell, 1994, p.117

One of the difficulties with Dumézil's tripartite ideology is that it does not always fit the Germanic evidence very closely, but this is rather a problem with the Germanic myths than with the system itself.[473] The war between the Æsir (F1 and F2, lords of magic and warfare) and the Vanir (F3, lords of produce and wealth) produced a truce which resulted in an exchange of hostages and therefore a combination of all three functions into a whole and wholesome society, no longer prey to the special vices of fratricide and incest. To this extent, the *idéologie tripartie* explains very well the story of the war in heaven in Norse mythology.

It should be noted – but is often overlooked – that Dumézil did not claim that Germanic, Celtic, Roman or any other historical social structure actually conformed in detail to this three-fold principle, but only that it was an *ideology*, a means of organising ideas and understanding the world.[474]

It is well known that the Germanic language group is anomalous within the Indo-European family: it shares a lot of common vocabulary relating to political and religious structures with the western languages of the Italic and Celtic groups (e.g. *teuta-* 'tribe', OE *þeod* 'folk, community') but it also has some ancient features which it shares only with the Anatolian group (e.g. Hittite), such as a very sparse two-tense system. A large part of Germanic vocabulary is also not drawn from Indo-European, but rather from some unrecorded language with peculiarities of its own.[475] The conclusion seems inescapable that the Germanic group is not a simple survival of late Proto-Indo-European in northern Europe but rather a mix of probably two different IE language groups and at least one other, non-IE group. What this means for Germanic mythology is that it fits with the IE type very closely in some places but hardly at all in others. To illustrate, we have only to look at the distribution of functions among the Norse gods:

F1 – kingship, rule of law	Týr (war, justice) + Óðinn (kingship)
F1 – priesthood, magical powers	Óðinn (wizard, runester)
F2 – aggressive warfare	Óðinn (warmaker)
F2 – defensive warfare	Þórr (storms, lightning, protection against giants) + Týr (justified aggression)
F3 – food production	Freyr (fertility) + Njörðr (fishing, seamanship) + Þórr (rainfall, harvests)

Some important Scandinavian gods, such as Ullr, Baldr, Loki and Heimdallr, do not fit into this system at all, while both Óðinn and Þórr seem to belong in more than one slot. Freyr is lord of fertility and is wealthy, but also has a reputation as a warrior and has some of the attributes of kingship.[476] The explanatory power of the three functions as a whole is not diminished by this poor match for the Germanic myths, but its usefulness in dealing with Germanic material is obviously reduced.

---

[473] Compton, 2006, p.231. Shaw, 2002, p.22-3, dismisses Dumézil's insights on the basis that they are drawn from mediaeval literary evidence, with the implication that such must be remote from the religious practices of the pre-Christian period. As a case in point, he cites the fact that only Tiw/Týr among the Germanic gods has a secure Indo-European etymology. While this is a salutary reminder of the limits of our knowledge, it remains the case that the individual names of the deities are not crucial, but rather their functions within the system as a whole.

[474] Scott Littleton, 1973; Woodard, 2006, p.21ff

[475] Ringe, 2006; Anthony, 2008

[476] Simek, 2004, p.87-9

Dumézil's work has been criticized both for being too narrow (relating with validity only to Sanskrit, Iranian and Greek myth) and for being too general (common to ancient societies everywhere in the world).[477] Other scholars have rejected the ideology outright and proposed alternative systems - notably Motz who suggested a different distribution of the three mythic functions.[478]

The three functions were more effective, persistent and persuasive than one might suppose. They were certainly influencing King Ælfred's thinking in the 9th c. prose translation of Boethius's *De Consolatio Philosophiæ*, where he says that he needs *gebedmen 7 fyrdmen 7 weorcmen* "praying men and fighting men and working men", since this division of labour is the ancient tripartite, trifunctional one.[479] Alfred's immediate source for this idea is not known. The idea of a tripartite division of society had some currency in the ancient world, as in Plato's discussion of the ideal society. King Alfred is usually considered to be the first mediaeval writer to use the concept.

A Gift from Heaven

Symbolic places and landscape features are frequently an important factor in social organisation. Typically, meetings (regulatory, judicial, commercial and social) take place at a certain spot which is believed to have some special significance in the history of the people: it may be the site of a great military victory, the burial place of a legendary or semi-divine ancestor, the spot where a saint worked a miracle or a god put forth his power. Often, the focus of attention is on a specific attribute of the location, be it a natural feature such as a hill, grove of trees, well-spring, prominent rock or a man-made marker such as a post, burial mound, stone column. Often the marker forms the central node from which property boundaries and political borders are laid out.

Some form of celestial authority is usually invoked as having set the marker. One such symbolic focal point is that of a stone pillar or column which has either been sent from heaven to earth, or is otherwise coincident with the arrival of the secular and religious powers.[480] A story often accompanies the establishment of the marker, clarifying where it originated, who placed it and the power it confers. Possession of the 'stone from heaven' legitimates the authority of the ruler. There are several variants of the tale, and the trifunctional nature of the traditions is set out here:

- in India, the stone or *linga* was placed prominently in the (F1) king's dwelling, and regarded as the (F3) phallus of the (F2) war-god, Shiva. The stone marked the point where heaven and earth connect;[481]

- in Ireland, the sacred stone or *Fál* was placed prominently on the sacred hill of Tara, where (F1) kingship ceremonies took place. It had been brought to Erin by the Tuatha Dé Danann, who arrived on clouds. It was also called (F3) *bod Fhearghais* 'Fergus's phallus' and would screech and cry out if the true king rode by. This 'Fergus' is identified with Fergus mac Róich, a great (F2) warrior-hero of Ulster;

- among the Scythians, three talismans fell from the sky in front of three brothers. The talismans were all made of gold and were a (F3) yoke-and-plough, a (F2) sword and a (F1) chalice;

- the Greeks claimed that Eteocles first offered sacrifice to the three Graces, and that some stones fell from heaven in his day and were erected in the temple at Orchomenus (the oldest Boeotian city). They were especially sought out by the (F1) wise, the (F3) beautiful and those (F2) famed for courage;

- for the Romans, the sign was the *ancile* or shield of Jupiter, which fell from heaven and was copied by his worshippers so that twelve such objects were used by the *Salii*, the public dancers, in the worship of (F1) Jupiter, (F2) Mars and (F3) Quirinus.

[477] Polomé, (ed.) 1996, *Introduction*
[478] Motz, 1995
[479] Pollington, 2002, p.29
[480] Woodard, 2006, p.61-3
[481] Woodard, 2006, p.66ff.

Among the common themes here is that of an object sent from heaven which endows sovereignty on the ruler (F1), and represents the virility or phallus (F3) of a warrior (F2). While none of the existing tales has exactly this form, it can be deduced from the variants which have survived.

The Indian *linga* is the *axis mundi* in Vedic cult, the point of contact for the sacred and the profane, the meeting point for the mundane world and the Otherworld. It is represented physically by the *yupa*, the stake to which a sacrifice is tied. It therefore has both a physical reality – stake or post used in religious rituals – and a cosmological significance. In Anglo-Saxon tradition, the post was probably called an *os* – a word meaning both 'pillar, beam of wood' and 'god, divine ancestor'.[482]

The Stone from Sutton Hoo

It is tempting to relate this knot of traditions to the stone bar found in the ship-burial at Sutton Hoo Mound 1.[483] It has been seen as a 'sceptre' or badge of (F1) authority, but it has the form and material of an object for sharpening (F2) weapons and is shaped in a rather (F3) phallic manner with a long shaft and a red globular excrescence on the end.[484] The bar and its complex fittings may reasonably be inferred to have had some important role in religious and social rituals. It may have conferred social and religious authority on the bearer. The careful workmanship applied to the creation of the piece – both in terms of design and of execution – strongly suggest that the 'sceptre-whetstone' was not something produced on a royal whim. It may have been an object of veneration in its own right, a point to which we shall return below (p.129).

The bar itself seems to be an invocation of authority – the impressive faces on the ends are not those of men to be trifled with. They may even be the faces of gods or divine ancestors. The OE term *os* has cognates in the Norse *áss* (pl. *Æsir*), and in Gothic *ansis* of whom Jordanes says:[485]

> *Tum Gothi haut segnes reperti arma capessunt primoque conflictu mox Romanos devincunt, Fuscoque duce exstincto, divitias de castris militum spoliant, magnaque potiti per loca victoria, jam proceres suos, quorum quasi fortuna vincebant, non puros homines, sed semideos, id est Ansis, vocaverunt. Quorum genealogia ut paucis percurram, vel quis quo parente genitus est, aut unde origo coepta, ubi finem effecit absque invidia qui legis vera dicentam ausculta: Horum ergo heroum ut ipsi suis in fabulis referent, primus fuit Gaut...*

> *"Then the Goths were aware, they took their weapons and soon overcame the Romans in the first clash, slew Fuscus, the commander, and looted the treasure from the camp of the army; because of the great victory they had gained in this region, they thereafter called their foremost men, through whose luck they had won, not mere men, but demigods, that is, 'Ansis'. Their lineage, as I shall briefly say, or who was born from which parent, and where it had its beginning and ending, to this they listen attentively when it is spoken. Of these heroes the first was Gaut, as they tell in their own stories ...."*

This notion that the worthy ancestors could become gods – could take their places in the heavenly halls among the holy powers - agrees with later Germanic notions of the king's *hæl* or divine favour, and also points to ideas about the Woden-sprung kingship of the Angles.

---

[482] Pollington, 2011a, p.85ff, 105

[483] Carver, Sanmark & Semple (eds.) 2010, p.13

[484] O'Connor (1991, p.48) does mention that, in the case of Irish whetstones, those used for sharpening blades often had particular design features, that is a flat back upon which to rest the stone and provide stable support, and a more curved and finely finished upper surface over which to pass the blade's edge to gain sharpness.

[485] *Getica*, ch.78. The events referred to took place in 86 AD. cf. Griffiths, 1996, p.26-7; North, 1997, p.136; Lindow, 2006, p.21; Tolley, 2009, p.209

Conclusion

It may be that the stone bar and its fittings were seen as an expression of authority, and that its possessor was distinguished by access to the power(s) which the object embodied. An important question following on from this is: in what, then, did the authority of the successor king reside?

It is of course tempting to invoke the conversion to Christianity at this point, and suggest that the East Anglian kings were encouraged to put away their pagan fetishes and look to the church for authority. While that must remain a possibility, there are other avenues to explore. We shall return to Rædwald's family below (see *Deified Ancestors?*).

III Possibilities and Conclusions

11. Analogues and Possibilities

Paul Mortimer and Stephen Pollington

There are many hundreds of analogues for the 'sceptre-whetstone', using the physical form, the supposed purpose(s) and the base material as the starting point for comparison. Examples include the many fragments of sharpening stone found in Anglo-Saxon and Scandinavian graves and settlements and the many depictions of human faces in Anglo-Saxon and northern European art. While we have examined many of these items for comparative purposes, in order to keep this paper manageable we have selected just a few objects and topics which seemed to us most likely to yield valuable results.

Sceptre, Whetstone or Neither?

The square-section bar is usually described as either a 'sceptre' or a 'whetstone' in the literature. Both descriptions are misleading in some respects. Whetstones typically are small, hand-held tools bearing the marks of use and even the larger carved examples (e.g. the small stone from Uncleby) are comparatively roughly worked in comparison with the stone bar from Mound 1, although the larger Uncleby stone (Figures 85 and 129) may prove to be an exception. Sceptres, likewise, are traditionally slender and often round-section, with an impressive finial and sometimes a counterweight below; while the stag and ring complex makes an impressive finial, in no other respect does the weighty bar resemble the wand of office mentioned in Roman and post-Roman contexts.

While these factors do not of themselves mean that the 'sceptre-whetstone theory' is invalid, they should encourage researchers to question on what basis the identification has been made. Bruce-Mitford, for example, immediately assumed that the bar must be a 'sceptre' without much further discussion: depending on how one defines a 'sceptre' (or 'whetstone') the stone bar with its metal fittings may approximate to a greater or lesser extent to that definition. Clearly, it is a thing of power, its weight and solidity give it immense presence, yet it is not an imposing stone monument in the way that a preaching cross or menhir is.

Sceptres do not appear frequently in Germanic art of the pre-Christian period. The 'Donar club' amuletic pendants occasionally found in later Roman contexts do not appear to replicate full-sized clubs, although the possibility cannot be excluded. The transformation of this 'club' into the 'hammer' of Þórr was already underway during the 5th and 6th centuries when long-shafted 'hammer' amulets began to appear in the graves of Kentish males.[486] The later version, *Mjölnir*, was short-handled whereas the Kentish examples are long and slender in the shaft and square in section.

Elsewhere in Germanic art, the supposed images of Balder on the 'three-god' bracteates (Figure 90) are accompanied by an object described as a 'sceptre', resembling a staff with a cross-piece at the upper end, sometimes with discoid terminals. Speidel has argued for an origin in the Greek *stylis* motif carried by the goddess Nike on gold stater coins issued by Alexander, mediated by debased central European coin issues.[487] However that may be, there is no clear indicaton that the 'sceptre' shown on the eight known

---

[486] Pollington, 2011a, p.209
[487] Speidel, 2012

examples of the three-god bracteates design is anything other than a symbolic implement; it does not appear to have been 'drawn from life' or designed to reflect any physical object then in use.

Figure 90 A three-god bracteate from Beresina.

(After Hauck)

Anglo-Saxon and Other Whetstones

Anglo-Saxon whetstones have been briefly discussed elsewhere in this volume (e.g. Brian Ansell's essay on the making of the reproduction stone) but are not a widely-researched topic. Evison's paper is one of the few to provide data on the stones themselves.[488] There have been many new finds from cemeteries and settlements subsequently excavated and Ellis's careful petrographic study has also informed much of the discussion.[489] According to Evison, citing Ellis, most whetstones from Anglo-Saxon sites were sourced locally, within a radius of 250 miles from the findspot. After about 900 AD this changed and a single source of schist in western Norway provided the bulk of the known finds until circa 1300 AD when local sourcing resumed.[490] Ellis attributed this change in sourcing to increased Scandinavian contact during the Viking period; while such may have been the impetus for the whetstone trade, it does not explain the 400 years of commercial connections which gave western Norway its advantage over other areas. It is possible that there was a cottage industry in cutting and shaping whetstones of proven good quality in the area and a cadre of merchants skilled in trading them, and that only later political and social developments interrupted this supply chain.

A remarkable undated (but probably before 450 AD) runic text appears on a whetstone found on an island in Strømfjord (Norway) in 1908.[491] The whetstone is flat, 14.5 cm long and 1.2 – 1.3 cm thick and at the widest it is 1.9 cm across. The texts appear on the narrow sides of the stone, reading (Side A) **watehalihinohorna** (Side B) **hahaskaþihaþuligi.** Remarkable is the repetition of the bindrune **ha** in four instances. The reading is usually taken as *wate hali hino, horna* 'wet stone this, horn' (i.e. Horn! Wet this stone!) *haha skaþi, haþu ligi* 'Sickle, scathe! Hay, lie!' (i.e. may the sickle cut, may the hay lie). The text is in the Germanic alliterative metre. The verse is probably to be understood as a charm exhorting the horn to wet the whetstone so that the blade may work well and the cut grass may fall. While an agricultural context is usually assumed, there is nothing in the text that prevents the whetstone's power being invoked to sharpen weapons so that their blades may do their work.

The long whetstone from Uncleby (Figure 85 and 129) was placed upright in the earth, in the south-eastern quadrant of the cemetery, about 10" (25cm) from the foot of grave 11, an adult male with a 18" (45cm) long *seax* on the hilt of which was placed a small whetstone (the only other example from a cemetery of nearly 70 individuals). The form of the *seax* suggests a 7th c. date for the grave, and indeed grave 11 may

---

[488] Evison, 1975; cf. Moore, 1978
[489] Ellis, 1969
[490] The source from Norway was located near Telemark, in fact from Eidsborg (Hansen, 2009, pp. 8, 18). This schist was of two main types. (Hansen, 2009, p. 23)
[491] Antonsen, 2002, p.155-61, 302-3; Pollington (forthcoming, b)

have been one of the last Angles buried here according to the traditional rites. If so, it may be that the burial in grave 11 was [492]

> "a grave of a man of some importance, that the large whetstone had a connection with grave 11, and that some special significance of ceremony or ritual was attached to it."

The whetstones and their proximity to the occupant of the grave were clearly of some importance. In her discussion of manufactured amulets, Meaney notes that:[493]

> "Some whetstones have been found in such a context or decorated in such a way that they almost certainly had virtues which transcended the purely practical – but yet they were hardly amulets."

Decoration of apparently mundane objects may not have been rare – there are many examples of whetstones and wooden items from the Danish bog sites which were clearly ornamented and personalised to an unnecessary degree for practical purposes of identification.

One remarkable find is reported from the 1874 discovery of a male grave at King's Field, Faversham, Kent with an iron sword. Embedded in the organic material of the sword's hilt were:[494]

> "a small greenish whetstone about 2 inches in length, a bivalve shell, the *mactra stultorum*, curiously marked, a small thin piece of purple glass, and a small incised flint. All these objects had, as I have stated, the appearance of having been inlaid in the sword-guard, and the little whetstone may have been placed there perhaps for the utilitarian purpose of sharpening the warrior's blade."

The tradition of carrying a whetstone did not cease: the last recorded English find is from a 9th c. burial at Harrold, Bedfordshire, where grave 3 also contained a sword, iron bucket, heckle, knife and spearhead.[495] The grave presumably reflects the interment of a male buried in the Scandinavian tradition.

Staves and Healing

In her authoritative and compendious work on symbolic stones in Anglo-Saxon contexts, *Anglo-Saxon Amulets and Curing Stones*, Meaney refers to two items which may have a bearing. In her discussion of jet, she notes:[496]

> "…jet may have had some symbolic or magic value among the continental Germans, to judge from two staffs, reminiscent in shape of the Sutton Hoo whetstone, one of which was found at Cologne and the other (no longer extant) at Tongeren in Belgium (Salin, IV, 82-90). Whether they were Roman or Frankish is disputed; but if Frankish they may have been 'staves consecrated according to the custom of the Franks' …"

For the example from Cologne, see below (p.158). The Tongeren example (Figure 91) appears to have featured a polyhedral finial at one end, and a dome or cup at the other. The shading in the engraved illustration suggests that it may have been octagonal in section, or perhaps the artist was trying to show that the section was square with chamfered edges.

---

[492] Evison, 1975, p.83
[493] Meaney, 1981, p.149
[494] Cited in Meaney, 1981, p.28
[495] Ellis, 1969; Meaney, 1981, p.196
[496] Meaney, 1981, p.73. The Salin reference is to Edouard Salin's *La Civilisation Mérovingienne*, 4 vols, Paris, 1949-59

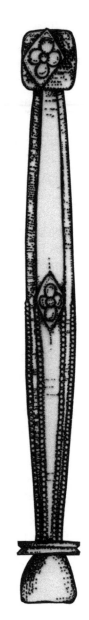

Figure 91 The jet staff from Tongeren, Belgium. (after Meaney, 1981)

Aside from this tradition, it is worth mentioning that a whetstone is involved in a curative procedure once in OE literature, in the *Lacnunga* manuscript, remedy no. 37. The *Lacnunga* manuscript (London, BL Harley 585) dating from around 1000 AD is a compendium of medical procedures. The title – meaning 'remedies' - was given by the work's first modern editor, Rev. Oswald Cockayne.[497] It is an unusual text in that it does not follow the head-to-toe order of most mediaeval medical works, and there is no real theme or ordering principle in the book overall, although some entries form distinct groups. It may never have been intended to be more than a private collection of jottings of various recipes and cures, as they came to hand, in one location. The relevant entry is as follows:[498]

> *To eahsealfe, nim aluwan 7 sidewaran, lawerberian 7 pipor, gescaf smale, 7 cubuteran fersce lege on wæter, nim þonne hwetstan bradne 7 gnid ða buteran on ðæm hwetstane mid copore þæt heo beo wel toh, do þonne sumne dæl þara wyrta þærto, clæm ðonne on arfæt, læt standan nygon niht, wende man ælce dæge, mylte siþþan on ðæm arfæte sylfan, aseoh þurh cla, do syþðan on swylc fætels swylce ðu wille, nyttige þonne þe þearf sy, þeos sealf mæg wið ælces cynnes untrumnysse ðe eagan eigliað.*

> *As an eye-salve: take aloes and zedoary, laurel berries and pepper; slice small, and lay fresh cow['s milk] butter on water; then take a broad whetstone and rub the butter on the whetstone with copper so that it be very stiff and then add some part of the plants to it; smear it then into a bronze vessel, let it stand nine nights and let it be turned each day, then let it be melted in the same bronze vessel; strain it out through a cloth; then put it into whichever vessel you want to; use then when it be needful; this salve has power against all kinds of infirmities which ail the eyes.*

The use of ingredients such as aloes, zedoary and pepper indicates that this remedy is not a native Anglo-Saxon one but copied or adapted from a Græco-Latin original; this is supported by the use of the word *copor* (from Latin *cuprum*) for 'copper' where OE regularly uses the word *ar* for this metal. In view of this, although interesting as a sidelight on the Anglo-Saxon adaptation of Mediterranean medical practice, the *Lacnunga* entry sheds little further light on the topic of the whetstone in Anglo-Saxon England.

---

[497] Cockayne, 1864-6
[498] From Pollington, 2000; cf. Waggoner, 2011, p.xxxvii

The Four-Faced God

The four surfaces of the bar, each with a pair of stern faces, recalls to some extent the four-faced pillars found in continental European contexts.

Here, Enright's insistence on the Pfalzfeld pillar as a precise analogue comes into play. The pillar shares with the stone bar from Sutton Hoo some characteristics: it is four-sided with a gently tapering profile; it bears a human mask on each face, staring outwards and thus unaware of its neighbours.[499] The resemblance is however far from compelling, for a number of reasons:

Pfalzfeld Pillar	Sutton Hoo Stone Bar
A stone pillar or stele, originally around 3m in height, placed prominently on a hill-top or -side	A stone bar, around 0.58m in length, hand-held and portable
Four masks placed midway along the (present) length of the four surfaces	Eight masks placed at the outer ends of the four surfaces
The surfaces flat and edges straight, covered with La Tène comma-leaf ornament, of which the masks form only a part	The surfaces and edges gently curved, plain and severe, the masks carved in isolation
The use of La Tène A style, dating the stele to the 5th c. BC[500]	The context of Mound 1 placing the stone bar in use in the later 6th-early 7th c. AD, (about a thousand years later than the stele)
The stele pyramidal, tapering away from a plano-convex base with circumferential ribbing (i.e. the rounded section joins the widest part of the stele)	The stone bar 'bi-pyramidal', tapering towards the bulbous terminals (i.e. the rounded section joins the narrowest part of the bar)

Taking all the above into account, the pillar is a far from close analogue for the stone bar, except in the matter of being formed with four flattish surfaces, each with a human mask. In the matter of these faces, there are other items for comparison.

In the Museum of Archaeology at Krakow, Poland, there is a tall four-sided stele or statue recovered from the River Zbruc (now in the Ukraine) (Figure 92). The stele stands 2.57 m high, and is carved with a human face at the top of each side, surmounted by a bell-shaped hat; the body of each head continues down the side, each with the right arm bent so that the hand rests on the chest, and the left extended so that the hand lies over the abdomen. The lower body of each face is kilted, with narrow, spindly legs; on one face, there is a sword in its scabbard placed diagonally across the hips and an incised figure of a horse below this. Below each figure is a separate panel depicting a robed figure (probably female due to the emphasis on the breasts), with arms extended to the sides of the panel so that they appear to link hands around the stele. The base on each face bears a D-shaped male face and traces of a cross-legged posture but the details are indistinct.

---

[499] Koch, 2006, p.1442

[500] Koch states that the pillar 'can be classified as belonging to the La Tène 'Early Style' of the 2nd half of the 5th century BC (La Tène A). The style shows an overlap of 'West Celtic' style characterized by floral patterns and 'east Celtic' bow and circles friezes. The various designs look as though they have been transferred from another medium, specifically from small ornamental metal jewellery to monumental stone carving.'

The figure is dated to the 9th c. AD, and is widely held to represent the presumed Slavic god *Svantovit* (with various spellings such as *Svetovid*, *Sutvid*, *Swiątowit*, etc.). Sadly, Slavic pre-Christian religion is not well documented and it is not certain whether the stele should be viewed as a single deity with four aspects (e.g. a deity connected to agriculture, fertility and food provision with different aspects for spring, summer, autumn and winter) or four separate gods sharing a single idol. Such other Slavic deities as Radegast, Perun, Svarog, Lada and Mokosh are all mentioned in early sources, although these references post-date the pagan period by many centuries.[501]

Figure 92 The four-faced stele from the River Zbruc in Krakow Museum

However, in discussion of the Slavic cult-site on the Baltic island of Rügen, Herrmann states that 'many-headed gods were characteristic of the Slavs. Svantevit sometimes had four heads. Other gods on Rügen had seven heads.'[502] 'In Arkona, the Rugian god Svantevit, is supposed to have been depicted with four heads. ... Triglaw, a three-headed god, stood in Brandenburg, and the town of Szczecin also had a Triglaw as its special communal god.'[503] He illustrates a 'double-headed cult-figure 1.7 metres high ... of oak, found at Fischerinsel near Neubrandenburg. The lower parts joined into an irregular seven-sided pillar.'[504] Further, 'pagan beliefs persisted among the Slavs well into the twelfth century, long after the rest of Europe had become Christian. Their gods had little in common with Germanic religion (though one remembers the quadruple heads on the Sutton Hoo sceptre).'[505]

Figure 93 Carved wooden figure with four faces from Wolin, Poland.

A group of four small four-faced wooden figures dating to the 9th or 10th c. are also known from the area of Wolin, Poland (Figure 93), close to the Baltic Sea.[506] These figures are formed with four tapering surfaces and stern male faces carved at the upper end; the lower is rounded. The length is about 6cm overall, and the design naïve. In the manner of execution they resemble the three alder-wood blocks found in the Nydam ship deposits, with the same impassive and forbidding expression.[507]

---

[501] Janse, 2004
[502] Herrmann, 1980, p.191
[503] Herrmann, 1980, p.206
[504] Herrmann, 1980, p.191
[505] Herrmann, 1980, p.190
[506] Herrmann, 1980, p.206; Müller-Wille, 1999, p.81
[507] Müller-Wille, 1999, p.53; Rieck, 2003 p.307

Figure 94 A 5th century hairpin from Eschborn, Germany

Many-headed figures are known in Germanic myth, although they do not have the prominence in Snorri's tales that they presumably had centuries before. One such figure is Þrívaldi (thrice-great, with the power of three), a giant with nine heads who is matched against Þórr; the god is known as *sundrkljúfr níu höfða Þrívalda* '(he) who cleaves apart the nine heads of Þrívaldi' in the *Skáldskaparmál*.[508]

A three-headed figure appears on the smaller Gallehus horn (Figure 95), where he seems to be brandishing an axe and leading a goat. The horns were stolen and melted down in the 19th c. but copies made at the time of discovery survive; these appear to be accurate i.e. they show that the artefacts were produced using the punched-point technique of Sösdala Style.[509] The runic inscription on one of the horns was uninterpretable at the time of its discovery, but is now agreed to be an example of 'North Sea Germanic' of the 4th-5th century AD.[510]

The most notable feature of the stone bar is its four-fold surfaces and the faces carved onto them (although from the carver's point of view the faces must have been laid out as part of the original design and could not be an afterthought). The stone appears to be a column or pillar, and may represent the column (or tree) which supports the vault of the skies. In ancient Indo-European tradition, the sky is considered to be the underside of a stone vault and the sky-god sometimes hurls pieces of this stone as thunderbolts.[511]

Figure 95 Three-headed figure on the smaller Gallehus horn.

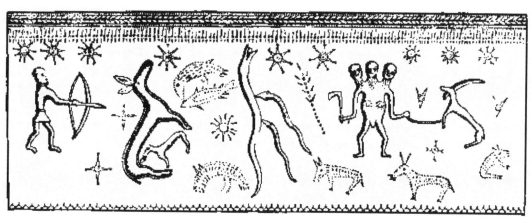

---

[508] West, 2007, p.299

[509] Pollington, Kerr & Hammond, 2010, p.84

[510] Nielsen, 1989, p.5 discusses the relationship between the earliest runic texts and the later West and North Germanic languages. See also Markey, 1976; Looijenga, 2003, p.167-8

[511] West, 2007, p.342-3. The Vedic *áśman* 'stone', Lithuanian *akmuo* 'stone' are derived from PIE *$h_2$ekmón* which also gives Old Persian *asman* 'heaven' and Proto-Germanic *hemenaz* 'heaven' (Gothic *himins*, OE *heofon*); Orel, 2003, *xemenaz*

The motif of four faces pointing in four directions is not unique to the stone bar, although it is not a common design in Germanic art and culture, while its formal symmetry means that a great many objects are made with four-fold alignments of their parts. Decoration based on an array of four elements includes the four-way knot and the swastika or hooked cross.

Figure 96   A (fragmentary) copper-alloy die for making pressblech plates, found near Chelmsford, Essex. The central design comprises four zoomorphs arranged in a four-way knot.

The principal four-fold division concerns orientation and the cardinal points. Conventionally, in religious rites, the speaker is regarded as facing towards the east, towards the rising sun at dawn, as in the OE charm *Æcerbot:*[512]

> *wende þe þonne eastweard and onlut nigon siþon*

> "turn to the east then and bow down nine times"

This automatically places the preferred, right (OE *swiðre* 'stronger') hand to the south and the path of the sun, while the left (OE *wynstre* 'weaker') hand aligns to the north, the direction of cold and death and the Underworld. The etymologies of the cardinal directions are interesting in this respect:

---

[512] Pollington, 2000, p.471, 477. Note here the use of the sacred number nine.

East	OE *east* from Proto-Germanic **austro-* 'sunrise' cognate with Latin *aurora* 'dawn'[513]
West	OE *west* from Proto-Germanic **west-* 'sunset' cognate with Latin *ves(per)* 'evening'[514]
North	OE *norð* from Proto-Germanic **nurþa-* 'on the left, downwards, below' cognate with Greek *enerthen* 'from beneath'[515]
South	OE *suð* from Proto-Germanic **sunþ-* from **sunn-* 'sun'[516]

The implication of facing east is in the word 'north' ('on the left') while the rising and setting sun is implicit in 'east' and 'west'. In Norse myth, cognates of these words are the names of four dwarfs who hold up the vault of the sky above *Miðgarðr* (middle-earth). There is no direct evidence for such a belief in Anglo-Saxon England, unless the words themselves and the quadripartite distribution of design elements (e.g. on disc brooches, pendants, etc.) were symbolic. Yet the consistent division of circles into quarters, for example in laying out disc brooch decoration, must imply that the idea of a four-fold division was already in circulation, although this does not necessarily mean that any mythological importance was attached to it.

The King's Number

In one of his early papers on Anglo-Saxon kingship, Chaney referred to an idea he termed 'the king's number'.[517] Writing of the earliest surviving Anglo-Saxon (Kentish) law-code – and in practice it must be regarded as the first such document ever composed – Chaney noted that Æthelbert's position as king was firmly and undeniably central to the society which the laws sought to regulate. The early society of Kent was, in Chaney's view, in transition from a youthful and dynamic patchwork of chiefdoms to a settled state – although there had been a demonstrable Germanic presence in that area of Britain for around two centuries at the time of Æthelbert's death in 616 AD. Kingship was still partly a priestly function:[518]

> In these frontiers of time and space, in which kingship stands hedged about with the nebulous divinity of folklore, the precision of later legal concepts of monarchic functions is looked for in vain, but the influence of historical continuity is not always confined to the precise. It is to the relationship of this royal figure of magic and fertility with the magic of number - the "king's number" - that our attention shall be confined.

He notes a curious anomaly in this early Kentish law: that a freeman who robs the king must compensate him to nine times the value of the thing stolen, while if he robs another freeman he must only compensate with three times the value. In contrast, in later West Saxon codes (e.g. that of King Ine), specific sums and punishments are set down which bear no direct relation to the value of the thing stolen.

The numbers three and nine relating to king and freeman have resonances elsewhere. In the 10th c. code *IV Athelstan*, a thief who seeks the king or archbishop or holy church shall have safekeeping for nine nights; Chaney saw this right of asylum as stemming not from constitutional law but from the king's position as priest and intercessor with the gods on behalf of his people.[519] The equation of the presence of the king with that of an archbishop is not sanctioned by ecclesiastical law, and must have its origin elsewhere. The same nine-night asylum is granted in the 11th c. text *Be Grithe and be Munde* in which the king's powers

---

[513] Orel, 2003, *austaz, austraz ~ austran*
[514] Orel, 2003, *westan*
[515] Orel, 2003, *nurþaz*
[516] Orel, 2003, *sunþiz*
[517] Chaney, 1962
[518] Chaney, 1962, p.154
[519] Chaney, 1962, p.155

relating to protection and safekeeping are established. We have already mentioned the extent of the king's *grið* above (p.119) with its three nines (miles, furlongs, acres) and three threes (feet, shaftments, barleycorns). Furthermore, Chaney notes that the use of the term *berecorn* in the OE document probably did not refer to a determined measurement (as its more modern usage does = 1/3"), but rather to the physical length of three such grains. Chaney then goes into more speculative territory when considering the significance of the barleycorn:[520]

> Its relationship to fertility is reflected in the North in "Lord Barleycorn" and "Lady Bean," servants of the fertility god Frey, the former of which, Byggvir, has been paralleled with the grain-spirit Beow, son of Scyld Scefing. As a symbol of the grain-spirit, the nine barleycorns in *Grith* echo the Germanic king's sacrificing on Mid-Winter's Day for good crops and his responsibility for peace and fertility far more than they do any Christian element.

Discounting the suggestion that the Anglo-Saxon law may have its roots in the Mediterranean culture of Christianity and Rome, he observes that no Roman laws specified nine-fold compensation for theft (but the principle of compensation as a multiple of the value of the thing(s) stolen was familiar in Roman law).

The number nine held great significance in the early Germanic world, and its position had not been entirely expunged with the advent of Judaeo-Christian religion and custom. In a wide-ranging discussion, Chaney invokes a number of apparently unrelated usages, for instance:[521]

- the *Lex Frisionum* (Law of the Frisians) requires a nine-fold *wergeld* for murder done in the court of the duke and for the murder of the duke's *missus* (envoy);

- in the West Frisian *Skeltana Riucht*, (probably 11th c.) in court a nine-fold testimony (a nine-fold ritual repetition), may invalidate the oath of a freeman while nine weeks is the longest time for which ordeal by battle may be postponed, and a defendant must be summoned to court nine times before the destruction of his house may lawfully be decreed against him;

- in the Frisian *Emsigo* code, a man wounded so that he cannot beget children is to be paid nine marks for the nine children he would have been able to father, and in the *Hunsigo* code a similar wound is compensated for by allowing its victim nine killings (death-blows, *niugen dadele*);

- in the *Leges Baiwariorum* (Laws of the Bavarians) nine-fold restitution ("*niungeldo . . . id est novem capita*") is payable if anything is stolen from a church, while the *Leges Alamannorum* (Laws of the Alamanni) prefer thrice nine-fold ("*tres novigildos*");

- in the *Leges Visigothorum* (Laws of the Visigoths) a law ascribed to King Chintaswinth decrees that a freeman who steals the property of another must pay to the owner nine times the value, while a slave pays six times the value of the property stolen, and each receives a hundred lashes;

- in the *Leges Alamannorum*, a particularly striking law decrees that if a man is killed by a dog, this is compensated by half the normal *wergeld*, but if the full *wergild* is demanded then all the doors of the house of the supplicant are to be closed except one, and the body of the dog is to be suspended nine feet from the sole usable door until the body rots away.

Many more instances are cited from across the Germanic world, all detailing a nine-fold compensation, or a multiple thereof. An early Scandinavian law (the *Older Gulathing Law*) requires that a minor theft had to be compensated by the thief running the gauntlet of his peers throwing stones and turf for the length of nine bows. In England, Francia and Frisia when a legal ordeal is decreed, the number nine is often involved – e.g. the number of paces the man must take with the hot iron in his hands.

---

[520] Chaney, 1962, p.156-7
[521] Chaney, 1962, p.159 ff.

Chaney next moves to a discussion of the significance of nine in early Icelandic literature, especially Snorri Sturluson: the nine worlds in the tree Yggdrasill; the nine mothers of Heimdall; the nine daughters of Ægir; the nine Valkyries; the nine black and nine white Dísir, and so on. Óðinn is surrounded by groups of nine: he hangs for nine nights on the tree, learns nine *fimbulljoð* 'songs of power', has a ring which drops eight more (becomes one of nine) every ninth night; etc. Furthermore, Adam of Bremen recalls a ceremony celebrated every nine years in which nine of every male creature were sacrificed at Uppsala to the gods. Thietmar of Merseburg tells of a nine-year cycle of festivals held at Lejre, Denmark, in similar terms.

The Anglo-Saxon verse from the *Lacnunga* manuscript known as the *Nine Herbs Charm* recalls the association between Woden and the number nine quite dramatically: [522]

> Ðas VIIII magon wið nygon attrum. Wyrm com snican, toslat he man; ða genam Woden VIIII wuldortanas, sloh ða þa næddran, þæt heo on VIIII tofleah.

> These nine (herbs) have power againt nine posions. A snake came crawling, he bit a man; then Woden took up nine rods of splendour then slew the adder so that it flew apart into nine pieces.

Nine-fold incantations and performances are common in Anglo-Saxon charms and medical procedures.[523] Likewise – although Chaney overlooked this evidence – Woden appears in prime position in many Anglo-Saxon king-lists, often as the 'ninth father' of (ninth generation above) a prominent founder king e.g. in relation to the West Saxon Cerdic in the *ASC* (*Parker Chronicle*) for 552.[524] Taking the obsession with threes and its multiples a stage further, one might see the relationship of stone bar to circle (1:27) as reflecting a triad of nines (3^3, or 3 x (3x3) in mathematical notation) as significant. Here again, and conceding that the evidence is suggestive rather than conclusive, the number 27 represents the nights in a lunation on which the moon should be visible and may have been selected as significant for this reason. Chaney concludes:[525]

> In a society in which the king "made" the year for his people and sacrificed for good crops and victory in battle, standing as an image of magic and fertility between them and the gods, it would perhaps be surprising if he were not associated with this number which was so integrated into the same areas of cosmic relationships. The early Anglo-Saxon laws concerning him may consequently reflect most strongly the recent ruler-centered paganism.

If the king-lists are interpreted in terms of groups of nine, then the presence of eight faces on the stone bar in Mound 1 might suggest that the eight faces there and the helmetted face of the king form a group of nine, with the helmet-wearer in the place of Woden the ninth father. However this interpretation is somewhat undermined by the presence of beardless faces at the bar's top – the faces of either youths or females, but hardly kings.

Images of the Gods

Quite a few writers have commented on the stylistic similarity between the man's face within the hip of the bird on the shield from Sutton Hoo (Figure 99) and the faces on the whetstone (Figure 100).[526] Both have piriform heads and what appears to be a surround, and both have some form of stop at the bottom of the surround underneath the chin; in the case of the whetstone heads, these are discs, but on the shield bird the corresponding object is of a similar shape to the mouth of the face - that is, two arcs meeting to form a lentoid shape. Whether there is any significance or not to the difference in shape between the two designs is not possible to ascertain, but it is certain that the jeweller who made the face on the shield could have made the stop circular had he wished to do so.

[522] Pollington, 2011, p.397
[523] Pollington, 2000
[524] Pollington, 2011, p.190ff
[525] Chaney, 1962,p.176
[526] Bruce-Mitford, 1978, Enright, 2006; Pollington, 2011a, p.206

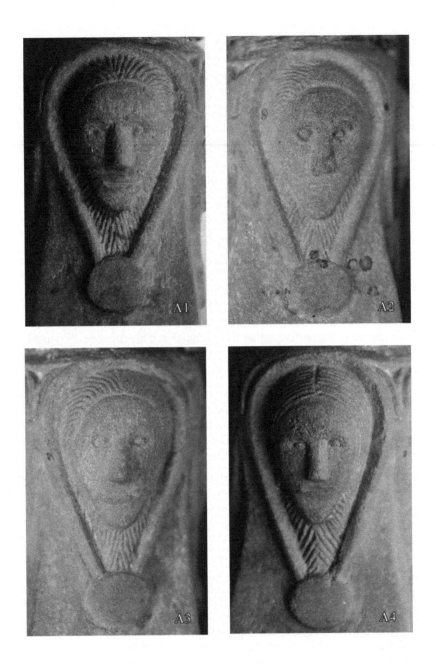

Figure 97 The faces from the original Sutton Hoo Stone, labelled as they were by Bruce-Mitford 1978. A1-4 are from the top of the stone. B1-4 are from the bottom. Note the careful treatment of the hair and that all the faces have convex eyes, except one of those from B1. The faces from the top have slender more gracile chins than the unbearded face from the bottom (B2).

140

B1   B1 left eye   B1 right eye

B2   B3   B4

Figure 98   Sutton Hoo stone. B1 right eye in profile is
convex. B1 left eye has been removed and re-worked,
note scarring under and around the eye.

If the shield bird is to be compared to the heads on the whetstone, then this may lead to some interesting conclusions - and it could be that there are ideological, symbolic and religious connections between the whetstone, the shield and the helmet from Mound 1.

Figure 99 A human mask executed in cloisonné, from the hip of the bird on the Sutton Hoo shield.

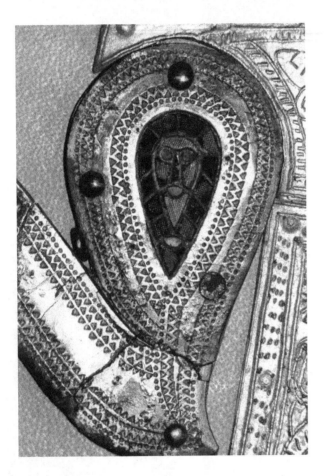

Figures 100 (below) The human mask from the hip of the bird on the Sutton Hoo shield (left). and (right) a face on the Sutton Hoo whetstone

It is generally thought likely that the decoration on the two figural *pressbleche* on the helmet is associated with Woden.[527] The rider motif with his smaller, probably supernatural, helper who appears to be guiding his spear, is possibly a depiction of the god; similar rider motifs are found on the helmets from Vendel, grave I, Valsgärde 7 and Valsgärde 8. Recently, rider designs were found in the Staffordshire Hoard.[528] The twin dancing warriors with 'horned hats' that appear on the front of the Sutton Hoo helmet and the cheekpieces are also generally thought to be referring to Woden; it is noticeable that the 'horns' terminate in birds' heads –and these could be symbolic of the two raven companions of Óðinn, in later Norse myths called *Huginn* and *Muninn*, 'thought' and 'memory'.[529] Other notable features of the helmet are the *wyrm* (serpent) that forms the crest or *walu*, which could refer to Óðinn's (Woden's) ability to take the shape of the serpent, and the male face presented by the faceplate.[530] The face can be looked at in at least two different ways: superficially, it is just the face of a man with a moustache, but when looked at more closely, the eyebrows form the wings of a bird, the nose the

---

[527] For example, Bruce-Mitford, 1978; Storms, 1973

[528] See Arwidsson, 1974; Arwidsson, 1954; Arne and Stolpe, 1927 and Mortimer, 2011 for more details.

[529] Helmbrecht, 2007 – 2008; Mortimer, 2011

[530] This story is in Sturluson's *Skáldskaparmál I*. Here, Óðinn takes the shape of a serpent in order to creep into the domicile of Suttungr, sleep with his daughter, Gunnloð, and sip the mead of poetry. There are other serpents in northern mythology and, of course, the *walu* serpent may refer to one or more of these.

body, and the moustache the tail; the head of the bird is the beast head above the eyebrows. Thus, there is a man's face on the helmet that becomes a bird, and on the shield there is a bird that contains a man's face in its hip. Is this the same theme portrayed in different ways on the two objects? And could it be referring to the shape-changing abilities of a shaman or, more specifically, of Woden? Snorri tells us that Óðinn could become an eagle when he escaped with the mead of poetry and was pursued by Suttungr, the giant from whom the god had stolen it.[531]

Figure 101 Detail of the eye apertures on the reproduction Sutton Hoo helmet.

What may clinch the argument as to the identity of the person represented on the helmet and the shield bird - and therefore possibly the whetstone faces - is another detail on the helmet. This is the fact that the two eyebrows are deliberately made to be different; the left eyebrow (from the wearer's point of view) has 21 garnets and the right 25, but the right eyebrow has golden, cross-hatched foils behind the garnets in order to reflect the light while in the left the foils are absent.[532] This could be a reference to the story where Óðinn gives his eye for a drink from Mimir's well and thus gains wisdom.[533] Incidentally, although this story was thought to be quite late, there is growing evidence of this not being the case as there are now several instances of figures, from the 5th to 7th centuries, on which a single eye has been altered, for example one of the dies from Torslunda (Öland) and a horned man figure from Uppåkra, both in Sweden.[534]

---

[531] This tale is also in *Skáldskaparmál I*. There are also features on the helmet which are likely to refer to other deities, for instance the boars' heads above the cheek guards; these may invoke the protection of *Ing* (Yngvi-Freyr).

[532] Bruce-Mitford, 1978, p.169; Mortimer, 2011; Price & Mortimer (forthcoming)

[533] The full story is in Sturlusson's, *Gylfaginning 14*; Pollington, 2011a, p.202

[534] For a fuller discussion of this feature see, Mortimer, 2011; Price & Mortimer (forthcoming)

So it is possible that at least one of the faces on the stone is that of Woden. It is possible, too, that the different heads reveal different aspects of the same god, even the presence of female faces would not prevent all the heads from representing Woden as it seems that there may once have been a story about him taking female form. This is hinted at in a tale from the *Elder Edda*, *Lokasenna* verse 24. Loki is at a gathering of the gods, there is much ale flowing and he takes part in a series of exchanges with other gods. In each Loki is insulting to the other deity. When it comes to Óðinn, Loki says:

> "Charms on Samsey, they say you worked,
> Wicked spells like a witch,
> Flew about in the form of a wizard
> And played a woman's part"[535]

The original tale of Óðinn's part in this is lost to us, but Óðinn's role as a shaman and his participation in the mostly feminine rituals of *seiðr* (magic) are more than enough to arouse doubts about how he may sometimes have appeared.[536]

It is also probable, as Simpson and Cohen have suggested, that the whetstone may be more appropriate to Thunor, the sky god. It may represent Thunor's thunderbolt, but its inability to strike sparks could be a hindrance to this concept, although it must be said that it is extremely unlikely that all stones reckoned to be 'thunderstones' are ready sparkers. There is, too, the legend of Þórr getting part of a whetstone lodged in his head, which is worth pursuing. Several commentators have mentioned the 'bulging' or 'staring' eyes of the heads and this can be a feature of Thor which is described as *ondótt*, 'fierce', 'frightening' in stanza 27 of *þrymskviða* (*Edda*, 115).[537]

However, Cohen noticed that the number four could be associated with Þórr and similar sky-gods in Eastern Europe (see above p.133). If Cohen is correct about the Trelleborg-type fortresses being linked to Þórr, then that is very significant indeed. Certainly, human sacrifice to Þórr is not unknown,[538] so the cases of sacrifice that Cohen mentions are possibly, as he says, for Þórr.

What is particularly interesting about the Trelleborg-type forts is the precision that went into their design; a similar precision, we now know, went into the way the whetstone was constructed although on a much smaller scale.[539] That this design of four equal sections can be carried over into Slavic and Baltic sanctuaries of sky gods is even more compelling.

Recent work on Trelleborg has indicated that many of the people buried there do not seem to have come from Denmark; strontium isotope analysis appears to point to origins from the Slavic lands and Norway.[540]

---

[535] Translation taken from Taylor and Auden, 1969. 137. Tolley, 2009, discusses Óðinn's loss of *ergi* and effeminate characteristics, p. 159-65. Þórr took on the appearance of a woman in *þrymskviða* in order to get his hammer back.

[536] Wallis, 2001, p.218; Tolley, 2009, p. 98, 100, 154-5, 160; Simek, 1984, p. 242

[537] For a full discussion on the qualities of Thor's eyes, and his prominent nose, see Perkins, 2001, pp.63, 102

[538] Perkins, 2001, p. 20-1. The examples that Perkins cites are from Dudo of St Quentin, who says that sacrifices were made to Thor for favourable winds. *Erbyggja Saga* also tells us of the Þórr stone where humans selected for sacrifice would have their backs broken over the stone. Pálsson and Edward (trans), 1973, p 50; Hreinsson (ed.), 1991, volume 5, p. 138

[539] The problem maybe that the sacrifices, as Cohen notes, are earlier than the fort at Trelleborg and the two may have little to do with each other. Christiansen, 2002, 81, also comments on the sacrifice of children at Trelleborg and the fact that their burnt bones were thrown into a pit along with the bones of pigs, cows and dogs. Cohen (1965, p.25) lists all the finds from two separate locations at Trelleborg. Besides the animal remains, the finds include vestiges of four children whose bones had all been charred. Cohen (1965, p.25) also lists the remains found at two other similar forts, Aggersborg and Fyrkat; there are vestiges of animal sacrifice but he could discern no human remains. Jones, 1968. 361, provides an excellent ground plan of the camp at Trelleborg.

[540] For details see Price, et al, 2011

Dobat has re-evaluated many of the artefacts and suggests that they show strong influences from Slavic areas, Norway and the Carolingians. Dobat feels that the construction methods of the forts show strong Slavonic influence.[541] These indications of eastern connections may add weight to Cohen's arguments.

That the swastika can be linked to Thunor/Þórr is very intriguing. A fairly recent instance is the find from the cremation cemetery at Sancton, East Yorkshire, where a cremation urn with swastikas upon it and a carefully crafted whetstone are within the same grave.[542] There does seem to be a connection between the number four and Thunor and, as we have already seen, the number has some importance in Anglo-Saxon art.[543] The Uncleby stone (Figure 85 and Figure 129) is also of four-sided (square) cross-section.

Although the Viking fortresses are of 10th and 11th century date, there are other structures with dates closer to the Mound 1 burial which may show some continuity of thought and ideology. One particular site is Ismantorp, on the island of Öland, Sweden. Recent work has shown that it was in use from circa 200 AD to the 7th century.[544] It appears to have been a multi-functional site but was never permanently inhabited. It is situated on a hill-top and consists of a roughly circular dry stone wall about 400 metres long. It has nine gates, but only three of these lead straight to the centre of the complex. Within the wall there are 95 houses arranged in 12 blocks that contain no sign of hierarchy - once inside, it would appear the occupants were equals.[545] In the centre is an open area where a large pit was discovered containing charcoal, earth and burnt bones. By the side of the pit were a fireplace and a smaller pit containing a spearhead. Also within the central space was a small semi-circular house that contained a small pit at its eastern end; this pit had an arrowhead deposited within it. To the east of the house was situated a large posthole, presumably for a pillar.[546]

Andrén interprets the fort as a martial complex, probably used for mustering, for training, for organising raids and ritualised warfare, a place where bonds could be reinforced, ranking ceremonies carried out, rituals performed and feasts held.[547] As he points out, making specific reference to Anglo-Saxon England, warfare was endemic throughout many parts of northern Europe throughout this period. He also says

"The clear cosmological and ritual aspects of figure nine (sic) means that Ismantorp can be interpreted as a representation of the world. The post in the centre of the fort corresponded to the world-tree, whereas the nine gates symbolised the nine worlds surrounding the tree."[548]

Andrén also reminds us of the importance of the figure nine to the northerners by referring to the writings of Adam of Bremen and Thietmar of Merseburg as well as the *Poetic Edda* and *Snorri's Edda*.

This theme of a sacred landscape overlaid on a natural one, which is hinted at by Cohen in regard to Trelleborg and the Slavic temples, finds fuller expression in work by Lotte Hedeager in reference to Gudme, Denmark and Asgard.[549] It is an interesting idea but we do not have the space to explore it any further in this work.

---

[541] Dobat, 2009

[542] Reynolds, 1980. This paper was written because Reynolds felt that this particular find directly supported the claims that Simpson, 1979, made regarding hones, Odin and Thor.

[543] Pollington, Kerr & Hammond, 2010, p.362, 377

[544] Andrén, 2006

[545] Andrén, 2006, p. 33

[546] Andrén, 2006. 33.

[547] Andrén, 2006. 34 and 36.

[548] Andrén, 2006. 36.

[549] Hedeager, 2011. 148 to 162.

Whetstones in Ritual

Evison has quite convincingly shown that there does seem to be a ritual context for whetstones in Anglo-Saxon graves.[550] Both the Uncleby and the Sutton Hoo ones were placed to stand upright within their cemeteries and this aspect may provide a further clue as to the function, not just of the Sutton Hoo example, but of whetstones once deposited in the earth - and perhaps before that, too

However that may be, the fact is that if the stone bar from Mound 1 is a sceptre, it is a very unusual one: no other known sceptre is of almost square cross-section, is made of stone and is as heavy. It looks increasingly unlikely that it is a sceptre, at least in its primary function.

One aspect of both the Uncleby and the Sutton Hoo stones is that there are stains on the long sides. These provoked Bruce-Mitford into suggesting that the stains are there due to the way that the stone bars were handled during their use as sceptres. There is a real problem with this idea - namely, that the greywacké both objects are made from is pretty much impervious to most liquids, including the oils and grease that would have come from a human hand. The stain is likely to have come from exposure, over a very long period, to something adjacent in the ground.

We (Brian Ansell, Paul Mortimer, Stephen Pollington, Hannah Simons, Angus Wainwright) recently (February 2012) examined the larger of the two Uncleby stones; the smaller one can no longer be located. It was very intriguing looking at the Uncleby stone in the light of what we have found regarding the construction methods and geometry of the Mound 1 stone. Brian Ansell ascertained that the dimensions are as follows:

Measured length: 47cm / 18½ inches

Measured depth: 46mm / 1 4/5 inches (Face bed)

Measured width: 51mm / 2 inches (Top bed)

Although not as finely finished as the Sutton Hoo stone, the find from Uncleby is a sophisticated example of the stonemason's art and is four-sided, as is the Mound 1 stone. The sides are not of the same width, so the cross-section is rectangular rather than square. Brian found that the diameters of the lateral curves are of two sizes, 22 feet / 6.7 metres (smallest) to 23 feet 4 inches / 7.1 metres, both larger than that on the Sutton Hoo stone. The ends of the stone are also quite finely shaped and are formed by a subtle three-centred arc following through from the curve of the main body allowing a smooth contour at both ends of the bar.

The large gouges in one face have been commented on by others. Some think they may be runes, but upon close examination they were revealed to be quite recent, probably caused by digging implements when the object was excavated. The revealed stone within these marks is of a much paler colour than other damage and hasn't suffered from a thousand years of being in the soil. There are similar but smaller marks on the stone which have taken on the same hue as the rest of the stone; these were presumably made prior to burial.

The general condition of the Uncleby stone shows that it may well have had a rough life before being buried, as it has many knocks and gouges all over it, especially along the edges; perhaps it has been frequently thrown as part of a ritual? There are no apparent signs of this whetstone being used to sharpen blades but, like the Sutton Hoo stone, it is harder than the metal that it would have been used to hone and, unless used a great deal, would not exhibit such signs.

As the pictures show (Figure 130) when positioned alongside the replica whetstone from Sutton Hoo, the Uncleby is very similar in scale and shape; it has not been so well looked after and does not have the heads and knobs at the ends. What it does have are many tiny flecks of red paint. As mentioned above[551] when looked at by the British Museum, this pigment was supposed to be of a type that was unavailable to the Anglo-Saxons; unfortunately, no further details have been forthcoming so it is not possible to pursue this

---

[550] Hansen, 2009, also mentions symbolic placement of whetstones in later Icelandic graves. It must be said that none of these resemble the one from Sutton Hoo or Uncleby. Hansen, 2009, pp. 28, 72.

[551] Evison, 1975, p.79

at the moment, but it would seem odd that anyone had painted the ends since its discovery, especially as the flecks of paint are mostly only found deep within small recesses.

The Uncleby stone is the nearest parallel to the Sutton Hoo stone, in time, in geography and in material, and it probably performed similar functions, despite being a poor relation in terms of decoration.

Saxo Grammaticus

In some ways it might have been more appropriate to look at a useful essay by Jan Peder Lamm in the section entitled *Review of Relevant Literature*; however, we will be using some of his evidence in our search for analogues and in attempting to focus the scope of future research, so it may be best to consider his comments about parallels for the whetstone here. Lamm does not actually say a great deal about the stone itself but he does have a lot to say about the cult of the multi-headed god and he amasses some impressive evidence. The first witness he calls upon is Saxo Grammaticus, in his work *Gesta Danorum*.[552]

Saxo provides an eyewitness report of the destruction of the Slavic sanctuary, Arkona, at Rügen in 1169 AD. We are told that the wooden idol of *Suantovitus* (*Światowit –Svantevit*) was massive, made of wood, that it had four heads and four necks, that the heads were clean shaven and crop-headed (cf. Figure). In the idol's right hand was a horn and the left held a bow; other items are mentioned that were associated with the deity, such as a saddle and a sword.[553]

There were more multiple-headed deities worshipped by the Slavs within the same town, although *Svantovit* was the most powerful. Others include a god named *Rugievithus* who had seven faces within its head, all covered with a single scalp; on a single belt the idol carried seven swords with an eighth in its right hand. Again, the figure was much bigger than a man.[554] *Porevithus* had five heads while *Porenutius* had four faces and a fifth let into its chest. All of these four deities were represented by superhuman-sized wooden idols of some complexity. Lamm mentions a fifth god, not included in Saxo's work but who was worshipped in Szczecin, Wolin and Brandenburg; he was three headed and his name was *Triglaw*.[555] The four sided, four headed stone idol found in the River Zbruc (Figure 92), a tributary of the Dniester, is in the same tradition and may represent *Svantovit*.

Lamm also mentions that small portable idols were carried around by the Slavs and one such is mentioned in *Hallfreðar saga* where an image of Thor, carved from walrus tusk, was kept in a purse.[556] There are survivals of little figures from England and parts of Scandinavia which appear to have been used for similar purposes - for instance the silver and gilt man from Carlton Colville (Figure 84), dated to the 7th century, which has phallic attributes and is one of ten or more figures that have been found by metal detectorists in recent years. There is also the bronze figure from Rällinge, Lunda parish, Södermanland, Sweden generally thought to be Freyr[557] and the figure of Þórr from Eyrarland, Iceland.[558] So the custom of carrying small portable idols in Germanic lands would seem to be well established and to have lasted for centuries.

---

[552] Saxo Grammaticus, Books X-XVI, BAR International Series 118 (i-iii), Oxford
[553] Lamm, 1987. 219 to 218. Lamm provides a full quote from Saxo book XII on the destruction of the temple, the detail is remarkable.
[554] Lamm, 1987. 221.
[555] Lamm, 1987. 221 to 222.
[556] Lamm, 1987. 222. Hreinsson, 1997. Volume 1, 238.
[557] Lamm, 1987. 222 although see Price, 2006, for reasons to exercise caution over the identity of this piece.
[558] Perkins, 2001. Perkins's book is about this image and he discusses several others of Þórr made from different materials, all small and portable. He discusses other god figures, too.

Lamm reports that a small wooden idol (9.3 cm high) with four bearded heads was found in Wolin, Poland. It is dated to the 9th century according to its stratigraphy.[559] In some ways the similarities between the heads on the Wolin piece and the way that the heads are portrayed on the Mound 1 whetstone are quite striking; the way that the small supporting pillar is shaped is similar to the stone bar, too. Lamm suggests that it may have been a 'whetstick' - that is, a piece of wood coated in fat and then having sand applied to use as a grinding material.[560]

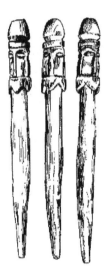 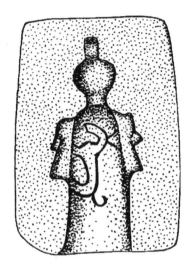 

Figure 102 A juniper-wood peg with three faces from Svendborg, Jutland,

Figure 103 A mould for casting small bells (?) with human faces and a stylised stag or horse incised to one face.

Figure 104 A cast mount for a pendant whetstone (?) from Wolin, Poland.

Another object from Wolin that could have a similar relationship is a small bronze terminal from a whetstone which has four simple faces on its four sides and a ring above them (Figure 104). Lamm tells us, too, of a mould found in Szczecin which was ostensibly for casting small bells with four bearded faces on, but he thinks it may actually be for casting whetstone terminals.[561] Lamm illustrates another mould, this time from Wolin, for casting bronze terminals, with only two heads but with a bulb above the heads and then a ring.[562]

---

[559] Lamm, 1987. 223. Noted, too, by Cohen.
[560] Lamm, 1987. 224. Noted, too, by Cohen.
[561] Lamm, 1987. 223.
[562] Lamm, 1987.225.

Lamm discusses the two miniature whetstones found in Svarta Jorden, Birka, Sweden, probably of Viking date. These show no signs of wear, like the Sutton Hoo example, and the larger (5 cm long) originally had a finial mount, which may have been of metal. The smaller one (2.5 cm) is shaped like a miniature Thor's hammer while the larger has a body shape not unlike that on the Mound 1 whetstone.[563] Lamm says

> "By analogy we may presume that the whole group of whetstone-like objects were (sic) used for cultic practices."[564]

Other objects Lamm discusses that may be pertinent to our exploration are (i) a three headed mace head of bronze (it could stylistically be Gallo-Roman) from Allinge, Bornholm, Sweden (Figure 105); (ii) the three headed image on one of the Gallehus horns from Denmark (Figure 90); a group of sculptured three-faced stone heads from Glejberg, Jutland, Denmark (dating unsure) (Figure 108); a three-headed bronze mounting from a bog at Hemdrup, Himmerland, Jutland (probably pre-Roman) (Figure 106); and a three-headed figure from the Skog tapestry, Hälsingland, Sweden (Figure 112).

Figure 105 A cast mace-head (?) from Allinge, Bornholm.

Figure 106 Cast bronze three-headed socketted mount from Hemdrup, Denmark

---

[563] Lamm, 1987. 223 and 224.

[564] Lamm, 1987. 224. Enright just dismisses all of Lamm's evidence and suggestions with "His (Lamm's) industry provides an impressive catalogue but it is based on the principle that multi-headedness is a motif that is relevant to the sceptre." Enright proceeds to criticise Lamm for choosing evidence from the "High Medieval Slavic" territories around the Baltic and claims that Lamm's methodological difficulties are "insurmountable" and inspire "little confidence". Enright, 2006. 28 to 29. We think Enright is incorrect; Bruce-Mitford disscuses the Birka stones, too. Bruce-Mitford, 1978. 361 to 362.

Lamm explains that there are no multi-headed deities known from Scandinavia but that there is a three headed *thurs* (a giant) in the *Edda* in the great spell of *Skirnismál*. In this account the god Freyr's herald, Skirnir, threatens his intended bride, Gerd and says that if she will not marry him she will have to accept the three-headed *þurs* (giant) instead. He tells us, too, of the discovery of a runic inscription, engraved on a bronze sheet, from Köpingsvik, Öland, Sweden, that has a spell engraved upon it in which a *þrihöftða þurs* is invoked to protect a woman.[565] It has been dated to the 11th or 12th century. A five headed creature is shown on a Gotlandic picture stone from Ardre VII - this may depict a *þurs* (Figure 107).

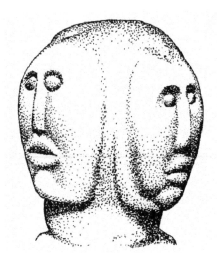

Lamm returns to the east with a 4.5 cm high bronze figurine from Perm, in the region of the Urals (Figure 119). This has four bearded heads with a saucer-like dish above them. It is very much like the arrangement at the bottom end of the whetstone from Sutton Hoo.[566]

Figure 107 Three-headed figure from Glejbjerg, Jutland, Denmark

Figure 108 Picture stone from Ardre, Gotland - a multi-headed þurs kneeling before a bearded assailant?

Figure 109 A pin-head with four radiating faces from Honsåkerskullen, Finland

---

[565] Lamm, 1987. 227. This is described in Macleod and Mees, 2006, as reading *þrymiandi þurs and* meaning a 'noisy ogre'. 123.
[566] Lamm, 1987. 228.

From Finland come another two items with four heads, both found in cremation graves. The first is the bronze pin-head from Kalmumäki, Finland, (Figure 110) which, although small, has a ring at the top and below that four inverted heads and below them another four heads in opposition to those at the top (that is, they are the right way up). An object from Hönsåkerskullen (Figure 109), also a pin-head, has four heads underneath an oblate sphere.

Erä-Esko also draws our attention to a broken terminal mount from one of the drinking horns from Taplow (Figure 111) with four heads at its end.[567] Erä-Esko believes that the pin-heads in particular were meant as miniature parallels to the Sutton Hoo whetstone and that the connections between Scandinavia and England were very close during the 5th to 7th centuries, as he dates the pin heads to around 500 AD.

The subject of amulets and miniature objects within graves and cremations is dealt with in full by Meaney.[568] She establishes that this was a customary ritual practice in Anglo-Saxon England before the conversion to Christianity.

Figure 110 A cast bronze pin-head from Kalmumäki, Finland

Figure 111 Drinking horn terminal from Taplow, Buckinghamshire

Figure 112 Motif from a tapestry from Skog, Hälsingland, Sweden

[567] Erä-Esko, 1965. 93 and plate XIV. Lamm, 1987. 227 to 228.
[568] Meaney, 1981

Figure 113 Bone handle (?)
from Tunby, Sweden.

Lamm returns to Scandinavia to discuss some objects carved in bone that have multiple heads. A four-headed piece from Tunby, St Illian's parish, Västmanland, Sweden (Figure 113) is rather damaged but was probably a handle. A similar item, but in much better condition, comes from Väsby, Vallentuna parish, Uppland (Figure 115) also possibly a handle with two of its originally four heads broken off. Both pieces are from cremation graves of around the 10th century.[569]

Lamm reports a peculiar silver dress pin from Borgholm, Öland which has six heads - at least it has six noses but only six eyes as the faces seem to overlap (Figure 114). It is likely to be Roman.[570]

Figure 114 A cast dress
pin from Borgholm

Figure 115 Bone object
from Väsby, Sweden.

---

[569] Lamm, 1987. 228 to 229.
[570] Lamm, 1987. 229.

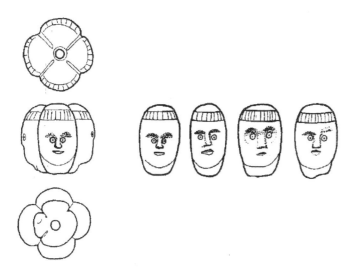

Figure 116 An amber 'melon' bead from Skåne

Figure 117 Male figure with two bearded faces on his chest, from Haglunda, Sweden. In some ways this figure resembles the description of the Slavic god Porenutius who had four faces and a fifth face let into his chest.

One intriguing piece reported by Lamm is a bronze terminal from Haglunda, Alböke parish, Öland, Sweden (Figure 117). It shows the head and upper body of a bearded man with two more men's faces on his chest. The figure recalls the idol of Porentius in Rügen, mentioned by Saxo, which had four heads and a fifth embedded on his chest. According to Lamm, the figure probably surmounted a wooden staff and is dated to the early Iron Age.[571] He includes an amber bead from Skåne, Sweden (Figure 116) which has been carved into the shape of four men's shaven heads. Unfortunately, its provenance is unknown. Finally, he mentions one more multi-headed piece from Praestegården, Bodin, Nordland in Norway (Figure 118). This is a bronze dress pin with four heads near the top of the shaft; the arrangement at the top above the heads appears to be broken and is difficult to interpret. The piece dates from the Viking age.[572]

Lamm has gathered evidence from a wide time-period and the whole of the Baltic area, demonstrating that multi-headed gods were known to the Slavs and may not have been strangers to the Scandinavians and, by extension, the Anglo-Saxons. It should be noted that some of the finds mentioned by Lamm are from Denmark and more particularly Jutland, the old home of the Angles. No multi-headed beings, apart from the *þurs*, are mentioned in the literature but that does not mean that they were absent from Germanic culture and belief systems, but simply not written about during later times; there certainly are images of them. He suggests that the cult of the multi headed god may actually have spread from the Scandinavians to the Slavs.[573]

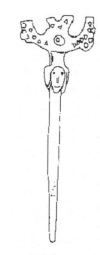

Figure 118 Bronze dress-pin from Bodin, Norway

---

[571] Lamm, 1987. 229. In Scandinavian contexts, this can include a date-range from ca.300BC to 1000 AD
[572] Lamm, 1987. 230.
[573] Lamm, 1987. 231.

Collecting other parallels such as the harness distributor from Bregentved, Denmark, (Figure 120) the 5th century silver pin from an Allemanic grave[574] and the bronze one from Hagestad, Denmark[575] we can build up a reasonably convincing picture that multi-headed beings were known and were important over a long period of time and a wide geographical area which includes Anglo-Saxon England during the 6th and 7th centuries, Scandinavia into the 10th century and parts of the Baltic much later. It may also point us in the direction of belief, rather than just political regalia as far as the whetstone from Mound 1 is concerned.

Religion in the Baltic Region

We would briefly like to return to the evidence of the West Slavic religion as there are one or two points that need to be made. Firstly, there is archaeological evidence of extensive trade and cultural exchange between Scandinavia and the west of Poland throughout the second half of the first millennium AD.[576] However, apart from a brief mention by Procopius during the sixth century, written sources about the area are almost completely absent until the 10th century.[577] So it could well be, as Lamm suggests, that the concept of multi-headed deities may have come to the Slavs from the Scandinavians, or it may be that both groups inherited them from an older shared heritage. What is important is that the two cultures enjoyed very similar sets of ideologies, but the Western Slavs kept theirs for much longer. There is even evidence that some of them – the Lutitians – turned against their rulers when the élite suggested it would be good to convert to Christianity; it seems the people objected to losing their customs and the fact that the élite would profit disproportionately compared to the bulk of the people.[578]

In western Slavic areas, the main centre of power was the temple and the one at Rhetra-Riedegost was, as Cohen points out, rectangular.[579] According to Thietmar the god worshipped there was called *Svarozic*, while Adam of Bremen says the name was *Riedegost*. Słupecki sees no problem with the two names and believes that they are both bynames of the same deity.[580] The site was a cult sanctuary for a number of tribes but the most powerful was the tribe who owned it, the *Redas*.

Svarozic ('son of Svarog') was a god of fire, the sun and heaven, in other words, a sky god; one of his attributes was a sacred white horse. It seems that sacrifice was made to the god, including humans. One notable sacrifice was the slaughter of Bishop John of Mecklenberg who was killed in November 1068 and specifically taken to Rhetra for the act to be carried out. He was beheaded, the head was probably taken into the shrine, while his body was left in the special field outside the sanctuary after the hands and legs were removed.[581]

Thietmar tells us that other gods were worshipped in the temple (but doesn't name them) and that their effigies were present in the sanctuary. The people's standards were kept in that sacred space, too, and only taken out for war. Apparently, the deity that the Luititians looked to for support in war was a goddess and her idol held a horn in its right hand which would be filled with liquid and used for divination.[582] Before any big decision was made, divination took place which involved drawing lots and watching where the sacred horse stepped over some crossed spears. There was also a sacred lake near the sanctuary with which boars were associated.[583]

---

[574] Ryan, 1992. 87 to 89.

[575] Cohen, 1966. 466 and plate II.

[576] See for instance, Paddenberg, 2006.

[577] Słupecki, 2006. 224.

[578] Słupecki, 2006. 224 to 225.

[579] Słupecki, 2006. According to Słupecki, Thietmar calls the place *Riedegost* while, Adam of Bremen calls it *Rhetra*. Cohen spells it *Rethra*.

[580] Słupecki, 2006. 224.

[581] Słupecki, 2006. 225.

[582] Słupecki, 2006. 226.

[583] Słupecki, 2006. 225 and 226. Paddenberg, 2006. 232 says that same happened at Parchim-Löddigsee.

Figure 119 Bronze socketted fitting from Perm, Russia

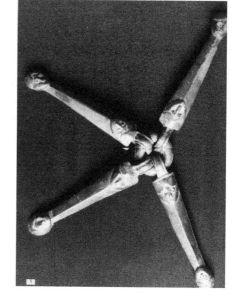

Figure 120 Horse harness strap distributor
from Bregentved, Denmark

Figure 121 Two small wooden objects from Wolin
mentioned by Lamm in his paper, perhaps whetsticks?

The sanctuary at Parchim-Löddigsee seems to relate a similar story. Its excavation began in 1975 and it is the only Slavonic sanctuary and settlement to have been completely explored.[584] It too has evidence of the horse-cult and the animal's use in divination; many horse skulls and skeletons have been found there.[585] Parchim-Lödiggsee was situated by a lake and trade was extremely important there, carried on close to the sanctuary - which is apparently unusual as more normally trade was carried out at some distance from the sacred space. Evidence for trade with Scandinavia and the Carolingians is present.[586]

Because of Saxo's account, the most famous Slavic sanctuary is at Arkona, modern Rügen. The archaeology has tended to confirm much of what Saxo has told us in relation to ritual activities.[587] Certainly, there are remains of animal and human sacrifice and evidence of ritual feasting. Beneath one pit were found human skulls belonging to between 8 to 11 individuals, some of whom, at least, died violently.[588] Together with the skull parts were animal bone, beads and arrows which allowed the pit to be dated to the 10th or 11th century.[589]

We have four-sided and multi-headed deities within the Slavic sanctuaries reportedly, by Saxo at least, made of wood, although the idol from Zbruc (Figure 92) is made of stone. We also have evidence of ritual activity involving the idols. We know that when the Christians came they destroyed the idols and, in the case of Arkona, used the wood to cook with in order to demonstrate the helplessness of the old gods; presumably that was more difficult with the stone from Zbruc which appears to have been dumped in the river. It is true that the Slavic evidence is comparatively late but there are some striking similarities between what we know of the earlier Germanic beliefs and the Slavic, and it may be that the evidence from Poland and eastern Germany is allowing us a glimpse of similar systems and activities that occurred further west in an earlier time.

Before we move on, we should consider one relevant piece of Germanic evidence from a later date. In 921 A.D., an Arab envoy, Ibn Fadlān, set out from Baghdad on a mission to meet *Almish ibn Yiltawar*, king of the *Bulghār*, near the Volga River. While there he was able to observe a group of *Rūs*[590] traders and carefully recorded what he saw. He relates that, "As soon as their boats arrive at this port, each of them disembarks, taking with him bread and meat, onions, milk and *nabīdh*, and he walks until he comes to a great wooden post stuck in the ground with a face like that of a man, and around it are little figures. Behind these images there are long wooden stakes driven into the ground. Each of them prostrates himself before the great idol, saying to it: 'Oh my Lord, I have come from a far country and I have with me such and such a number of young slave girls, and such and such a number of sable skins…' and so on, until he has listed all the trade goods he has brought [Then he adds:] 'I have brought you this gift' Then he leaves what he has with him in front of the wooden post [and says] 'I would like you to do the favour of sending me a merchant who has large quantities of *dīnārs* and dirhams and who will buy everything that I want and not argue with me over my price'"[591] Fadlān tells us more, that the little figures are the wives and sons of the god and that, after successful trading, sheep and cattle may be slaughtered for these gods and the heads of the beasts and some of the meat hung from the wooden stakes behind the idols. Fadlān makes a scathing comment about the conclusion to all this effort, he says that during the night the dogs will come and eats the sacrifices, but that the supplicant will say in the morning, "My Lord is pleased with me and has eaten the gift that I brought him"[592] It is highly likely that Fadlān, as a Moslem, is missing the point here and that the *Rūs* would feel that

---

[584] Paddenberg, 2006. 229. There are actually 18 known temple sites for the Western Slavs – see map Paddenberg, 2006. 230.

[585] Paddenberg, 2006. 230.

[586] Paddenberg, 2006. 232.

[587] Tummuscheit, 2006. 236.

[588] Tummuscheit, 2006. 235.

[589] Tummuscheit. 2006 235.

[590] The *Rūs* are often referred to as Vikings, they were certainly mostly Scandinavian traders.

[591] Fadlān, 2012. 48 to 49.

[592] Fadlān, 2012. 49.

the dogs were either the embodiment of the deities, or had been sent by them; in any case the incident shows that Scandinavians were worshipping headed idols as late as the 10th century.

The Oath-Ring?

The presence of eight implacable faces around the whetstone-sceptre might suggest that these are the (male and female) divine ancestors of the Wuffing line. We discussed this idea elsewhere (see p.77 and p.161) but did not find it compelling.[593] The ring which forms the greater part of the upper fitting may have served as the leader's oath-ring on which vows of loyalty were traditionally sworn.[594] If so, then the use of this powerful symbolic item on top of the stone may have encouraged the idea that both the sentinel stag and the divinities shown on its surfaces were witnesses to the words spoken while holding the sacred ring.

A close connection between rings and oaths is apparent in much OE verse, where the ring (*hring, beag*) symbolises the reciprocity in the lord-warrior bond (see *Beahgifa, Brytta, Maððumgiefa, Sincgiefa*). This is clear in *Beowulf*:

> *"Ic ðæt mæl geman, þær we medu þegun,*
> *þonne we geheton ussum hlaforde*
> *in biorsele, ðe us ðas beagas geaf,*
> *þæt we him ða guðgetawa gyldan woldon ..."*

> *"I recall that time where we tasted the mead,*
> *when we promised to our lord*
> *in the beer-hall – to him who gave us rings -*
> *that we would repay him for the wargear ...."*
>
> *Beowulf, l.2633-6*

Likewise, during Alfred's wars with the Danes, the oath-ring played an important part in exacting binding undertakings:[595]

> *Her hine bestæl se here into Wærham ... 7 siððan wið þone here se cyning frið nam 7 him þa gislas sealdon þe on þam here weorþuste wæron to þam cyninge 7 on him þa aðas sworon on þam halgan beage þe hi ær nanre þeode don noldon þet hi hredlice of his rice foron...*

> *876. Here the enemy army stole into Wareham ... and afterwards the king made peace with the enemy army, and they then gave hostages, who were the most honoured [men] in the army, to the king and then swore oaths to him on the hallowed ring, which before they would not do for any people, that they would quickly go from his kingdom...*
>
> *ASC* MS 'E' s.a.876

Rings evidently could be used to invoke the gods (among the heathen Danes, and so plausibly among the pre-Christian Angles) as witnesses to oaths freely taken. A collection of 65 rings was found at the site Lille Ullevi (Uppland Sweden) in 2007, understood to be oath-rings from a temple: *Ullevi* is 'Ullr's sacred place', the sanctuary of the god Ullr.[596] The site began to be used from the 5th c. onwards, and showed signs of increased activity in the Vendel and Viking periods (i.e. circa 500-1000 AD).

---

[593] Ellis Davidson, 1988, p.127-9. The heads have been seen as those of defeated foes. The Irish tradition whereby a king puts the head of a slain foe under his thigh is noted, but it does not seem especially relevant to either the whetstone or the corresponding image on the shield.
[594] Pollington, 2002, p.122
[595] Pollington, 2002
[596] Reported at www.archeurope.com/index.php?page=lilla-ullevi.

Sword-Rings

The correlation of a symbolic ring and a public oath is significant since the ring-hilted sword has elsewhere been linked to the practice of ritual oath-swearing, whereby the warrior laid his hand on the hilt of his lord's sword while swearing his loyalty.[597] Rings – in the form of *kolben* armrings – were a badge of loyalty and distinction used among the eastern Germanic peoples in the 4th century AD and after; they may derive from the military rings worn by Roman army veterans, called *armillae*.

It is possible that this symbolic use of the ring as a badge of honour was transferred to the pommel of the sword.[598] Ring-hilted swords, with or without runic text, are a feature of mainly Kent and the south-east in the 6th and 7th c. where it has been suggested their presence shows that the Kentish kings were influenced by contemporary Merovingian Frankish customs.[599] Indeed, some Frankish kings included the Jutes (of Kent?) among their tributary peoples. This interlude of Frankish hegemony is usually ascribed to the period 520x30 – 560x70 AD, a time of consolidation in southern Britain in which chiefdoms were coalescing around powerful kinship groups. Identical customs are found in Kentish cemeteries such as Ash Gilton and Faversham and Frankish ones such as St. Dizier.[600] The characteristic style of hilt fitting is called the 'Bifrons-Gilton pommel' due to the early finds from Kent. The contemporary

Figure 121a
Restoration of a
ring-hilt from
Biffrons. Kent

finds of ring-swords in Västergotland (Sweden) and Westphalia (Germany) may be considered outliers of this cultural group, either local chiefs adopting an attractive foreign custom or, perhaps more probably, a small group of warriors settled and embedded in a distant land perhaps as followers to an exiled lord or retainers to a bride given in exogamous marriage.

Sceptres

The parallels for royal sceptres in the Germanic world are not plentiful. The late Roman forms of sceptre mainly consisted of a rod surmounted by a figure, usually an eagle but sometimes in combination with a warrior figure, modelled in the round and in classical style. A lathe-turned wooden rod found with a princely burial beneath Cologne cathedral has also been seen as a sceptre, although this is no more than an assumption since the item is very plain and rather slender, and carries no feeling of physical or symbolic weight.[601] In this it rather resembles the thin gold-mounted wand from Sutton Hoo Mound 1 with its decorative wolf-motif plaque.

.

---

[597] Pollington, 2002

[598] Hedeager, 2011 p.205

[599] Fischer & Soulat, 2007; cf. James, 1989, p.28. The evidence for Merovingian dominance of Kent is contrasted with that for a strong Anglo-Saxon presence in north-east Francia.

[600] Truc, 2007

[601] Bruce-Mitford, 1978, fig.257 showed various late Roman sceptres depicted in ivory diptychs; p.352-7 dealt with northern European sceptres in archaeology and iconography. Henig, 1995, p.174-5 saw the Sutton Hoo sceptre as a direct copying of Roman symbolism. Price, 2003, p.181-204 treated the archaeological evidence for ceremonial or magical staves in Scandinavian contexts. Kuznetsov, 2005, interpreted the Yamna culture cudgel-sceptre (a copper bar worked into a cudgel) as the source of the mythological *vajra* weapon in Indian mythology.

The Favour of Woden?

The faces on the whetstone are not identical, but feature definite variations and it must be assumed that it was the sculptor's intention to show eight individual persons or aspects of a single personality.[602]

Face	Top	Bottom
1	short hair, centre parting, no beard	long hair, centre parting; long forked beard
2	short hair back-combed, no beard	long hair back-combed, moustache, forked beard
3	long hair, centre parting, no beard	long hair back-combed, moustache, forked beard
4	long hair, back-combed, no beard	long hair, centre parting, no beard

The dimensions of the respective heads are also consistently different:

Face	Top	Bottom	Variance
1	38 mm	41 mm	3mm
2	38.5 mm	40 mm	1.5 mm
3	37 mm	42 mm	5 mm
4	38.5 mm	42 mm	3.5 mm

As this scheme shows, the stern male faces all appear at the bottom of the stone while at the top the faces are carved to appear somewhat softer and beardless, which suggests female features; with the stone placed vertically on a flat surface, the 'female' faces would be the right way up and the 'males' inverted. In addition, the chins on the top faces are more gracile than that of the shaven face at the bottom; this could be because the faces at the top represent the faces of women.[603]

The presence of a beard on some faces is deduced from the fact that no chin is visible on them. All the faces have some kind of linear hatching feature beneath the jaw-line which might represent a beard worn off the face, as shown in some Anglo-Saxon manuscript pictures, or a hairstyle gathered on the chest in plaits; however, the possibility remains that it is simply a hatched infill to complete the design. Some faces have a definite parting with the hair falling sideways, while others have lines running straight back from the brow as if the hair were combed and tied back. The faces each have a triangular chin which is parallelled on the cloisonné shield mount from Mound 1, where the bird's hip is represented as a human face.[604]

In the long hair pulled round from the sides under the chin, one might see an allusion to the story of the origin of the Lombards (*Langobardi*) as told in the *Origo Gentis Langobardorum* of Paul the Deacon, written in the 8th century and recording the early history of the nation.[605] The tribe was originally called the *Winniles*, and was active in seeking new lands in the south due to overpopulation in their homeland. Their route into Italy was blocked by the powerful tribe of the Vandals, who demanded tribute from the Winniles to allow them to pass through their lands; this the Winniles refused. The Vandals prepared for war and consulted Godan (the god Woden), who answered that he would give the victory to those he saw

---

[602] Smedley & Owles, 1967; Bruce-Mitford, 1978, p.316-23, 372-3; Walton-Rogers, 2006, p.218-9

[603] Bruce-Mitford, 1978. 326.

[604] Bruce-Mitford, 1974, p.45. The lentoid motif below the chin is also present on the shield-mount. While it is possible that it represents some article of apparel, the possibility cannot be excluded that it is merely a part of the decorative frame.

[605] Bóna, 1976; Pohl, 2006, p.147 refers to the fact that it is the *females* who win the Winniles their change of fortune, assisted by Frea, the *goddess wife* of Godan.

first at sunrise. The Winniles' powerful seeress, Gambara, sought help from Frea (the goddess wife of Godan), who advised them to ensure that their women tie their hair in front of their faces like beards and prepare for war alongside their husbands. Godan asked his wife about the identity of these approaching 'long-beards' (*Langobardi*) and she promptly reminded him that he must supply a gift to go with the name he had just bestowed. The gift for the Lombards was victory in their struggle with the Vandals.

However, there is nothing in the surviving literature to link this tale to the East Angles, nor anything in the ship burial known to be of specifically Lombard origin, so the dressing of the hair in this manner on the whetstone faces may be fortuitous.

Figure 122 The appliqué bird from the Sutton Hoo
shield. Its hip is executed in closionné garnets, and
features a male face similar to those on the
whetstone-sceptre. See also Figure 99

The Stag and Animal Transformation

As we noted above (p.113), the stag may then have had an importance for the heathen Angles in Suffolk which dates back millennia, based not solely on primitive hunting rituals but rather on an understanding of animals as mediators between the worlds of gods and men (cf. the stag on the Skrydstrup bracteate, (Figure 86). This idea is amplified further by Bolin:[606]

> "In my opinion it is possible that the elk-human figure depicted in the upper right part of the rock painting at Hästskotjärn … can be associated with a form of out-of-body-journey whereby a human assumes the form of a mythical animal in order to enter the spiritual world."

If this is so, then the stag may have been a means of mediation between the world of men and the Otherworld.

This would reinforce the close association between the human masks on the stone and the human mask on the hip of the bird on the shield from the same grave (Figure 122), which must suggest that a similar form of man-animal transformation formed part of the religious traditions of the East Angles.[607]

Stag figurines cast in bronze are found across the ancient world from as far away as Luristan; examples from Britain include the find from Gateholm (Pembrokeshire, Wales) and part of a similar one from Traprain Law (East Lothian, Scotland).[608] In Germanic contexts, we have already mentioned the bronze stag figurine found at Høyland (Denmark).

Deified Ancestors?

As noted above (p.51), Karl Hauck suggested that the stone bar might be an 'ancestor-staff' (*Ahnenstab*) with the faces of the Anglian kings placed around it. We touched on this earlier (p.127) when we suggested that these ancestral figures were in fact deified or regarded as members of the family of the gods.

The idea of an 'ancestor-staff' apparently began with Hauck: it was not a recognised artefact-type before he coined the word *Ahnenstab*. This makes discussion of the stone in these terms exceedingly difficult: the sample size (i.e. one example) is too small for valid conclusions to be drawn.

The stone bar was buried, presumably with its last owner. It was no longer an active part of the 'regalia' of the East Anglian kings, and it was honourably retired. Like the king himself, it went into the Otherworld where its power could be available to successors.

If, as Jordanes implies in respect of the Goths (p.127), successful ancestors were elevated to the status of demigods or lesser divine beings, then the putting aside of the carved divine-ancestral images may represent a break in the biological succession. That is to say, the successor to the occupant of Mound 1 (be it Rædwald or whoever else) may not have been a blood kinsman of the previous king. Bede is fairly clear in his assertions that Rædwald succeeded his father, Tytla, and that he was succeeded in turn by his son, Eorpwald.

At some time during the 590s Rædwald married an unnamed woman who, Bede implies, was heathen, as was Rædwald himself at this time. With her, he fathered at least two sons, Rægenhere and his younger brother Eorpwald. The brothers also had an older kinsman, Sigeberht, whose name is unusual in the East Anglian tradition. It is in fact typical of the neighbouring East Saxon dynasty, whose names overwhelmingly alliterate on S-. William of Malmesbury, in the 12th century, indicated that Sigeberht was not Rædwald's own son but a stepson; his source for this is unknown. He would thus have been the son of Rædwald's queen, conceived in a previous marriage. However, when Sigeberht and Rædwald fell out, the former took himself off to Francia, so it is equally possible that the prince was a member of the

---

[606] Bolin, 2000, p.164

[607] Brentjes, 2000, explores the role of animal art in Eurasian shamanic societies.

[608] Burley, 1956, item 267. It is worth repeating that this stag figurine is of doubtful provenance and unknown date.

Merovingian family, many of whom also bore names beginning with the element *Sigi-* e.g. Sigibert, Sigamber, Sigimand, Sigivald, Sigila, etc. Rædwald's queen may then have been either been born as a member of that dynasty, or have previously married into it.

Frankish power was already dominant in Kent at this time, with King Æþelberht married to a Frankish princess, Bertha, and a bishop installed in Canterbury in the late 6th century. Kent was the most economically powerful state in Britain, benefitting from its proximity to Francia and the easy maritime passage from its southern shore to the continent. The pre-eminence of the Kentish court and its satellite in Essex may have caused concern among the Angles who were unwilling to accept Kentish-Frankish hegemony. Carver has suggested that the spate of burial mound construction in East Anglia may have been a reaction to the perceived Frankish threat, with its new ideologies of centralised kingship, literacy and Christianity.[609]

The Workman's Output

One of the many mysteries surrounding the stone bar is its uniqueness. The craftsman who designed and executed this stunning piece of stonework was clearly a master of his profession, with access to very accurate measuring equipment and finely made stoneworking tools. He had served an apprenticeship and progressed to the level of a master craftsman (see p.42). The metal components, which have to be viewed as integral to the piece, are likewise very accomplished and finely-made pieces of work The result was the product of a collaboration between designer, metalworker and stoneworker.

Our brief survey of Anglo-Saxon whetstones (p.130) has shown that Anglo-Saxon stonecarving in the 6th century was capable, but there is little evidence for monumental stonework in the Roman tradition. Many early Anglo-Saxon churches routinely use existing squared blocks e.g. Bradwell-on-Sea (Essex), constructed out of the ruins of the Roman fort of *Othona*, or Escomb (County Durham) robbed from nearby Binchester. Some of the earliest date to the 7th century.

The presence of Bishop Liudhard in Canterbury as chaplain to Queen Bertha, and later the arrival of Augustine's mission, prompted re-use of Roman buildings for Christian worship. Liudhard and Bertha used St. Martin's, Canterbury, as a private chapel, believing that it had been a church in Roman times. In this context, an interest in stoneworking and masonry grew up in Christianised areas but there is no certain example of an Anglo-Saxon stone building or free-standing monument from the pre-Christian period.

Free-standing preaching crosses in wood and stone were used in some areas, the earliest dating to the 8th century – Ruthwell (Dumfriesshire) and Bewcastle (Cumbria) are the best known, both with extensive runic texts. These monuments formed an important symbol of religious conversion for the communities they served. It is known that non-Christian areas had wooden god-posts, and that they served a similar purpose as a focus of religious devotion for heathen communities.[610] The crosses are all square or rectangular in section, with tapering sides and a tall finial; in this they resemble the Svantovit pillar from Zbruc (Figure 92).

We do not know enough about when the stone and its fittings were made to indicate the context of its design and manufacture. The workmen who created them were highly skilled and confident in their use of tools and materials. The central question is: where are the other products of their collaboration?

As there is no other certain example of such high-quality workmanship in stone in Anglo-Saxon England from the early period, three possibilities present themselves:

> The work no longer exists. It may have been deliberately destroyed by Christian zealots in the conversion to Christianity; by heathens during the Danish assault on East Anglia in the 9th century; by Normans during the dismantling of Anglo-Saxon buildings in the later 11th century; by Tudor zealots at the Reformation; by Puritan zealots during the Civil War. Equally, it may have been buried and still await discovery.

[609] Carver, 1998; Pollington, 2008
[610] Pollington, 2011a, p.101, 117-20

The work was carried out by a stoneworker who only stayed in East Anglia for the duration of the commission. A craftsman of such skill would have been in demand, and in common with most masons and stonecarvers over the last two millennia, he may have completed his commission, taken his payment and left. In all likelihood he would have been trained in a classical school, possibly in the Byzantine-dominated region, and would only have expected to remain among the East Angles while the work was in progress.

The work was carried out on the continent and was an heirloom of the Wuffings when they established hegemony in East Anglia. The stonecarving is egregious and cannot be linked firmly to the 'Insular Germanic' tradition (or any other tradition presently recognised). The carving cannot be dated by conventional means, and the metalwork does not bear any of the hallmarks of standard Early Anglo-Saxon material – Style I ornament or mercury gilding, for example. Nor does it appear to form part of any recognised stoneworking tradition from contemporary Europe. Some of the manufacturing techniques used – cast bronze bars, swaged bronze strips and the like – are familiar from Anglo-Saxon contexts and formed part of the metalworker's repertoire.

It is perfectly possible that the metalworker was also responsible for the shield-fittings, pressblech ornaments for the horns, helmet, cups and flasks found in Mound 1, and the similarity of the carved heads on the stone bar to the one on the hip of the bird shield-fitting suggests that they were either conceived together or one was copied from the other. In the nature of the case, the stone bar is a more durable object although we cannot be sure that it predates and thus formed the model for the metal shield fitting (Figure 122).

Yet the metal fittings clearly form a unity with the stone bar, which is undatable. In that case, the bar and its set of fittings may have been in use as ritual objects for decades or even centuries before they entered the ship-burial.

Gothic Connections?

One might ask: what bearing does the attitude of the Goths in the 5th century have on East Anglian kingship in the 6th-7th century? What connection is there between the Ostrogothic kingdom in Italy, or the Visigothic in Spain and southern France, and the East Anglian kingdom in Britain?

The wide connections of the East Angles as evidenced in the assemblage in Mound 1 are well documented: Byzantine silverware, Frankish coins, a British hanging bowl, garnets from central Europe or further afield, weapons and tableware with Scandinavian connections were all brought together for the funerary display.

Yet there is a possible connection to the Ostrogoths in particular, and specifically to their royal family. In about 540 AD, after a protracted war in Italy, the Ostrogothic King Witigis was captured by the Eastern Empire's general, Belisarius. On the orders of Emperor Justinian I, the Roman general took both Witigis and his wife Matasuntha as captives to Byzantium. The king died there, having failed to leave any children. After his death, the widowed Matasuntha married the patrician Germanus Justinus, a nephew of Justinian I by his sister Vigilantia.

Back in Italy, the Ostrogoths were leaderless. The noble families chose to raise one of their promising young men to the throne: a kinsman of Theudis, the sword-bearer of King Theoderic the Great, called Baduila. The young king took the name Totila as his royal title. Totila reversed the tide of war with the eastern Empire and by 543 AD had managed to regain most of the territories in Italy the Eastern Roman Empire had seized in 540 AD. After Belisarius retreated to Byzantium in 549 AD, King Totila recaptured Rome, and by the end of 550 AD, only Ravenna and a small pocket of land surrounding it had not been regained. In further conflict, Totila was mortally wounded at the battle of Taginae in 552 AD and the Ostrogoths suffered a huge defeat. Resistance to the Eastern Empire continued until 560 AD, reinforced by assistance from the Franks and Alamanni, but the combined forces of the Eastern Empire with its Lombard, Gepidic and Herulian allies overran Italy and severely weakened Ostrogothic power; the incoming Lombard leader, Alboin, assumed control and absorbed the remnants of the Ostrogothic state.

In East Anglia, King Rædwald died circa 625, having been born probably around 575; his father was thus probably born around 550 at the time when Totila's power was at its greatest. Rædwald's father, Tytla, bears a name which is an anglicised version of the Gothic name Totila - i.e. in the OE of the 6th century, *Tutila.

It is possible that stories of the successful Ostrogothic king were circulating around the North Sea and across Germanic-speaking Europe at this time. Certainly, tales of the Lombard King Alboin were widely known, as Paul the Deacon says:[611]

> *Alboin vero ita praeclarum longe lateque nomen percrebuit, ut hactenus atiam tam aput Baioariorum gentem quamque et Saxonum, sed et alios eiusdem linguae homines eius liberalitas et gloria bellorumque felicitas et virtus in eorum carminibus celebretur.*

> *Truly, the famous name of Alboin was spread far and wide so that even now his openhandedness and glory, luck and courage in war are celebrated in songs among the Bavarian folk and the Saxons, as among other men of the same language.*

This was evidently true, as the OE poem *Widsith* (l.70-4) does indeed record this name (OE Ælfwine) in connection with generous gifts, and that of his father, Audoin (OE Eadwine):[612]

> *Swylce ic wæs on Eatule mid Ælfwine*
> *se hæfde moncynnesmine gefræge*
> *leohteste hond lofes to wyrcenne,*
> *heortan unhneaweste hringa gedales,*
> *beorhtra beaga, bearn Eadwines.*

> *Thus I was in Italy with Ælfwine*
> *who, as I have heard, of mankind*
> *had the lightest hand to create a good name*
> *a heart most generous in the sharing of rings,*
> *bright circlets – the son of Eadwine.*

Clearly, Alboin's generosity was known to the English poet, centuries after the king had died in 565 AD, having led his people from Noricum (modern Hungary) to overthrow the Gepid king, Þurismod, and then onward to conquer Italy. The notion that 'the same language' was in use among Lombards, Bavarians, Saxons and more distant peoples was evidently commonplace at this time.

We might assume some form of dynastic link between the Anglian royal line and the Ostrogothic, although there is no firm evidence for this unless we ascribe the presence of the Byzantine silverware in Mound 1 to either diplomatic exchange or a share in the loot taken by Totila from General Belisarius. Perhaps more likely is the notion that the fame of a powerful and lucky ruler was sufficient for royal parents to name their own children after him?

Scandinavian Connections?

One intriguing possibility is that the stone ensemble may not have been made in England at all but may have been designed and created elsewhere, perhaps in Scandinavia. Many commentators, not least Bruce-Mitford, have noted the many similarities between several of the artefacts found in the Mound 1 grave at Sutton Hoo and others, particularly, from graves at Vendel and Valsgärde in Sweden.[613] It is, at present, impossible to take this suggestion any further.

---

[611] Pollington, 2011a, p.42-3
[612] Chambers, 1912
[613] Most notably the helmet, shield fittings and sword pommel. See Mortimer, 2011 for a full discussion.

Figure 123   Eyrar Thors statue (National Museum of Iceland)

12. Some Conclusions

A Graven Image?

As mentioned above, there are no known 'sceptres' from antiquity that are of square section and made almost entirely of stone. The only stone parallels that are also square in section, the Pfalzfeld pillar included, appear to have been idols, objects of religious veneration. [614]

One clue that could have meant that the Mound 1 stone also functioned as an idol is that fact that the bronzes at the top of the stone enclosing the bulb have been replaced. As mentioned above,[615] this may have been because of a poor casting, but it could be due to the whetstone being knocked over from an upright position and the arms of the cage shattering or deforming on impact. If the arms of the cage had been well cast such damage probably would not have happened but, as we have seen, getting a good casting is difficult.

Why would the stone be upright? If it spent most of its time in a shrine, then part of its magic would perhaps be that it would stand on its base, almost miraculously defying gravity. As we have already seen, Bruce-Mitford's assertion (based on his trials with a plaster replica) that the stone would be unstable if stood on its pedestal, were wrong. It appears, too, that like the Uncleby stone, the Sutton Hoo was placed upright within the grave.[616]

As for who the faces represent and which gods were involved, we must remember that being heathens the Anglo-Saxons worshipped many gods. The stone could represent one god (e.g. Thunor, Woden, Ing or others) or it could represent all of them. The possibility that the heads at the top are female while those at the bottom are male has been mentioned before and this could reflect another idea - that of the holy marriage, the *hieros gamos*, between the sky-god and mother-earth, perhaps Woden and Frige. The fact is that the heads at the top are not only unbearded, but have also been deliberately made smaller than those at the bottom and with more slender chins than the shaven figure at the bottom. As for the red-painted knobs, they could represent phases of the sun, perhaps the rising and setting sun, or even, as Enright suggests, divine furnaces. It may well be that there were multiple uses for the stone and multiple meanings, that the designer incorporated a set of complex concepts that would have real significance to the Anglo-Saxons and possibly other Germanic peoples.

A clue to the meaning of the stone was recently discovered by Brian Ansell and Hannah Simons while considering Hannah's photographs. They noticed that the left eye on the face (labelled 'B1' by Bruce-Mitford) does not appear to be the original eye; it seems that it has been struck off and a new eye, rather crudely, carved in its place. This eye is larger than all the others and has a very rough surround, particularly below the eye itself. (See Figures 98 & 124)

However, Hannah Simons and Brian Ansell also noted that three of the faces, A1, A4 and B4 appear to have red pigment residues in their hair and B4 may have it in the beard, too. (Figures 97 & 98) If this is the case, then that is very curious indeed and could add another dimension to the enquiry: for instance, Thor, in later accounts is well known for having red hair and a red beard; he also famously dressed as a woman in the episode of his hammer's theft and recovery related in *Þrymskviða*.

This could, of course, be poor workmanship, or the result of an accident, just as the helmet's eyebrow and the bird's eye without foils could just be the result of a repair. We have to some extent explored the Woden imagery

---

[614] Schutz, 1983. 281 to 283, provides a picture of another stone pillar, of similar vintage (5th century BC) to the Pfalfeld from Holzgerlingen, near Stuttgart, Germany. This is four sided but has the figure of a man on two sides and the head is of the 'Janus' type, including the 'leaf crown' that is depicted on the Pfalzfeld. It is about 2.25 metres tall.

[615] This volume, p.14ff

[616] Bruce-Mitford, 1978. 311 to 312. Carver, 2005. 187 to 199. This discussion includes useful drawings.

of the helmet and the shield above (Figure 122) but we would just like to extend the idea a little further with reference to two other objects from Mound 1. Thor Ewing reports that on the purse, the left one of the men-between-two-beasts figures has had some damage done to its left eye; it is as if it has been struck, although the garnet is still present.[617] These are so tiny that most people have never noticed them and Bruce-Mitford did not mention the defect. Once again, this could be through accidental damage within the tomb or even before burial. However, it may be going beyond coincidence when it is realised that in each case, it is the left eye that is affected; that goes for the helmet, the bird, the figure on the purse lid and the eye of the B1 face.

Figure 124 The B1 face from the Sutton Hoo whetstone.

The final piece - or rather, two pieces - is the two sword decorations from the scabbard of the Mound 1 sword, usually referred to as 'sword bosses'. These are of gold and garnets, precisely made, backed by a white material that makes them look like eyes; possibly the 'eyes in the sword'.[618] They are superficially similar, but the one on the wearer's left is smaller than the other.[619]

So what does all this mean? Well, if these aren't all coincidences, then at least one of the faces on the stone is a clear reference to the god with the altered eye, almost certainly Woden.

---

[617] Ewing, 2008. p 94. However, Ewing is in error when he states that an eye has been removed - it has merely been struck and the gold around it deformed. It must also be said that the right eye of this same figure has a very small dent above it.

[618] For a full discussion of this feature, see, Mortimer, 2011. 112 to 115.

[619] Price and Mortimer, in preparation, makes it quite clear that the one eye feature is not consistently left or right on items from other places, but it certainly appears to be the left which is stressed in the Sutton Hoo material.

13. Further Research

Paul Mortimer and Stephen Pollington

Figure 125 From the Sutton Hoo purse lid a figure of a man between two canids. His left eye has suffered damage but the socket has been filled in during conservation.

The notion that the whetstone-sceptre is a completely 'one-off' object, *sui generis*, is deeply unsatisfactory. The quest for understanding the object and its meaning lies, at least in part, in finding valid analogues and then developing and testing theories to account for the similarities and differences between them.

Figure 126 The picture of the Sutton Hoo sword bosses, shows that the left one (wearer's left and right in the picture) is smaller than that on the wearers right.

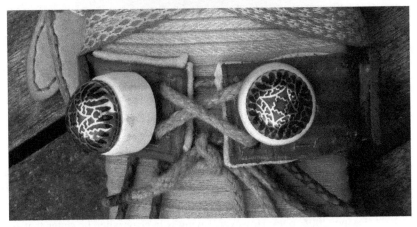

We have presented some ideas about possible analogues above (p. 129) and are conscious that many more must lie in the archaeological records of northern Europe. The number of many—faced objects from the Baltic area set out above (*Images of the Gods*) indicates that there would be merit in investigating this topic further and in a broader geographical setting. Janiform objects are not unusual in the Roman world, and a comparison of the two object-classes might yield interesting results.

Another possibility that could be explored further is the tradition of the *Irminsul*, or World Pillar which is a concept common to many European societies and possibly elsewhere. The relationship of the stone bar with its obelisk-like profile to the wooden *Irminsul* columns needs investigation. Unfortunately, as far as we know, no such pillar is extant and we can only rely on the observations recorded in the literary sources and, perhaps, objects like the Zbruc Pillar and the one from Pfalzfeld - unless objects like the whetstone represent miniature versions of the pillar.

An area that may bear fruit is a systematic review of all the 'idol' figures that are known to exist from the 4th to the 10th century in the northern world, including wooden figures as well as the portable metal objects such as the Carlton Colville figure, the small statue from Eyrarland and the parts of staffs that have survived. Perhaps, too, a consideration of the way faces are portrayed on objects such as brooches and belt buckles from the period, could be included? There are certainly many clues there, it just takes a 'key' to unlock some of them and maybe some form of correspondence analysis.

In this study we have begun a consideration of ideas of measurement and number but there may be other relationships yet to be unravelled in the way that houses and halls were built and what this may tell us about how measurement and number related to the world-view of the northern peoples. It would be useful, too, if others considered the measurements contained within the whetstones from Sutton Hoo and Uncleby; and reviewed other whetstones and portable objects to see if there are other geometric relationships that may help to understand them.

An incidental but important field of research concerns vernacular ecclesiastical architecture in northern Europe. Church steeples appear to have rather mysterious origins and were largely confined to northern Europe. We know that the early Christian missionaries were instructed to take over heathen temples and sanctify them; did they take over the tradition of the steeple, too? Were steeples part of that earlier tradition? Even today some Christian sects refuse to use them, claiming that they have pagan origins,[620] are connected with sun worship and are phallic. The exploration of the pagan temple at Uppåkra, in Sweden, seems to indicate that it had some form of steeple. Likewise, there is place-name evidence to consider. It may be that such high structures represent the world pillar.

Cohen draws our attention to the Pershore censer which has a particular kind of "Rhenish" steeple above a colonnade and which he believes may be of some relevance to the Sutton Hoo whetstone. There are indeed churches in England with this type of steeple - for instance, St Mary's Church, Sompting in Sussex. St Mary's existing steeple is dated to the 14th century but there are indications that it is based on an older structure. The Pershore censer does in some ways echo the temples of Greece and Rome with their semi-outdoor nature and it may be that sanctuaries of this type were a little more widespread than is usually thought, but perhaps made of more perishable material than stone.

A comparison with concepts of measurement and number within the classical world may give us further insights into the origins of the stone carver and his training. Cohen was convinced that there was a relationship between the Sutton Hoo stone's form and the building plans of sanctuaries, particularly at the pre-Trelleborg type fort sites in the original homeland of the Angles and Jutes; further research could provide more information about the significance of any relationship between sacral areas and the whetstone. The apparent connection between the sky/thunder god and the number four and its multiples is intriguing.

Another aspect related to the sky god is the concept of the thunderbolt and how it connects to certain stones, which may or may not include the Sutton Hoo stone. 'Thunderstones' appear to have been an active concept in many parts of Europe and this is another area of research which needs to be brought into the overall picture of stones and their significance to religion. There is the further consideration that most of the Icelandic stories in which a whetstone is mentioned also include the act of throwing a whetstone to cause something to happen. Are there similar stories in other cultures that could perhaps tell us more?

---

[620] See for instance this website: http://www.adventistbiblicalresearch.org/documents/steeples.htm

Figure 127
Pershore Censer

Incidentally, Simpson overlooked at least one saga reference to whetstones or hones, the account found in *Egil's Saga*, where Egil has to save his head from being taken by King Erik Bloodaxe by making up a poem in praise of Erik. Egil calls a sword *heinsöðul* the 'hone's saddle' which is a curious kenning for the weapon and may have deeper meaning.[621]

The idea that a thunderstone may actually be the end-product of a lightning strike, rather than its initiator requires further consideration; this would mean, that the fact that the stones made from greywacké cannot produce a spark when struck is of little significance.

Mitchell's explanation regarding the linguistics of whetting terminology in relation to the Sutton Hoo whetstone and the ability to speak in public and persuade others needs developing further. Unfortunately, there is not the space within this volume to provide the treatment that this very interesting idea requires.

An intriguing idea that we have not been able to pursue is that of the 'judgement sceptre'[622] used in mediaeval Germany as a symbol of justice; it would be valuable to know how far back this tradition goes,

---

[621] Hreinsson (ed.), 1997 p.108
[622] Bruce-Mitford, 1978, 175

where it comes from and what form the sceptre took. Several of our source commentators have related the stone to a king's justice, including Simpson and Enright.

Enright was very keen on the idea that the red terminal knobs may represent furnaces, perhaps one celestial and the other mundane; it is certainly a concept that has possibilities, bearing in mind what we know of the semi-magical position of the smith and of the mysteries surrounding the making of metal in northern cultures.

Incidentally, the colourant used on the knobs has not - as far as we know - ever been analysed, and its composition is unknown. It would be useful to see if it can be determined using modern techniques and whether the red residues affecting the hair of some of the faces are of the same material and have not just been caused by mineral deposition within the grave.

Several of those who have written about the whetstone have said that it is one of, if not the most important and significant objects within the Mound 1 tomb and it for the time being will have to remain so.[623] We have perhaps narrowed the possibilities for viable theory to the best of our ability; it will have to be left to others to draw all the secrets from the stone!

---

[623]Storms, 1978. 323, Wallace-Hadrill, 1975. 47, Enright, 2007. 8.

Appendix 1. The Uncleby Whetstone

Brian Ansell. Masons' Report. 22nd February 2012

The information gained from the visit assisted with an invaluable insight into the creation of this rare and remarkable artefact.

Initial studies revealed in-depth details of its creation and for the benefit of actual dimensions the bar was measured by ruler, square and tracing its form on white paper.

> Measured length: 47cm
> Measured depth: 46mm (Face bed)
> Measured width: 51mm (Top bed)

Allowing for slight variances in the bar's overall form - which could possibly be due to a combination of either minor errors in its creation, natural bedding weaknesses in the stone, erosion, accidental or deliberate damage - the following geometric assessments were taken.

Overall and from the smallest to the largest diameter of the circles creating the segments for the bar's curved surfaces, based on its present condition, gives a variance of 16 inches with the measured diameters which range from 22 feet (smallest) to 23 feet 4 inches (largest) giving an average diameter of 22 feet 8 inches. The larger fits four out of the eight sides (two sides to each corner) quite well.

The leading edges of the bars' curved length are badly impaired in places, which is very common with ancient artefacts especially in this type of work when the surfaces meet at an angle of ninety degrees. Even so, with just a few physical points of reference of the original surfaces, it's a relatively simple matter to accurately recreate its shape and dimensions.

As I have said in the Sutton Hoo Whetstone reports (above, 2. The Sutton Hoo Whetstone-Sceptre Project: Stone Sculpture by Direct Carving) it is essential for all regular stonework to begin with a plan. Even with a relatively simple piece of work such as this it is evident that a basic setting out system has been applied and a template used.

The treatment of the sides of the bar proved similar in design and craftsmanship to the Sutton Hoo stone in that they are deliberately rounded in cross section. The slight rounding is marginally more evident on the 'face bed' or narrower side of the stone because it is fractionally denser than the 'top bed' or the wider side which, depending on its sited position, can be slightly more prone to the processes of erosion.

The end of the bar (Figure 128) clearly showing the consistency of the round-shouldered surfaces and the tapering curve towards the bar's end. The numerous minute 'stun' marks remain as a natural result of the mason's tooling during the shaping process indicating that this was its intended form. I have mentioned many times in other texts that these ancient tool marks are a true record of the human motion that created them!

The rounded ends of the wider face of the bar are formed by a subtle three-centred arc following through from the curve of the main body allowing a smooth contour a both ends of the bar.

The wider face of the bar curves away towards the ends springing from the centre line of the larger circle and naturally terminates as an edge meeting the rounded forms of the ends. (Figure 129)

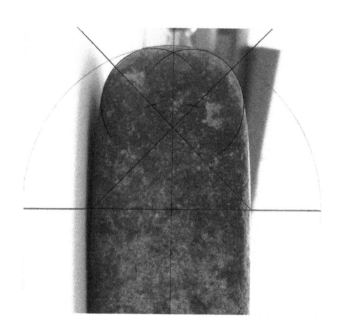

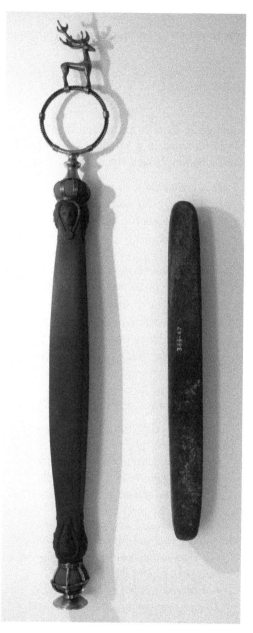

Figure 128 (top) The Uncleby whetstone from the end

Figure 130 A replica Sutton Hoo Stone with the Uncleby Stone

Figure 129 (bottom)   Three centres indicated by the 'Y' on centre line. This is the basic geometric layout for a three-centred (relevant segments of three circles) arc set out on an enlarged photo of the original stone bar.

Appendix 2 The York Legend

Brian Ansell

As an aside, there is a tradition that the craft of masonry was introduced in the reign of King Athelstan. This is recorded in a Middle English poem (circa 1390 AD), the so-called *York Legend*. The first verse records the king's concern:

Thys craft com ynto Englond as yow say
Yn tyme of good kynge Adelstonus' day
He made tho bothe halle and eke bowre
And hye templus of gret honowre
To sportyn him yn bothe day and nygth,
An to worsehepe hys God with alle hys mygth.
Thys goode lorde loved thys craft ful wel
And purposud to strengthyn hyt every del,
For dyvers defawtys that yn the crayft he fonde
He sende aboute ynto the londe
After alle the masonus of the crafte
To come to hym ful evene strayfte
For to amende these defautys alle
By good consel gef hyt mytgth fallen

This skill came into England as you say
In the days of good King Athelstan
He then made both halls and bowers
And high temples of great honour
In which to be seen both day and night
And to worship his God with all his might
This good lord loved skill greatly
And decided to strengthen it in every part
For the various faults that he found in the skill
He sent about in the land
For all the masons of the craft
To come to him straight away
In order to correct al those faults
By good advice it might turn out so.

Whatever the source for this tradition, it sets the introduction of skilled masons into England during the 10th c., long after some of the most remarkable Anglo-Saxon buildings had been completed (e.g. Jarrow, Hexham, Brixworth, etc.). It may nevertheless record a renewed interest in architecture during the 'golden age' of Athelstan's reign when there was a resurgence in Anglo-Saxon confidence after more than a century of warfare with the Danes.

Appendix 3 The Word *Greywacké*

The stone used for the bar is of a type called by masons 'greywacké' or in US usage 'graywacke'; despite its acute accent on the final vowel, the term is not French but derived from the German term *Grauwacke* denoting a conglomerate of grey-coloured grit. The accent, which is occasionally found in acute (é) and grave (è) versions, presumably serves to show that the final –*e* has to be pronounced as a separate syllable.

Figures 131 & 132

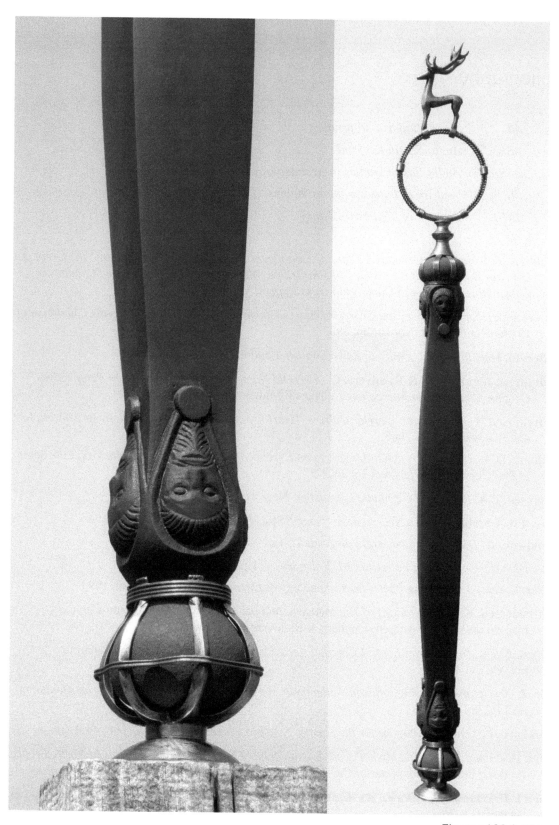

Figures 133 & 134

Bibliography

AJ   *The Antiquaries Journal*
ASE   *Anglo-Saxon England*
ASSAH   *Anglo-Saxon Studies in Archaeology and History*
JIES   *Journal of Indo-European Studies*
JMH   *Journal of Medieval History*

Alföldi, A. & Ross, M.C. *Cornuti: A Teutonic Contingent in the Service of Constantine the Great and Its Decisive Role in the Battle at the Milvian Bridge. With a Discussion of Bronze Statuettes of Constantine the Great* in *Dumbarton Oaks Papers*, Vol. 13, 1959

Almgren, B. *Helmets, Crowns and Warriors' Dress – from the Roman Emperors to the Chieftains of Uppland* in Lamm & Nordström, 1983

Anderson, E.R. *Folk-Taxonomies in Early English*, London, 2003

Andrén, A., Jennbert, K. & Raudvere, C. (eds) *Old Norse Religion in Long-Term Perspectives, Origins, Changes and Interactions*, Vägar till Midgard 8, Lund, 2006

Andrén, A. *A World of Stone: Warrior Culture, Hybridity and Old Norse Cosmology* in Andrén, Jennbert and Raudvere, (eds.), 2006.

Anthony, D.A. *A New Approach to Language and Archaeology: The Usatovo Culture and the Separation of Pre-Germanic* in *JIES*, vol.36, 2008

Antonsen, E.A. *Runes and Germanic Linguistics*, New York, 2002

Arne, T.J & Stolpe, H.J. *La Necropole de Vendel*, Stockholm, 1927

Arwidsson, G. *Die Gräberfunde von Valsgärde II: Valsgärde 8,* Uppsala, 1954

-   *Die Gräberfunde von Valsgärde III: Valsgärde 7,* Uppsala, 1977

Baker, C. (ed.), *Under Your Feet. The Archaeology of Dartford District*, Dartford, 1993

Bek-Pedersen, K. *Interpretations of Ynglingasaga and the Mabonigi – Some Norse-Celtic Correspondences* in Andrén, Jennbert, & Raudvere (eds), 2006a

Bettess, F. *The Anglo-Saxon Foot: A Computerized Assessment* in *Mediaeval Archaeology*, vol.XXXV, 1991

Blair, J. *Grid-planning in Anglo-Saxon Settlements: the Short-Perch and the Four-Perch Module* in *ASSAH*, vol.18, 2013

Blinkhorn, P. *Tolerating Pagans for the Sake of Trade* in *Current Archaeology*, no. 44, London, 1999

Bolin, H. *Animal Magic. The Mythological Significance of Elks, Boats and Humans in North Swedish Rock Art* in *Journal of Material Culture*, 2000

Bóna, I. *The Dawn of the Dark Ages. The Gepids and the Lombards in the Carpathian Basin*, Budapest, 1976

Bradley, R. and Fábregas Valcarce, R. *Crossing the Border: Contrasting Styles of Rock Art in the Prehistory of North-west Iberia* in *Oxford Journal of Archaeology* 17(3), 1998

Brentjes, B. *'Animal Style' and Shamanism Problems of Pictorial Tradition in Northern in Central Asia* in Davis-Kimball, Murphy, Koryakova & Yablonksy (eds.), 2000

Bruce-Mitford, R. *Aspects of Anglo-Saxon Archaeology. Sutton Hoo and Other Discoveries*, London, 1974

- *The Sutton Hoo Ship-Burial. Excavations, Background, The Ship, Dating and Inventory,* volume 1, London, 1975

- *The Sutton Hoo Ship Burial: Arms, Armour and Regalia*, volume 2. London, 1978

Burley, E. *A Catalogue and Survey of the Metal-Work from Traprain Law* in *Proceedings of the Society of Antiquares of Scotland*, 1955-56

Cabouret, B. Groslambert A.& Wolff, C. *Visions de l'Occident Romain - Hommages à Yann le Bohec*, vol. 2, Paris, 2012

Campbell, A. *Old English Grammar*, Oxford, 1987

Campbell, J. *The Anglo-Saxon State*, New York, 2000

Carver, M. (ed.), *The Age of Sutton Hoo*, Woodbridge, 1992

- *Sutton Hoo – Burial Ground of Kings?* London, 1998

- *Sutton Hoo: a Seventh Century Princely Burial Ground and its Context*, London, 2005

Carver, M., Sanmark, A. & Semple, S. *Signals of Belief in Early England. Anglo-Saxon Paganism Revisited*, Oxford, 2010

Chambers, R.W. *Widsith: A Study in Old English Heroic Legend*, Cambridge, 1912

Chaney, W.A. *Aethelberht's Code and the King's Number* in *American Journal of Legal History*, Vol. 6, No. 2, 1962

- *The Cult of Kingship in Anglo-Saxon England*, Manchester, 1970

Christiansen, E. (trans.) *Saxo Grammaticus Gesta Danorum*, Books X-XVI, BAR, International Series, vol.118, Oxford, 1980-1

- *The Norsemen in the Viking Age*, Oxford, 2002

Clark-Hall, J.R. *A Concise Anglo-Saxon Dictionary*, Ontario, 1984

Coblenz, W. *Kunst und Kunstgewerbe aus der Ur- und Frühgeschichte Sachsens,* Berlin, 1975

Cockayne, T. O. *Leechdoms, Wortcunning and Starcraft of Early England*, 3 vols. London, 1864–6

Cohen, S.L. *Viking Fortresses of the Trelleborg Type*, Copenhagen, 1965

- *The Sutton Hoo Whetstone* in *Speculum*, volume 41, 1966

Compton, T.M. *Victims of the Muses: Poet as Scapegoat, Warrior and Hero in Greco-Roman and Indo-European Myth and History,* Hellenic Studies 11, London, 2006

Corby, D.D.B. & Mitchell, J.G. *A Survey of British Metamorphic hone stones of the 9th to 15th centurise A.D. in the light of potassium-argon and natural remnant studies* in *Journal of Archaeological Science* volume 14 issue 5, 1987

Coutts, H. (ed.) *Golden Warriors of the Ukrainian Steppes*, Edinburgh, 1993

Davis-Kimball, J., Murphy, E.M., Koryakova, L. & Yablonksy, L.T. (eds.), *Kurgans Ritual Sites, and Settlements - Eurasian Bronze and Iron Age*, BAR International Series, Oxford, 2000

Dobat, A.S. *The State and the Strangers: the Role of External Forces in a Process of State Formation in Viking-Age South Scandinavia (c. ad 900--1050)* in *Viking and Medieval Scandinavia* 5, Turnhout, 2009

Einarsson, B. *Egil's Saga*, London, 2003

Ekwall, E. *The Concise Oxford Dictionary of English Place-Names*, 4th edition, Oxford, 1960

Ellis, S. E. *The Petrography and Provenance of Anglo-Saxon and Medieval English Honestones, with Notes on Some Other Hones* in *Bulletin of The British Museum (Natural History) Mineralogy*, Volume 2 no.3, London, 1969

Ellis Davidson, H.R. *Myths and Symbols in Pagan Europe,* New York, 1988

Enright, M.J. *The Sutton Hoo Whetstone Sceptre: a Study in Iconography and Cultural Milieu* in *Anglo-Saxon England*, vol.11, pp 119-134, Cambridge, 1982

- *The Lady With a Mead Cup; Ritual, Prphecy and Lordship in the European Warband from La Tène to the Viking Age*, Dublin, 1995
- *The Sutton Hoo Sceptre and the Roots of Celtic Kingship Theory*, Dublin, 2006

Erä-Esko, A. *Germanic Animal Art of Salin's Style I in Finland*, Helsinki, 1965

Evison, V.I. *Pagan Saxon Whetstones* in *AJ*, London, 1975

- *Dover Buckland Anglo-Saxon Cemetery*, London, 1987

Ewing, T. *Gods and Worshippers in the Viking and Germanic World*, Stroud, 2008

Fadlan, Ibn. *Ibn Fadlan and the Land of Darkness; Arab Travellers in the Far North.* Translated with an Introduction by Paul Lunde and Caroline Stone. 2012.

Fanning, S. *Bede, Imperium, and the Bretwaldas* in *Speculum* vol. 66 No. 1, 1991

Farrell, R. and Neuman de Vegvar, C. (eds) *Sutton Hoo: Fifty Years After*. Oxford, 1992

Fernie, E.C. *Anglo-Saxon Lengths and the Evidence of the Buildings* in *Mediaeval Archaeology*, vol.XXXV, 1991

Filmer-Sankey, W. *The 'Roman Emperor' in the Sutton Hoo Ship Burial* in *The Journal of the British Archaeological Association*, vol.149, 1995

Fischer, S. & Soulat, J. *Runic Swords and Raw Materials – Anglo-Saxon Interaction with Northern Gaul* in *Sachsensymposium* vol.58, 2007

Forsberg, L. *En kronologisk analys av ristningarna vid Nämforsen* in Forsberg and Larsson (eds.) 1993

Forsberg L. & Larsson T. (eds) *Ekonomi och näringsformer i nordisk bronsålder*, Umeå: Arkeologiska Institutionen, 1993

Franceschi, G., Jorn, A. & Magnus, B. *Ten Thousand Years of Folk Art in the North*: vol. 1, *Men, Gods and Masks in Nordic Iron Age Art*, Köln, 2005a

- vol. 2 *Bird, Beast and Man in Nordic Iron Age Art*, Köln, 2005b

Frodsham, P. *Forgetting Gefrin: Elements of the Past in the Past at Yeavering* in *Northern Archaeology*, vol.17/18, 1999

Frodsham, P. & O'Brien, C. (eds.) *Yeavering – People, Power & Place*, Stroud, 2005

Gamber, O. *The Sutton Hoo Military Equipment – an Attempted Reconstruction*, in *The Journal of the Arms and Armour Society,* volume V, 1966

Glob. P.V. *The Bog People. Iron Age Man Preserved*, London, 1969

Greis, G.P. & Geselowitz, M.N. *Sutton Hoo Art: Two Millennia of History* in Kendall & Wells, 1992

Griffiths, B. *Aspects of Anglo-Saxon Magic*, Hockwold-cum-Wilton, 1996

Grigsby, J. *Warriors of the Wasteland*, London, 2002

- *Beowulf and Grendel*, London, 2005

Gunnell, T. *The Origins of Drama in Scandinavia,* Woodbridge, 1995

Hallström, G. *Monumental Art of Northern Sweden from the Stone Age*, Stockholm, 1960

Hansen, S.C. *Whetstones from Viking Age Iceland as Part of the Trans-Atlantic Trade in Basic Commodities*, Thesis Sigillum Universitatis Islandiae, Rekjavik, 2009

Haslam, J. *The Metrology of Anglo-Saxon Cricklade* **in** *Mediaeval Archaeology*, vol.XXX, 1986

Hedeager, L. *Iron Age Myth and Materiality: An Archaeology of Scandinavia AD 400-1000*, Abingdon, 2011

Helmbrecht, M. *Innere Strukturen von Siedlungen und Gräberfeldern als Spiegel gesellschaftlicher Wirklichkeit?* in *57th Internationalen Sachsensymposions vom 26. bis 30. August 2006,* Münster, 2006.

- *Figures with horned headgear. A case study of context analysis and social significance of pictures in Vendel and Viking Age Scandinavia,* in *Lund Archaeological Review* 13-14 (2007-2008). Lund, 2008

Helskog, K. *Maleness and Femaleness in the Sky and in the Underworld – and in between* in K. Helskog and B. Olsen (eds.) *Perceiving Rock Art: Social and Political Perspectives*, Oslo, 1995

Henig, M. *The Art of Roman Britain*, London, 1995

Herrmann, J. *The Northern Slavs* in Wilson, D.M. (ed.), 1980

Herzog, R. and Koller; A. *Die Alamannen*, Stuttgart, 2001

Hicks, C. *The Birds on the Sutton Hoo Purse* in *ASE*, vol. 15, 1986

- *Animals in Early Medieval Art*, Edinburgh, 1993

Hills, C. *The Anglo-Saxon Cemetery at Spong Hill, North Elmham. Part I. Catalogue of Cremations nos. 20-64 and 1000-1690*, East Anglian Archaeology Report no. 6, Gressenhall, 1977

Hines, J. A New Corpus of Anglo-, Saxon Great Square Headed Brooches, Woodbridge. 1997.

Hinton, D. *The Fifth and Sixth Centuries: Reorganization Among the Ruins* in Karkov, (ed.), 1999

- *Gold and Gilt, Pots and Pins: Possessions and People in Medieval Britain,* Oxford, 2005

Hodges ,H.,1964. Artefacts. London

Holthausen, F. *Altenglisches Etymologisches Worterbuch*, Heidelberg, 1974

Hope-Taylor, B. *Yeavering – An Anglo-British Centre of Early Northumbria*, Dept of the Environment Archaeological Reports, no. 7, London, 1977

Hreinsson, V. (general editor), *The Complete Sagas of the Icelanders,* 5 vols, Reykjavik, 1997

Huggins, P.J. *Yeavering Measurements: An Alternative View* in *Mediaeval Archaeology*, vol.XXV, 1981

- *Anglo-Saxon Timber Building Measurements: Recent Results* in *Mediaeval Archaeology*, vol.XXXV, 1991

James, E. *Burial and Status in the Early Medieval West* in *Transactions of the Royal Historical Society,* vol.39, 1989

Janse, H. *Kultföremål - En kritisk granskning av arkeologins förhållande till religion mot bakgrund av fynd från Novgorod, Gorodische och Staraja Ladoga,* Uppsala, 2004

Jensen, R. *Härjedalen och Jämtland* in *Hällristningar och hällmålningar i Sverige,* Stockholm, 1989

Jones, G. *A History of the Vikings,* Oxford, 1968

Jørgensen, L., Storgaard, B. & Thomsen, L.G. (eds.) *The Spoils of Victory – The North in the Shadow of the Roman Empire,* Copenhagen, 2003

Karkov, C.E. The *Archaeology of Anglo-Saxon England: Basic Readings,* London, 1999

Kaul, F. *Ships on Bronzes.* Copenhagen, 1998

Keary, C.F. (ed. Poole, R.S.) *A Catalogue of English Coins in the British Museum. Anglo-Saxon Series.* Volume 1, London, 1887

Kendall, C.B. & Wells, P.S. (eds) *Voyage to the Otherworld – the Legacy of Sutton Hoo,* Minneapolis, 1992

Kendrick, Thomas. *The Sutton Hoo Finds* in The British Museum Quarterly 13 no. 4. 1939.

Kershaw, K. *The One-Eyed God. Odin and the (Indo-)Germanic Männerbünde,* JIES Monograph, no. 36, Washington, 2000

Keynes, S. *Rædwald The Bretwalda* in Kendall and Wells, (eds.), 1992

Kitchingham, G. *The Saxon Period* in Baker, (ed.), 1993

Koch, J.T. *Celtic Culture: A Historical Encyclopedia,* London, 2006

Kuznetsov, P. *An Indo-Iranian Symbol of Power in the Earliest Steppe Kurgans* in *JIES,* vol. 33, nos. 3/4, 2005

Laing, L. *The Mote of Mark and the Origins of Celtic Interlace* in *Antiquity,* vol. XLIX, 1975

Lamm, J.P. *On the Cult of Multiple-Headed Gods in England and in the Baltic Area* in *Przegląd Archeologiczny,* Volume 34, 1987

Lamm, J.P. & Nordström, H.-Å., *Vendel Period Studies. Transactions of the Boat-Grave Symposium in Stockholm, February 2-3, 1981,* Stockholm, 1983

Lass, R. *Old English: A Historical Linguistic Companion,* Cambridge, 1994

László, G. *The Art of the Migration Period,* London, 1970

Lieberman, A. *Berserkir: A Double Legend* in *Brathair* vol. 4, no. 2, 2004

Lindow, J. *Murder and Vengeance Among the Gods: Baldr in Scandinavian Mythology,* FF Communications vol.CXVI no.262, Helsinki, 1997

- *Narrative Worlds, Human Environments and Poets. The Case of Bragi* in Andrén, Jennbert, & Raudvere (eds), 2006a

Lindqvist, C. *Fångstfolkets bilder. En studie av de nordfennoskandiska kustanknutna jägarhällristningarna,* Stockholm: Dissertation, 1994

Livingston, M. *The Roads to Brunanburh* in Livingston (ed.), 2011

- (ed.) *The Battle of Brunanburh. A Casebook,* Exeter, 2011

Looijenga, T. *Texts and Contexts of the Oldest Runic Inscriptions,* Leiden, 2003

Loyn, H.R. *The Term Ealdorman in the Translations Prepared at the Time of King Alfred* in *The English Historical Review*, vol.68, 1953

Lucy, S. *Early Medieval Burial at Yeavering: A Retrospective* in Frodsham & O'Brien, 2005

Lyttleton, J. *Loughpark 'Crannog' Revisited* in *Journal of the Galway Archaeological and Historical Society*, Vol. 50, 1998

MacLeod, M. & Mees, B. *Runic Amulets and Magic Objects,* Woodbridge, 2006

Magoun, F.P. Jr. *The Sutton Hoo Ship-Burial: A Chronological Bibliography*, in *Speculum*, volume 29, 1954

Mallory, J.P. & Mair, V.H. *The Tarim Mummies. Ancient China and the Mystery of the Earliest Peoples from the West*, London, 2000

Malmer, M. *Har nordlig och sydlig hällristningstradition påverkat varandra – och i så fall hur, och varför?* in *Arkeologi i norr* 3, Umeå, 1992

Marek, L. *Early Medieval Swords from Central and Eastern Europe; Dilemmas of an Archaeologist and a Student of Arms*, Wroclaw, 2005

Markey, T.L. *A North Sea Germanic Reader*, München, 1976

Mayr-Harting, H. *Charlemagne, the Saxons, and the Imperial Coronation of 800* in *The English Historical Review*, Vol. 111, No. 444, 1996

Meaney, A. *Anglo-Saxon Amulets and Curing Stones,* B.A.R. British Series, no.96, Oxford, 1981

Menghin, W. *Das Schwert im Frühen Mittelalter*, Stuttgart, 1983

- *Frühgeschichte Bayerns: Römer und Germanen, Baiern und Schwaben, Franken und Slawen,* Stuttgart, 1990

Mitchell, Stephen A. *The Whetstone as Symbol of Authority in Old English and Old Norse* in Scandinavian Studies The Journal of the Society for the Advancement of Scandinavian Study since 1911. Volume 57 no. 1. 1985.

Moore, T.D. *The Petrography and Archaeology of English Honestones*, in *Journal of Archaeological Science* vol. 5, 1978

Mortimer, P. *Woden's Warriors: Warfare, Beliefs, Arms and Armour in Northern Europe during the 6th and 7th Centuries*, Ely, 2011

Motz, L. *The King, the Champion and the Sorceror: A Study in Germanic Myth*, Studia Medievalia Septentrionalia no.1, Vienna, 1995

Mulk, I-M. *Nyfunna hällristningar avbildar samiska segelbåtar* in *Poulär Arkeologi*, Nr. 4, 1998

Müller-Wille, M. *Opferkulte der Germanen und Slawen*, Stuttgart, 1999

Myres, J.N.L. *The English Settlements,* Oxford History of England, vol.1b, Oxford, 1989

Newton, S. *The Origin of Beowulf and the Pre-Viking Kingdom of East Anglia*, Cambridge, 1993

Nielsen, H.F. *The Germanic Languages. Origins and Early Dialectal Interrelations*, London, 1989

Noble, T.F.X. (ed.), *From Roman Provinces to Medieval Kingdoms*, London, 2006

North, R. *Heathen Gods in Old English Literature*, Cambridge Studies in Anglo-Saxon England, 22, Cambridge, 1997

O'Connor, L. Irish *Iron Age and Early Christian Whetstones* in *The Journal of the Royal Society of Antiquaries of Ireland*, vol. 121, 1991

Orel, V. *A Handbook of Germanic Etymology*, Leiden, 2003

- *Paddenberg, D. Parchim-Löddigsee, Late Slavonic Temple and Trading Site* in Andrén, Jennbert, Raudvere (eds.), 2006

Owen-Crocker, G.R. *Hawks and Horse-Trappings* in Scragg (ed.), 1991

Pálsson, H. &Edwards, P. *Eyrbyggia Saga*, Edinburgh, 1973

Perkins, R. *Thor the Wind Raiser and the Eyrarland Image*, London, 2001

Pesch, A. *Goldbrakteaten der Völkerwaderungszeit – Thema und Variation*, Berlin, 2007

Petrie, F. *Weights and Measures*, London, 1934

Pheifer, J.D. (ed.) *Old English Glosses in the Épinal-Erfurt Glossary*, Oxford, 1974

Pluskowski, A. *The Beast Within? Breaching Human – Animal Boundaries in Anglo-Saxon Paganism* in *Saxon*, no. 45, 2007

Pohl, W. *Telling the Difference. Signs of Ethnic Identity* in Noble, (ed.), 2006

Pollington, S. *Leechcraft - Early English Charms, Plantlore and Healing*, Hockwold-cum-Wilton, 2000

- *The English Warrior from Earliest Times till 1066*, 2nd edition, Hockwold-cum-Wilton, 2002

- *Meadhall – The Feasting Tradition in Anglo-Saxon England*, Hockwold-cum-Wilton, 2003

- *Anglo-Saxon Burial Mounds: Princely Burials in the 6th & 7th Centuries,* Swaffham, 2008

- *The Elder Gods – The Other-World of Early England*, Ely, 2011a

- *The Meadhall Community* in *JMH* vol.37, 2011b

- *The English Warrior*, 3rd edition (forthcoming)

- *Runes in Context* (forthcoming, b)

Pollington, S., Kerr, L. & Hammond, B. *Wayland's Work: Anglo-Saxon Art, Myth and Material Culture from the 4th to the 7th Century*, Ely, 2010

Polomé, E. (ed.), *Old Norse Literature and Mythology: A Symposium*, Austin, 1969

- *Essays on Germanic Religion*, *JIES* monograph 6, Washington, 1989

- (ed.) *Indo-European Religion After Dumézil*, *JIES* monograph 16, Washington, 1996

Price, N. (ed.) *The Archaeology of Shamanism*, London, 2001

- *The Viking Way. Religion and War in Late Iron Age Scandinavia*, AUN 31, Uppsala, 2003

- *What's in a name? An archaeological identity crisis for the Norse gods (and some of their friends)* in Andrén, Jennbert, Raudvere (eds.), 2006

Price, N. & Mortimer, P. *An Eye for Odin? Divine role playing at Sutton Hoo,* (in press)

Price, T.D., Frei, K.M., Dobat, A.S., Lynnerup, N. & Bennike, P. *Who was in Harold Bluetooth's Army? Strontium isotope investigation of the cemetery at the Viking Fortress of Trelleborg, Denmark* in *Antiquity* volume 85 no. 328, 2011

Raleigh Radford, C.A. *The Saxon House: A Review and Some Parallels* in *Mediaeval Archaeology*, vol.I, 1957

Ramqvist, P. *Ångermanland, Västerbotten och Lappland* in *Hällristningar och Hällmålningar i Sverige*, Stockholm, 1989

Raynor, K. *The Rempstone Mount,* East Leake, 2010

Redin. M. *Studies in Uncompounded Personal names in Old English*, Uppsala, 1919

Reynolds, N. *The Kings's Whetstone: A Footnote*, in *Antiquity* vol.LIV, 1980.

Rieck, F. *The Ships from Nydam Bog* in Jørgensen, Storgaard, & Thomsen (eds.), 2003

Ringe, D. *From Proto-Indo-European to Proto-Germanic, A Linguistic History of English*, volume 1, Oxford, 2006

Rives, J.B. (trans.) *Tacitus – Germania*, Oxford, 1999

Robinson, F.C. *Beowulf and the Appositive Style,* Knoxville, 1985

Russell, J.C. *The Germanization of Medieval Christianity. A Sociohistorical Approach to Religious Transformation*, Oxford, 1994

Ryan, M. *The Sutton Hoo Ship Burial and Ireland: Some Celtic Perspectives* in Farrell and Neuman de Vegvar, (eds.) 1992

Salin, E. *La Civilisation Mérovingienne*, 4 vols, Paris, 1949-59

Scarfe, N. *Suffolk in the Middle Ages*, Woodbridge, 1986

Schichler, R.L. *Glæd man at Heorot: Beowulf and the Anglo-Saxon Psalter* in *Leeds Studies in English*, vol. 27, 1996

Schön, M.D. *Feddersen Wierde, Fallward, Flögeln. Archäologie im Museum Burg Bederkesa, Landkreis Cuxhaven*, Bad Bederkesa, 1999

Schutz, H. *The Prehistory of Germanic Europe*, London, 1983

Scott Littleton, C. *The New Comparative Mythology. An Anthropological Assessment of the Theories of Georges Dumézil*, Berkeley, 1973

Scragg, D.J. (ed.) *The Battle of Maldon*, Manchester, 1981

- *The Battle of Maldon AD 991*, Oxford, 1991

Shaw, P. *The Uses of Wodan – The Development of his Cult and of Medieval Literary Responses to It* (Ph.D.thesis), 2002

  - *The Origins of the Theophoric Week in the Germanic Languages* in *Early Medieval Europe*, vol. 15, 2007

Sherley-Price, L. *Ecclesiastical History of the English People*, Harmondsworth, 1990

Słupecki, L. *The Temple at Rhetra-Riedegost* in Andrén, Jennbert and Raudvere, 2006

Simek, R. *Dictionary of Northern Mythology*, Cambridge, 1993

Simpson, J., *The King's Whetstone* in *Antiquity* 53, Cambridge, 1979

Smedley, N. & Owles, E.J. *A Sherd of Ipswich Ware with Face-Mask Decoration* in *Proceedings of the Suffolk Institute of Archaeology*, vol. XXX part 1, 1967

Snyder, C.A. *An Age of Tyrants. Britain and the Britons A.D. 400-600,* Stroud, 1998

Bibliography

Speidel, M.P. *Ancient Germanic Warriors – Warrior Styles from Trajan's Column to Icelandic Sagas*, London, 2004

- *Balder and Loki on Germanic Silver Coins of the First Century B.C.* in Cabouret, Groslambert & Wolff, 2012

Storms, G. *The Sutton Hoo Ship Burial: An Interpretation* in *Berichten van de Rijksdienst voor het Oudheid Kundig Bodemonderzoek*, vol. 28, 1978

Sturlusson, S. (trans.Young, J.I.) *Prose Edda*, London, 1954

Sundqvist, O. *Freyr's Offspring: Rulers and Religion in Ancient Svea Society*, Uppsala, 2002.

Suzuki, S. *Anglo-Saxon Button Brooches: Typology, Genealogy, Chronology*: 10 Anglo-Saxon Studies. Woodbridge, 2008

Swanton, M. (trans. & ed.) *The Anglo-Saxon Chronicles*, London, 1996

Sweet H. (ed. Whitlock, D.) *Sweet's Anglo-Saxon Reader in Prose and Verse*, Oxford, 1967

- (ed.Hoad, T.F.) *A Second Anglo-Saxon Reader: Archaic and Dialectal*, Oxford, 1979

Taylor, P.B. and Auden W. H. (trans.), *The Elder Edda*, London, 1969

Tilley, C. *Material Culture and Text. The Art of Ambiguity*, London, 1991

Timby, J. *Sancton I Anglo-Saxon Cemetery Excavations Carried Out Between 1976 and 1980* in *AJ*, vol. 150, London, 1993

Tolley, C. *Shamanism in Norse Myth and Magic*, Helsinki, 2009

Truc, M.-C. *Les Tombes Aristocratiques Franques de Saint Dizier* in *Archéopages* vol. 18: *Migrations*, Paris, 2007

Tummuscheit, A. *Pre-Christian Cult at Arkona* in Andrén, Jennbert and Raudvere, 2006

Vang Petersen, P. *Warrior Art, Religion and Symbolism* in Jørgensen, Storgaard & Thomsen, (eds.), 2003

Waggoner, B. (trans. & ed.) *Norse Magical and Herbal Healing. A Medical Book from Medieval Iceland*, Newhaven, 2011

Wallace-Hadrill,J. M. *Early Medieval History*, Oxford, 1975

Wallis, R.J. *Waking Ancestor Spirits: Neo-Shamanic Engagements with Archaeology* in Price (ed.), 2001

Walton Rogers, P. *Cloth & Clothing in Early Anglo-Saxon England, AD 450-700*, CBA Research Reports, London, 2006

Wells, P.S. B*eyond, Celts, Germans and Scythians – Archaeology and Identity in Iron Age Europe*, London, 2001

West, M.L. *Indo-European Poetry and Myth*, London, 2007

Wilson, D. *Anglo-Saxon Paganism*, London, 1992

Wilson, D.M. (ed.) *The Northern World. The History and Heritage of Northern Europe*, London, 1980

Woodard, R.W. *Indo-European Sacred Space. Vedic and Roman Cult*, Urbana, 2006

Some of our other title

Please see www.asbooks.co.uk for latest availability and prices

First Steps in Old English
An easy to follow language course for the beginner
Stephen Pollington

A complete and easy to use Old English language course that contains all the exercises and texts needed to learn Old English. This course has been designed to be of help to a wide range of students, from those who are teaching themselves at home, to undergraduates who are learning Old English as part of their English degree course. The author has adopted a step-by-step approach that enables students of differing abilities to advance at their own pace. The course includes practice and translation exercises, a glossary of the words used in the course, and many Old English texts, including the *Battle of Brunanburh* and *Battle of Maldon*.

£16-95   272 pages

Old English Poems, Prose & Lessons   2 CDs
read by Stephen Pollington

These CDs contain lessons and texts from *First Steps in Old English*.

Tracks include: 1. Deor. 2. Beowulf – The Funeral of Scyld Scefing. 3. Engla Tocyme (The Arrival of the English). 4. Ines Domas. Two Extracts from the Laws of King Ine. 5. Deniga Hergung (The Danes' Harrying) Anglo-Saxon Chronicle Entry AD997. 6. Durham 7. The Ordeal (Be ðon ðe ordales weddigaþ) 8. Wið Dweorh (Against a Dwarf) 9. Wið Wennum (Against Wens) 10. Wið Wæterælfadle (Against Waterelf Sickness) 11. The Nine Herbs Charm 12. Læcedomas (Leechdoms) 13. Beowulf's Greeting 14. The Battle of Brunanburh 15. A Guide to Pronunciation.
And more than 30 other lessons and extracts of Old English verse and prose.

£15   2 CDs - Free Old English transcript from www.asbooks.co.uk.

Learn Old English with Leofwin
Matt Love

This is a new approach to learning old English – as a *living language*. Leofwin and his family are your guides through six lively, entertaining, topic-based units. New vocabulary and grammar are presented in context, step by step, so that younger readers and non-language specialists can feel engaged rather than intimidated. The author has complemented the text with a wealth of illustrations. There are listening, speaking, reading and writing exercises throughout. Free soundtracks available on the Anglo-Saxon Books website.

£14.95 160 pages

Wordcraft: Concise English/Old English Dictionary and Thesaurus
Stephen Pollington

This book provides Old English equivalents to the commoner modern words in both dictionary and thesaurus formats. The Thesaurus presents vocabulary relevant to a wide range of individual topics in alphabetical lists, thus making it easily accessible to those with specific areas of interest. Each thematic listing is encoded for cross-reference from the Dictionary. The two sections will be of invaluable assistance to students of the language, as well as to those with either a general or a specific interest in the Anglo-Saxon period.

£9.95   256 pages

An Introduction to the Old English Language and its Literature
Stephen Pollington

The purpose of this general introduction to Old English is not to deal with the teaching of Old English but to dispel some misconceptions about the language and to give an outline of its structure and its literature. Some basic knowledge of these is essential to an understanding of the early period of English history and the present form of the language.

£5.95   48 pages

Monasteriales Indicia
The Anglo-Saxon Monastic Sign Language
Edited with notes and translation by Debby Banham

The *Monasteriales Indicia* is one of very few texts which let us see how evryday life was lived in monasteries in the early Middle Ages. Written in Old English and preserved in a manuscript of the mid-eleventh century, it consists of 127 signs used by Anglo-Saxon monks during the times when the Benedictine Rule forbade them to speak. These indicate the foods the monks ate, the clothes they wore, and the books they used in church and chapter, as well as the tools they used in their daily life, and persons they might meet both in the monastery and outside. The text is printed here with a parallel translation. The introduction gives a summary of the background, both historical and textual, as well as a brief look at the later evidence for monastic sign language in England.

£5.95   96 pages

Woden's Warriors
Warfare, Beliefs, Arms & Armour in Northern Europe
during the 6-7th Centuries
Paul Mortimer

This book explores some of the resources available to warriors in Anglo-Saxon England and northern Europe during the 6th and 7th centuries. In this time of great change, the remains of old empires were still visible but new ideas and methods of organisation were making possible the growth of centralised kingdoms which became the nation states that dominated Europe for the next thousand years.

It was also a time of great artistry and wealth, much of which was devoted to the creation of works of art devoted to war and warfare. It is a time when traditional symbols of identity and the old gods were mingling with new patterns of belief.

The aim of this book is to try and provide the reader with glimpses of what it was like to be part of a warrior society.

£45 305 black & white and colour illustrations - large format hardback 304 pages

The Battle of Maldon: Text and Translation
Translated and edited by Bill Griffiths

The Battle of Maldon was fought between the men of Essex and the Vikings in AD 991. The action was captured in an Anglo-Saxon poem whose vividness and heroic spirit has fascinated readers and scholars for generations. *The Battle of Maldon* includes the source text; edited text; parallel literal translation; verse translation; a review of 103 books and articles.

This edition has a helpful guide to Old English verse.

£5.95   96 pages

Beowulf: Text and Translation
Translated by John Porter

The verse in which the story unfolds is, by common consent, the finest writing surviving in Old English, a text that all students of the language and many general readers will want to tackle in the original form. To aid understanding of the Old English, a literal word-by-word translation is printed opposite the edited text and provides a practical key to this Anglo-Saxon masterpiece.

£6.95   192 pages

Tastes of Anglo-Saxon England

Mary Savelli

These easy to follow recipes will enable you to enjoy a mix of ingredients and flavours that were widely known in Anglo-Saxon England but are rarely experienced today. In addition to the 46 recipes, there is background information about households and cooking techniques.

£5.95   80 pages

An Introduction to Early English Law

Bill Griffiths

Much of Anglo-Saxon life followed a traditional pattern, of custom, and of dependence on kin-groups for land, support and security. The Viking incursions of the ninth century and the reconquest of the north that followed both disturbed this pattern and led to a new emphasis on centralized power and law, with royal and ecclesiastical officials prominent as arbitrators and settlers of disputes. The diversity and development of early English law is sampled here by selecting several law-codes to be read in translation - that of Æthelbert of Kent, being the first to be issued in England, Alfred the Great's, the most clearly thought-out of all, and short codes from the reigns of Edmund and Æthelred the Unready.

£5.95 96 pages

English Heroic Legends

Kathleen Herbert

The author has taken the skeletons of ancient Germanic legends about great kings, queens and heroes, and put flesh on them. Kathleen Herbert's extensive knowledge of the period is reflected in the wealth of detail she brings to these tales of adventure, passion, bloodshed and magic.

The book is in two parts. First are the stories that originate deep in the past, yet because they have not been hackneyed, they are still strange and enchanting. After that there is a selection of the source material, with information about where it can be found and some discussion about how it can be used.

£9-95 268 pages

Peace-Weavers and Shield-Maidens: Women in Early English Society

Kathleen Herbert

The recorded history of the English people did not start in 1066 as popularly believed but one-thousand years earlier. The Roman historian Cornelius Tacitus noted in *Germania*, published in the year 98, that the English (Latin *Anglii*), who lived in the southern part of the Jutland peninsula, were members of an alliance of Goddess-worshippers. The author has taken that as an appropriate opening to an account of the earliest Englishwomen, the part they played in the making of England, what they did in peace and war, the impressions they left in Britain and on the continent, how they were recorded in the chronicles, how they come alive in heroic verse and riddles.

£5.95 64 pages

Anglo-Saxon Runes

John. M. Kemble

Kemble's essay *On Anglo-Saxon Runes* first appeared in the journal *Archaeologia* for 1840; it draws on the work of Wilhelm Grimm, but breaks new ground for Anglo-Saxon studies in his survey of the Ruthwell Cross and the Cynewulf poems. It is an expression both of his own indomitable spirit and of the fascination and mystery of the Runes themselves, making one of the most attractive introductions to the topic. For this edition new notes have been supplied, which include translations of Latin and Old English material quoted in the text, to make this key work in the study of runes more accessible to the general reader.

£5.95 80 pages

Looking for the Lost Gods of England

Kathleen Herbert

Kathleen Herbert sifts through the royal genealogies, charms, verse and other sources to find clues to the names and attributes of the Gods and Goddesses of the early English. The earliest account of English heathen practices reveals that they worshipped the Earth Mother and called her Nerthus. The tales, beliefs and traditions of that time are still with us in, for example, Sand able to stir our minds and imaginations.

£5.95 64 pages

Rudiments of Runelore

Stephen Pollington

This book provides both a comprehensive introduction for those coming to the subject for the first time, and a handy and inexpensive reference work for those with some knowledge of the subject. The *Abecedarium Nordmannicum* and the English, Norwegian and Icelandic rune poems are included in their original and translated form. Also included is work on the three Brandon runic inscriptions and the Norfolk 'Tiw' runes.

£5.95   88 pages

Anglo-Saxon FAQs

Stephen Pollington

125 questions and answers on a wide range of topics.

Are there any Anglo-Saxon jokes? Who was the Venerable Bede? Did the women wear make-up? What musical instruments did they have? How was food preserved? Did they have shops? Did their ships have sails? Why was Ethelred called 'Unready'? Did they have clocks? Did they celebrate Christmas? What are runes? What weapons and tactics did they use? Were there female warriors? What was the Synod of Whitby?

£9.95   128pages

Dark Age Naval Power

A Reassessment of Frankish and Anglo-Saxon Seafaring Activity

John Haywood

In the first edition of this work, published in 1991, John Haywood argued that the capabilities of the pre-Viking Germanic seafarers had been greatly underestimated. Since that time, his reassessment of Frankish and Anglo-Saxon shipbuilding and seafaring has been widely praised and accepted.

In this second edition, some sections of the book have been revised and updated to include information gained from excavations and sea trials with sailing replicas of early ships. The new evidence supports the author's argument that early Germanic shipbuilding and seafaring skills were far more advanced than previously thought. It also supports the view that Viking ships and seaborne activities were not as revolutionary as is commonly believed.

'The book remains a historical study of the first order. It is required reading for our seminar on medieval seafaring at Texas A & M University and is essential reading for anyone interested in the subject.'

F. H. Van Doorninck, *The American Neptune*

£16.95 hardback 224 pages

English Martial Arts

Terry Brown

Little is known about the very early history of English martial arts but it is likely that methods, techniques and principles were passed on from one generation to the next for centuries. By the sixteenth century English martial artists had their own governing body which controlled its members in much the same way as do modern-day martial arts organisations. It is apparent from contemporary evidence that the Company of Maisters taught and practised a fighting system that ranks as high in terms of effectiveness and pedigree as any in the world.

In the first part of the book the author investigates the weapons, history and development of the English fighting system and looks at some of the attitudes, beliefs and social pressures that helped mould it.

Part two deals with English fighting techniques drawn from books and manuscripts that recorded the system at various stages in its history. All of the methods and techniques shown in this book are authentic and have not been created by the author. The theories that underlie the system are explained in a chapter on *The Principles of True Fighting*. All of the techniques covered are illustrated with photographs and accompanied by instructions. Techniques included are for bare-fist fighting, broadsword, quarterstaff, bill, sword and buckler, sword and dagger.

Experienced martial artists, irrespective of the style they practice, will recognise that the techniques and methods of this system are based on principles that are as valid as those underlying the system that they practice.

£16.95 220 photos 240 pages

Plain English – A Wealth of Words
Bryan Evans

The message here is not that we should strive in a narrow-minded way to scorn and drive out all borrowed words – it is that, if we stop and think, we can probably find a plain English word for what we want to say. We will thus keep plain English alive and help it thrive. We have been given a great gift, let us wherever possible use it and keep it safe.

This wordbook outlines the story of English then it offers 'A hundred words to start you off' (*shorten* rather than *abbreviate*, *speed up* instead of *accelerate*, *drive home* rather than *emphasize*, and so on). In the main part of the book will be found over 10,000 English words that are still alive and well, then a list of some 3,600 borrowed words, with suggestions about English words we might use instead. It is hoped that this book will help readers think about the words they use, and in doing so speak and write more clearly.

£9.95   328 pages

A Guide to Late Anglo-Saxon England
From Alfred to Eadgar II 871–1074
Donald Henson

This guide has been prepared with the aim of providing the general readers with both an overview of the period and a wealth of background information. Facts and figures are presented in a way that makes this a useful reference handbook.

Contents include: The Origins of England; Physical Geography; Human Geography; English Society; Government and Politics; The Church; Language and Literature; Personal Names; Effects of the Norman Conquest. All of the kings from Alfred to Eadgar II are dealt with separately and there is a chronicle of events for each of their reigns. There are also maps, family trees and extensive appendices.

£9.95   6 maps, 3 family trees, 208 pages

The English Elite in 1066 - Gone but not forgotten
Donald Henson

The people listed in this book formed the topmost section of the ruling elite in 1066. It includes all those who held office between the death of Eadward III (January 1066) and the abdication of Eadgar II (December 1066). There are 455 individuals in the main entries and these have been divided according to their office or position.

The following information is listed where available:

What is known of their life;

Their landed wealth;

The early sources in which information about the individual can be found
Modern references that give details about his or her life.

In addition to the biographical details, there is a wealth of background information about English society and government. A series of appendices provide detailed information about particular topics or groups of people.

£16.95   272 pages

Tolkien's *Mythology for England*
A Guide to Middle-Earth
Edmund Wainwright

Tolkien set out to create a mythology for England and the English but the popularity of his books and the recent films has spread across the English-speaking world and beyond.

You will find here an outline of Tolkien's life and work. The main part of the book consists of an alphabetical subject entry which will help you gain a greater understanding of Tolkien's Middle-Earth, the creatures that inhabit it, and the languages they spoke. It will also give an insight into a culture and way-of-life that extolled values which are as valid today as they were over 1,000 years ago.

This book focuses on *The Lord of the Rings* and shows how Tolkien's knowledge of Anglo-Saxon and Norse literature and history helped shape its plot and characters.

£9-95 hardback 128 pages

The Origins of the Anglo-Saxons
Donald Henson
This book has three great strengths.

First, it pulls together and summarises the whole range of evidence bearing on the subject, offering an up-to-date assessment: the book is, in other words, a highly efficient introduction to the subject. Second – perhaps reflecting Henson's position as a leading practitioner of public archaeology (he is currently Education and Outreach Co-ordinator for the Council for British Archaeology) – the book is refreshingly jargon free and accessible. Third, Henson is not afraid to offer strong, controversial interpretations. The Origins of the Anglo-Saxons can therefore be strongly recommended to those who want a detailed road-map of the evidence and debates for the migration period.

Current Archaeology

£16..95 296 pages

The Elder Gods – The Otherworld of Early England
Stephen Pollington
The purpose of the work is to bring together a range of evidence for pre-Christian beliefs and attitudes to the Otherworld drawn from archaeology, linguistics, literary studies and comparative mythology. The rich and varied English tradition influenced the worldview of the later mediaeval and Norse societies. Aspects of this tradition are with us still in the 21st century.

£35 70 illustrations 528 pages

Anglo-Saxon Riddles

Translated by John Porter
Here you will find ingenious characters who speak their names in riddles, and meet a one-eyed garlic seller, a bookworm, an iceberg, an oyster, the sun and moon and a host of others from the everyday life and imagination of the Anglo-Saxons. Their sense of the awesome power of creation goes hand in hand with a frank delight in obscenity, a fascination with disguise and with the mysterious processes by which the natural world is turned to human use. This edition contains **all 95 riddles of the Exeter Book in both Old English and Modern English.**

£5.95 144 page

English Sea Power 871-1100 AD

John Pullen-Appleby
This work examines the largely untold story of English sea power during the period 871 to 1100. It was an age when English kings deployed warships first against Scandinavian invaders and later in support of Continental allies.

The author has gathered together information about the appearance of warships and how they were financed, crewed, and deployed.

£9.95 hardback 114 pages

Anglo-Saxon Burial Mounds
Princely Burials in the 6th & 7th centuries
Stephen Pollington

This is the first book-length treatment of Anglo-Saxon Barrows in English. It brings together some of the evidence from Sutton Hoo and elsewhere in England for these magnificent burials and sets them in their historical, religious and social context.

The first section comprises the physical construction and symbolic meaning of these monuments. The second offers a comprehensive listing of known Anglo-Saxon barrows with notes on their contents and the circumstances of their discovery. The five appendices deal with literary and place-name evidence.

£16.95   272 pages

Leechcraft: Early English Charms, Plantlore and Healing
Stephen Pollington

An unequalled examination of every aspect of early English healing, including the use of plants, amulets, charms, and prayer. Other topics covered include Anglo-Saxon witchcraft; tree-lore; gods, elves and dwarves.

The author has brought together a wide range of evidence for the English healing tradition, and presented it in a clear and readable manner. The extensive 2,000-entry index makes it possible for the reader to quickly find specific information.

The three key Old English texts are reproduced in full, accompanied by new translations.

Bald's Third Leechbook; *Lacnunga*; *Old English Herbarium*.

£25   28 illustrations   536 pages

Anglo-Saxon Attitudes – A short introduction to Anglo-Saxonism
J.A. Hilton

This is not a book about the Anglo-Saxons, but a book about books about Anglo-Saxons. It describes the academic discipline of Anglo-Saxonism; the methods of study used; the underlying assumptions; and the uses to which it has been put.

Methods and motives have changed over time but right from the start there have been constant themes: English patriotism and English freedom.

£5.95   hardback   64 pages

The Hallowing of England
A Guide to the Saints of Old England and their Places of Pilgrimage
Fr. Andrew Philips

In the Old English period we can count over 300 saints, yet today their names and exploits are largely unknown. They are part of a forgotten England which, though it lies deep in the past, is an important part of our national and spiritual history. This guide includes a list of saints, an alphabetical list of places with which they are associated, and a calendar of saint's feast days.

£5.95   96 pages

Anglo-Saxon Food & Drink
Production, Processing, Distribution, and Consumption
Ann Hagen

Food production for home consumption was the basis of economic activity throughout the Anglo-Saxon period. Used as payment and a medium of trade, food was the basis of the Anglo-Saxons' system of finance and administration.

Information from various sources has been brought together in order to build up a picture of how food was grown, conserved, distributed, prepared and eaten during the period from the beginning of the 5th century to the 11th century. Many people will find it fascinating for the views it gives of an important aspect of Anglo-Saxon life and culture. In addition to Anglo-Saxon England the Celtic west of Britain is also covered.

This edition combines earlier titles – *A Handbook of Anglo-Saxon Food* and *A Second Handbook of Anglo-Saxon Food & Drink*.

Extensive index.

£25   512 pages

The English Warrior from earliest times till 1066
Stephen Pollington

This is not intended to be a bald listing of the battles and campaigns from the Anglo-Saxon Chronicle and other sources, but rather it is an attempt to get below the surface of Anglo-Saxon warriorhood and to investigate the rites, social attitudes, mentality and mythology of the warfare of those times.

> "An under-the-skin study of the role, rights, duties, psyche and rituals of the Anglo-Saxon warrior. The author combines original translations from Norse and Old English primary sources with archaeological and linguistic evidence for an in-depth look at the warrior, his weapons, tactics and logistics.
>
> A very refreshing, innovative and well-written piece of scholarship that illuminates a neglected period of English history"
>
> *Time Team Booklists* - Channel 4 Television

Revised Edition
An already highly acclaimed book has been made even better by the inclusion of additional information and illustrations.

£16.95   hardback   304 pages

The Mead Hall   The feasting tradition in Anglo-Saxon England
Stephen Pollington

This new study takes a broad look at the subject of halls and feasting in Anglo-Saxon England. The idea of the communal meal was very important among nobles and yeomen, warriors, farmers churchmen and laity. One of the aims of the book is to show that there was not just one 'feast' but two main types: the informal social occasion *gebeorscipe* and the formal, ritual gathering *symbel*.

Using the evidence of Old English texts - mainly the epic *Beowulf* and the *Anglo-Saxon Chronicles*, Stephen Pollington shows that the idea of feasting remained central to early English social traditions long after the physical reality had declined in importance.

The words of the poets and saga-writers are supported by a wealth of archaeological data dealing with halls, settlement layouts and magnificent feasting gear found in many early Anglo-Saxon graves.

Three appendices cover:
- Hall-themes in Old English verse;
- Old English and translated texts;
- The structure and origins of the warband.

£16.95   24 illustrations   296 pages

Organisations

Centingas

Centingas is a living history group devoted to the Anglo-Saxon way-of-life. The core of our membership is in the South East of England but it is constantly expanding. We have set ourselves the task of gaining expertise in the widest possible range of period crafts and skills. Our specialist areas include textiles, language and weapons.

We provide displays and information for schools and museums, and take part in re-enactment events around England.

For latest details and information visit www.centingas.co.uk

Þa Engliscan Gesiðas (The English Companions)

Þa Engliscan Gesiðas is a historical and cultural society exclusively devoted to Anglo-Saxon history. The Fellowship publishes a quarterly journal, *Wiðowinde,* and has a website with regularly updated information and discussions. Local groups arrange their own meetings and attend lectures, exhibitions and events. Members are able to share their interest with like-minded people and learn more about the origins and growth of English culture, including language, literature, archaeology, anthropology, architecture, art, religion, mythology, folklore and material culture.

For further details see www.tha-engliscan-gesithas.org.uk or write to:

Membership Secretary, The English Companions, PO Box 62790, London, SW12 2BH

Regia Anglorum

Regia Anglorum is an active group of enthusiasts who attempt to portray as accurately as possible the life and times of the people who lived in the British Isles around a thousand years ago. We investigate a wide range of crafts and have a Living History Exhibit that frequently erects some thirty tented period structures.

We have a thriving membership and 40 branches in the British Isles and United States - so there might be one near you. We especially welcome families with children.

www.regia.org   *General information* eolder@regia.org   *Membership* join@regia.org

The Sutton Hoo Society

Our aims and objectives focus on promoting research and education relating to the Anglo Saxon Royal cemetery at Sutton Hoo, Suffolk in the UK. The Society publishes a newsletter SAXON twice a year, which keeps members up to date with society activities, carries resumes of lectures and visits, and reports progress on research and publication associated with the site. If you would like to join the Society please see website: www.suttonhoo.org

Wuffing Education

Wuffing Education provides those interested in the history, archaeology, literature and culture of the Anglo-Saxons with the chance to meet experts and fellow enthusiasts for a whole day of in-depth seminars and discussions. Day Schools take place at the historic Tranmer House overlooking the burial mounds of Sutton Hoo in Suffolk.

For details of programme of events contact:-

Wuffing Education, 4 Hilly Fields, Woodbridge, Suffolk IP12 4DX
email education@wuffings.co.uk   website www.wuffings.co.uk
Tel. 01394 383908 or 01728 688749

Places to visit

Bede's World at Jarrow

Bede's world tells the remarkable story of the life and times of the Venerable Bede, 673–735 AD. Visitors can explore the origins of early medieval Northumbria and Bede's life and achievements through his own writings and the excavations of the monasteries at Jarrow and other sites.

Location – 10 miles from Newcastle upon Tyne, off the A19 near the southern entrance to the River Tyne tunnel. Bus services 526 & 527

Bede's World, Church Bank, Jarrow, Tyne and Wear, NE32 3DY

Tel. 0191 489 2106; Fax: 0191 428 2361; website: www.bedesworld.co.uk

Sutton Hoo near Woodbridge, Suffolk

Sutton Hoo is a group of low burial mounds overlooking the River Deben in south-east Suffolk. Excavations in 1939 brought to light the richest burial ever discovered in Britain – an Anglo-Saxon ship containing a magnificent treasure which has become one of the principal attractions of the British Museum. The mound from which the treasure was dug is thought to be the grave of Rædwald, an early English king who died in 624/5 AD.

This National Trust site has an excellent visitor centre, which includes a reconstruction of the burial chamber and its grave goods. Some original objects as well as replicas of the treasure are on display.

2 miles east of Woodbridge on B1083   Tel. 01394 389700

West Stow Anglo-Saxon Village

An early Anglo-Saxon Settlement reconstructed on the site where it was excavated consisting of timber and thatch hall, houses and workshop. There is also a museum containing objects found during the excavation of the site. Open all year 10am (except Christmas) Last entrance summer 4pm; winter 3-30pm. Special provision for school parties. A teachers' resource pack is available. Costumed events are held on some weekends, especially Easter Sunday and August Bank Holiday Monday. Craft courses are organised.

For further details see www.weststow.org or contact:

The Visitor Centre, West Stow Country Park, Icklingham Road, West Stow,
Bury St Edmunds, Suffolk IP28 6HG   Tel. 01284 728718